The Gift
of Self

Marion D. Hanks

The Gift of Self

MARION D. HANKS

Published by
BOOKCRAFT, INC.
Salt Lake City, Utah

Library of Congress Catalog Card Number: 74-75166
ISBN 0-88494-211-2

4th Printing, 1975

LITHOGRAPHED IN U.S.A.
PUBLISHERS PRESS
SALT LAKE CITY, UTAH

TO MY WIFE

in whom
giving of self
is a natural
and unflawed
quality of grace

Publisher's Foreword

At the time this book is published it is more than twenty years since Elder Marion D. Hanks was called to be a General Authority—first as a member of the First Council of the Seventy, latterly as an Assistant to the Twelve. During that time he has stood before countless gatherings of the Saints declaring "a reason of the hope that is in [him]."

It has been our observation that Elder Hanks' outstanding background of experience, reading, and gospel study has combined with a talent for eloquent expression to produce addresses and writings of exceptional appeal and merit. Illuminating and stimulating to the mind and the soul, they are delivered with a compassionate understanding that lifts the heart. The skill with words which they portray delights the responsive hearer and reader, yet this factor is secondary to the deep significance of the message itself—a potent reminder of our responsibilities in relation to the great issues of life and an inspired urging of the compelling reasons for fulfilling them.

It has long been our opinion that a selection of these powerful gospel messages ought to be made available to Church members in the permanent form of a book, and we have now prevailed upon Elder Hanks to permit this. We are confident that Church members everywhere will be well pleased with the result.

Bookcraft takes much pride and pleasure in offering Elder Marion D. Hanks' first book—*The Gift of Self.*

BOOKCRAFT PUBLISHERS

Contents

CONTENTS

IV. GIVE OBEDIENCE

V. GIVE LEADERSHIP

VI. GIVE LOVE

The Gift of Self

The least disciple cannot say
There are no alms to give away,
If love be in thy heart.

—Rita Snowden

It is always rewarding to read again the Lord's story of the Samaritan who rescued from the wayside of the Jericho road the traveler who had been plundered and wounded and left half dead by thieves; and it is aways encouraging and inspiring to recall what he did for the unfortunate man after the priest and the Levite passed him by, on their way no doubt to what they conceived to be weightier matters. His immediate needs were cared for, and a promise made of continued concern. It scarcely seems possible that an even greater gift was bestowed than these, and yet of course there was, for because of the Samaritan the traveler not only survived his ordeal, he came through it with renewed and enhanced faith in men.

Like the Samaritan's, every worthwhile life will involve a generous measure of giving. There will be experience also in receiving, which, like giving, if the full blessing is to be enjoyed, requires graciousness, sincerity, and love. (We do not know what motivated the Samaritan to his selfless act when others, presumably subjected to and susceptible to good instruction and generous impulses, passed by. But somehow he understood, and the reasonable supposition is that he had

1

been taught.) But the emphasis in such a life will be on giving, for that is why we are here. The instinct of the human heart, the yearning of the human spirit, are to give. God so loves us that he gave his dearly beloved Son, and thus the example of sacrificing that which is precious to us. Christ willingly surrendered his life for us, and thus blessed us with the lofty lesson of a matchless gift of love.

What of us? How can we express the heart's intention? What can we give? Where can we begin?

Perhaps we have some material substance to share. In the Bible we read Isaiah's admonition to "deal thy bread to the hungry," and "when thou seest the naked, cover him." (Isaiah 58:7.) One of Christ's most beautiful lessons taught us to care for those who hunger or thirst or have other temporal wants. There is the greatest need for sharing the material blessings we enjoy, for there are many who have insufficient for their needs.

But there is much more than this. The great Hebrew prophet taught that it is our obligation as humans to "satisfy the afflicted soul," to "bring the poor that are cast out to thy house . . ." We are to "undo the heavy burdens . . . let the oppressed go free . . . ," "break every yoke," "loose the bands of wickedness," ". . . hide not thyself from thine own flesh." (Isaiah 58:6, 7, 10.) Christ's loving lesson taught us our obligation not only to the hungry, thirsty, and naked, but to the stranger, the sick, the imprisoned, and thus, of course, to all men who have needs. We are to give to others as we would be grateful to have them give to us if our circumstances were reversed.

Whatever others receive from us must be given in the right spirit, for the right reasons, in the right way. It must be given at the right time, when the need exists, not always at our convenience. It is written that the manner of giving shows the character of the giver more than the gift itself. Said Seneca, "The benefit is not in what is done or given, but in the intention of the giver or doer."

Once I had an experience with an eight-year-old young lady and her parents just before her baptism was to be performed. She had come to my office to talk about the sacred experience ahead. As our visit ended I took from my desk a letter-opener with the sculptured likeness of Abraham Lincoln on the handle.

"I have loved Abraham Lincoln all of my life," I said to the young lady. "He was my hero when I was a boy. This letter-opener in the very front of my desk drawer has reminded me of him constantly for years. I treasure it very much. Now, because it means so much to me, I would like to give it to you as a remembrance of this important day."

Her parents were embarrassed and alarmed that I would part with something I valued so highly, and they began to intervene. But their child, quietly and very firmly, responded to their concern. "Momma," she said, "when you give something to someone it should be something that is important to you."

She understood.

When my young friend carried away her gift she held it tightly in her hand. Over the years I have heard from her periodically as she has reported her progress. We have all remembered that day, not because a gift was given—gifts and giving should be forgotten by those who share—but because something more important occurred; a true principle was practiced and comprehended.

A great nation fell to the enemy with unanticipated ease in World War II. One of those involved in her leadership later explained the tragedy as he saw it:

> Our spirit of enjoyment was greater than our spirit of sacrifice. We wanted to have more than we wanted to give. We tried to spare effort, and we met disaster. (Henri Petain.)

So will it be with each of God's children who suffers the same sorrowful, selfish misunderstanding. There is a certain risk to service, but if we seek to shelter ourselves from the vulnerability involved we will surely miss some of life's greatest blessings. If we protect ourselves from possible rejection by refusing the exposure genuine concern requires, if we center our attentions on ourselves and refuse to give, we will lose that which Jesus died to make available to us; we will lose life on its highest level, abundant life, eternal life, life with God.

When the Lord was born, each who had followed the star laid at the foot of the manger what he had to give. The kings bestowed costly possessions, the shepherds their obeisance and love; all who were true worshippers gave their hearts. In the scriptures it is recorded that each of us must give "according to that which he hath . . . ." (Mosiah 4:26.) The recognition that "the least disciple" among us has much to give, the translation of the instinct of the heart into the act of giving, these are the keys that open the door to meeting the real needs of others. If we have not a penny to offer, can there be any blessing more vital to the afflicted soul than faith and hope and love? To share compassion, dispel doubt, make a timely suggestion, awaken faith, instill hope, strengthen courage, lift over a rough spot, offer forgiveness, suggest a helpful idea, convey kindness, renew confidence, give comfort, speak a word of appreciation, express understanding, restore self-respect—this is to deal that which cannot be bartered but only given away. Bestowed in gracious manner, in a timely way, with tender feelings, these gifts effect the giving of the giver with the gift. They are tied with heartstrings, conveying heart-strengths; they come from deep wellsprings of common humanity and a common eternal heritage of brotherhood. They can make life bearable, purposeful, beautiful. They are gifts of the mind, the heart, and the spirit. They carry with them comprehension of the admonition of the Lord:

> For whosoever will save his life shall lose it; and whosoever will lose his life for my sake shall find it. (Matthew 16:25.)

I.
Give
Appreciation

We need the current companionship of the sweetest and most gracious and godly One who ever lived. We need the assurance that comes with the reading anew of the problems he faced, the tragedies he endured, the patience and forgiveness and love he manifested in times of trial. We need to think again of his triumph and his purposes for us.

Purposeful Happiness

On my desk at this moment is the cover of a leading news journal with this headline: "GOOD TIMES—BUT PEOPLE ARE UNHAPPY." The story within reported the results of a survey made to determine *why* people are unhappy in good times. The reasons given are substantially the same as those produced by any responsible inquiry:

> Lack of meaning or purpose in life; anxiety, fear, poor self-image, doubting one's capacity to love or worthiness to be loved, not accomplishing anything, bad conscience; inability to form lasting relationships, unsatisfactory home life, loneliness; no sense of belonging, little giving of self; and the summation of them all: *Lack of life-directing relationships with God and Christ.*

Men without God and the living Christ in their lives lack center, and thus lack the joy they could have.

Hundreds of years before Christ, God confronted the willful ignorance of Israel in these words: "My people are destroyed for lack of knowledge: because thou hast rejected knowledge, I will also reject thee . . . seeing thou hast forgotten the law of thy God." (Hosea 4:6.) The knowledge for lack of which they suffered is plainly explained by Hosea:

> The Lord hath a controversy with the inhabitants of the land, because there is no truth, nor mercy, nor knowledge of God in the land.

Address given at General Conference, April 1972.

7

> For I desired mercy, and not sacrifice; and the knowledge
> of God more than burnt offerings. (Hosea 4:1, 6:6.)

In a poem of pessimism which he wrote soon after World War I, Yeats described the widening circle—the gyre—in which the falcon flew away from the falconer:

> Turning and turning in the widening gyre,
> The falcon cannot hear the falconer,
> Things fall apart, the center cannot hold,

And he finished:

> The best lack all conviction, while the worst
> Are full of passionate intensity.

When the falcon is not heard, the falcon is lost. So do men lose direction when they cannot or will not hear the voice of the Master. Things fall apart in human life; the center cannot hold; trouble is born; and the "worst," who are "full of passionate intensity," do their own thing, follow their own base appetites and wayward wills, and impose upon those who are less intense and involved—particularly the young—false constructions and interpretations of the meaning of life.

It is well to consider where we are with respect to our Creator. If we are out of touch, if we have moved away from him, we are not as happy as we could be. Something is missing. Epictetus said: "God hath made all men to be happy." And a prophet wrote: "Men are that they might have joy."

Wherein have we erred if we are not happy? Why are we less happy than we could be? How can we have more joy? May I offer six simple observations.

I

When I was a boy growing up in a home with a widowed mother, I heard a simple story which touched me and which has had much more meaning since I have had the blessing of having a son of my own. A youngster was assigned by his father to see to the moving of a large rock. He tugged, he pushed, and he lifted and struggled without avail. Some friends were enlisted, but together they could not move it. Reluctantly he reported to his father that he could not budge the rock. "Have you done all you could?" asked the father. "Yes," said the little boy. "Have you tried everything?" persisted the father. "Yes," said the boy, "I've tried everything." "No, son, you haven't," said his dad. "You haven't asked me."

Why do so many of us, "heirs of God, joint heirs with Christ," fail to go to him, to keep in touch with our Father? He is anxious to help, but he wants us to learn our need for him, to open the door to him. "And therefore," said the prophet, "will the Lord wait, that he may be gracious unto you, and therefore will he be exalted, that he may have mercy upon you." (Isaiah 30:18.)

II

For some of us, a reason for unhappiness is, as the poet said:

> The world is too much with us; late and soon,
> Getting and spending, we lay waste our powers.
>
> (Wordsworth.)

Material objectives consume too much of our attention. The struggle for what we need, or for more than we need, exhausts our time and energy. We pursue pleasure or entertainment, or become overinvolved in associations or civic matters. Of course, people need recreation, need to be achieving, need to contribute, but if these come at the cost of friendship with Christ, the price is much too high.

"For my people have committed two evils," said the Lord to Israel; "they have forsaken me the fountain of living waters, and hewed them out cisterns, broken cisterns, that can hold no water." (Jeremiah 2:13.)

The substitutions we fashion to take the place of God in our lives truly hold no water. To the measure we thus refuse the "living water," we miss the joy we could have.

9

Luke records Christ's well-known story to the Pharisees:

> A certain man made a great supper, and bade many: And
> sent his servant at supper time to say to them that were bidden,
> Come; for all things are now ready. And they all with one con-
> sent began to make excuse. The first said unto him, I have bought
> a piece of ground, and I must needs go and see it: I pray thee
> have me excused. And another said, I have bought five yoke of
> oxen, and I go to prove them: I pray thee have me excused. And
> another said, I have married a wife, and therefore I cannot come.
> (Luke 14:16-20.)

Other guests were invited to take their places at the supper.

III

Some of us may be less happy than we should be or could
be because of arrogance or pride. We think we are sufficient
unto ourselves. We think we do not need God or his Christ.
We may be, as President Joseph F. Smith once wrote, lazy,
or "among the proud and self-vaunting, who read by the lamp
of their own conceit, interpret by rules of their own contriving
. . . become a law unto themselves, and so pose as the sole
judges of their own doings."

To recreant Israel, God said:

> This is a rebellious people, lying children, children that will
> not hear the law of the Lord; which say to the seers, See not;
> and to the prophets, Prophesy not unto us right things, speak
> unto us smooth things, prophesy deceits. (Isaiah 30:9-10.)

From the prophet Jacob in the Book of Mormon comes
this sobering warning, well known to students in the Church:

> O that cunning plan of the evil one! O the vainness, and
> the frailties, and the foolishness of men! When they are learned
> they think they are wise, and they hearken not unto the counsel
> of God, for they set it aside, supposing they know of themselves,
> wherefore, their wisdom is foolishness and it profiteth them not.
> And they shall perish. But to be learned is good if they hearken
> unto the counsels of God. (2 Nephi 9:28-29.)

Paul, the brilliant author who wrote the letters which constitute a major part of the New Testament, assured the Corinthians that he had been sent not to satisfy those who required a sign or were seeking after worldly wisdom. He determined to preach nothing but Jesus Christ and him crucified, and he did it, so he said, "in weakness, and in fear, and in much trembling . . . . in demonstration of the Spirit and of power: that your faith should not stand in the wisdom of men, but in the power of God." (1 Corinthians 2:3-5.)

It is not enough, is it, to know the scriptures about prayer or the motions of prayer or the words of prayer? The man who will not humble himself—really humble himself—before the Lord "receiveth not the things of the Spirit of God," wrote Paul, "for they are foolishness unto him: neither can he know them, because they are spiritually discerned." (1 Corinthians 2:14.)

The truths of eternal life, the Prophet has written, "are only to be seen and understood by the power of the Holy Spirit, which God bestows on those who love him, and purify themselves before him; to whom he grants this privilege of seeing and knowing for themselves." (D&C 76:116-117.)

IV

There are those who lose faith because of personal tragedies or troubles. Faced with problems akin to Job's, they have in effect accepted the invitation to curse God and die rather than to love God and gain the strength to endure their trials. In the promises of God there is, of course, no warrant that we will avoid the very experiences which we came here to undergo and through which we can learn reliance on the Lord. Jesus said, "In the world ye shall have tribulation: but be of good cheer; I have overcome the world." (John 16:33.) *He* had tribulation, and overcame. And so may we, with his help.

Some years ago I became acquainted with a young family whose little son was tragically ill with cancer. Every night the

11

father sat with his boy, holding him in his arms. The pain seemed less when daddy held him close. The father slept on a mattress on the floor beside his son so that he could reach him whenever the boy cried out. The parents bore their sorrow with courage. They prayed, they loved, they served. Faith gave them strength to meet the test.

V

Sometimes we turn from the Lord because other people have made or are making mistakes. I don't want to forget the story of the farmer who felt he had been wronged in the distribution of irrigation water and that the watermaster was at fault. Having angered himself into distraction over the seeming unfairness, he sought out the watermaster, grasped him by the shirt and bitterly said, "Tom, as long as you are watermaster, I won't take another drop out of that ditch." What happened to that farmer? Well he was a stubborn man. He kept his foolish vow, and he and his property dried up and blew away.

That we have not found perfection in men or organization, or that we hear reports of imperfection—these are not reasons to cease seeking or serving or worshipping. The frailties or failings of others can never be appropriate reason for our losing the blessings we might have if we ourselves are doing our duty.

VI

And, finally, perhaps the saddest of all reasons for failing ourselves and the Lord is that we choose to disqualify ourselves because of our own mistakes. We know that sin and failure to obey tend to keep us from God and prayer. We refuse to receive the soul-saving gift of forgiveness because *we have sinned*. But this is the larger failure. To reject the Lord and his love and his redeeming sacrifice is to deny the efficacy of God's love and his graciousness. All men are capable of mistakes, and have made some, but all of us too can have the cleansing forgiveness that comes with repentance and devotion. We are all like Paul—sometimes tortured by an inability to do consistently and faithfully that which we know we should do. "For to will is present with me," he said, "but how to perform that which is good I find not. For the good that I would I do not: but the evil which I would not, that I do." (Romans 7:18-19.) But Paul knew Jesus. He knew him as the Lord, and he accepted his pardon, gave him his life and died for him.

To me, there comes perhaps the most personal and encouraging expression of all from Nephi, sincere servant of God, who, bearing his witness of gratitude and delight in the Lord, is honest enough to say:

> Nevertheless, notwithstanding the great goodness of the Lord, in showing me his great and marvelous works, my heart exclaimeth: O wretched man that I am! Yea, my heart sorroweth because of my flesh; my soul grieveth because of mine iniquities. I am encompassed about, because of the temptations and the sins which do so easily beset me. And when I desire to rejoice, my heart groaneth because of my sins. (2 Nephi 4:17-19.)

And then he cried out to the Lord for help: "Wilt thou make me that I may shake at the appearance of sin? . . . O Lord, I have trusted in thee, and I will trust in thee forever. I will not put my trust in the arm of flesh." (2 Nephi 4:31, 34.) And Nephi gave his life to the Lord.

Our strength and our peace and our happiness are in the Lord. In this world of trial and affliction, we have need of the comforting and qualifying assurances that come with faith in God, and repentance, and service to his cause. If we will acknowledge him, be thankful, serve him, love his children, and accept the responsibilities of being truly Christian, we will be happy notwithstanding problems or troubles. Said the apostle John, "If ye know these things, happy are ye if ye do them." (John 13:17.)

There *is no* lasting joy in possessions. There *is no* peace here or hereafter in pride. There *is* comfort and understanding in the loving arms of him whose every act of courage, of

13

mercy, and of love was performed in the shadow of a cross he knew was ahead for him, and in a world "shot through with moral flaws." We cannot permit the mistakes of others nor our own mistakes to mislead us from our own joy. Jesus died for our personal sins. He is the Savior and Redeemer to whom we belong.

Faith in God and Christ make for righteousness in the world, and for happiness. One who knows has said:

> God exists in the world. He exists wherever men let him in. Perhaps it is only humble men, men in search of him, men with a great need for him, who really let him in. And God comes to such men not only because of their great need for him, but also because of his great need for them as his allies in the divine task of creating a better world, a better human society, a real kingdom of God. (P. A. Christensen.)

Martin Buber helps us: "You know always in your heart that you need God more than anything else. But do you not know too that God needs you . . . in the fulness of his eternity he needs you?"

Said the Lord to ancient Israel: "If ye will obey my voice indeed, and keep my covenant, then ye shall be a peculiar treasure unto me . . . for all the earth is mine." (Exodus 19:5.)

> World, O world, of muddled men,
> Seek the Peace of God again:
> In the humble faith that kneels,
> In the hallowed Word that heals:
> In the courage of a tree,
> In the rock's integrity;
> In the hill that holds the sky,
> The star you pull your heart up by;
> In the laughter of a child,
> Altogether undefiled;
> In the hope that answers doubt,
> Love that drives the darkness out . . .
> Frantic, frightened, foolish men,
> Take God by the hand again.
>
> (Joseph Auslander.)

Why Jesus Christ

If the Lord will bless me, I would like to talk about the meaning of this day which we celebrate with all Christians everywhere, a day signal and significant, a day pivotal in the whole history of mankind.

Perhaps I can do that best by reading a few words that came to my mind as I stood not long ago in the catacombs outside Rome on the Appian Way, where multitudes of Christians gave their lives rather than relinquish their convictions or their faith. This is one of the things I remembered and was pleased to look up and read again on my return. It is a letter written by Cyprian, a martyr in the third century, to his friend Donatus. He wrote from Carthage:

> This seems a cheerful world, Donatus, when I view it from this fair garden under the shadow of these vines. But if I climbed some great mountain and looked out over the wide lands, you know very well what I would see—brigands on the high roads, pirates on the seas, in the amphitheaters men murdered to please applauding crowds; under all roofs misery and selfishness. It is really a bad world, yet in the midst of it I have found a quiet and holy people. They have discovered a joy which is a thousand times better than any pleasure of this sinful life. They are despised and persecuted, but they care not. They have overcome the world. These people, Donatus, are the Christians and I am one of them.

Address given at General Conference, April 1969.

And then in a magazine some years ago I read and was deeply moved by another account. It had come freshly to view after centuries of being hidden.

On May 13, A.D. 303, in the Algerian city of Cirta (now Constantine), one Munatus Felix, high priest of the emperor, personally led a raid on a Christian worship service. He took with him a stenographer, whose report, taken in shorthand, sounds disconcertingly familiar to modern ears.

"Bring out whatever scriptures you have got," commanded Felix, after his men had collected all the evidence they could find. A subdeacon brought only one large book, explaining that the lectors kept the rest. Felix said to them, "Identify the lectors." They said, "We are not informers. Here we stand. Command us to be executed." Felix said, "Put them under arrest."

And the editorialist noted:

> No one knows how many thousands were rounded up in such raids and executed. They could easily have saved their skins by staying home and saying their prayers in comfortable privacy. But they insisted on the right to come together [in the name of Christ].

Easter is the day when those who believe in and accept his name gratefully worship the risen Redeemer. Men of good will everywhere join in the solemn celebration. What was so important about him? Why the total commitment of Cyprian and the saints at Cirta? In outline form, let me offer an answer.

His was a redemptive story.

> For God so loved the world, that he gave his only begotten Son, that whosoever believeth in him should not perish, but have everlasting life. (John 3:16.)

He was a God, a member of the Godly council, a Son delegated by his Father for a holy mission. He was a God who came to earth and walked among men and suffered more

16

than any man could suffer, because this was his mission, and in him was the love which made it possible for him to do what he had to do.

He was a creator, indeed the Creator of this world, under the direction of his Father.

> And there stood one among them that was like unto God, and he said unto those who were with him: We will go down, for there is space there, and we will take of these materials, and we will make an earth whereon these may dwell. (Abraham 3:24.)

> For by him were all things created, that are in heaven, and that are in earth. (Colossians 1:16.)

> God . . . . hath in these last days spoken unto us by his Son, whom he hath appointed heir of all things, by whom also he made the worlds. (Hebrews 1:1-2.)

He was the Firstborn in the spirit.

> I was in the beginning with the Father, and am the Firstborn. (D&C 93:21.)

His mission was prophesied long before he was born into the world.

> Behold, a virgin shall conceive, and bear a son, and shall call his name Immanuel. (Isaiah 7:14.)

He was the Only Begotten in the flesh, on this earth the only one begotten of a Divine Father and an earthly mother.

> I beheld his glory, as the glory of the Only Begotten of the Father. (D&C 93:11.)

He alone was without blemish, and yet he learned.

> Though he were a Son, yet learned he obedience by the things which he suffered. (Hebrews 5:8.)

17

He was tempted, but would not yield. It isn't so hard to us to identify, is it, with one who was tempted, even as we are tempted?

> For in that he himself hath suffered being tempted, he is able to succour them that are tempted. (Hebrews 2:18.)

After Christ had fasted for forty days and nights, he was invited to use his marvelous powers to serve himself, to satisfy himself, to save his own life, to turn stones into bread, and he would not. The tempter said to him, in effect, "Win the plaudits of the crowd; it will be easy for you. Please them, gain their acceptance. Cast yourself down. Then they will listen to your important message." But he would not. He was offered power and glory in exchange for his soul, and he would not yield.

We have similar temptations in our own time, and so we can identify with Christ.

He was the servant of all. One of his last earthly acts was to wash the feet of his disciples.

He suffered in both body and spirit.

> For behold, I, God, have suffered these things for all, that they might not suffer if they would repent. (D&C 19:16.)

He died willingly, alone, for this was how it must be. There had to be a propitiation, by one of his unique qualifications, for the sins of men—our sins—payment for which, through the love of God and the love of his Son, was made on Calvary's hill.

> Thinkest thou that I cannot now pray to my Father, and he shall presently give me more than twelve legions of angels? But how then shall the scriptures be fulfilled, that thus it must be? (Matthew 26:53,54.)

> My God, my God, why hast thou forsaken me? (Matthew 27:46.)

I bear testimony and thank God for this Good Friday—tragic as are the events which it commemorates—and for what it means to me and to all men, for what it lays before men of a future; for this day had to happen in order that Easter and its glorious events could come to pass.

The pure in heart shall see God. Those who become the manner of man he was, who walk in the Spirit, will see him, and will be his.

I pray God to bless us, that all the good and wholesome and sweet feelings of the Christian world at this sacred season may motivate us and all who worship his name and seek to do his will to the kind of commitment spoken by Cyprian; to the kind of courage and devotion known by those who died in the catacombs so long ago—they who loved him well and paid whatever price was necessary to demonstrate that love.

Your Gift to Mother

The thought has before been expressed that each of our great national holidays is in reality a *memorial day*—a day in which to remember, appreciate and pay homage. This is certainly true of Christmas, of Thanksgiving, of Lincoln's and Washington's birthday anniversaries, of Independence Day, and of others. So is it of Mother's Day, for this is a day to remember mother, to be grateful for all she has meant to us and to pay our respects to her or to her sacred memory.

And how shall we honor and give tribute to mother? What may we fittingly do?

Some sons and daughters have chosen to remember mother with costly monuments over the place she rests. Some have established foundations or named hospitals or endowed charities or dedicated books in her name. Most of those who still have a mother and the chance to honor her while she is yet with them seek to remember her with flowers or candy or other gifts. Some write appreciative letters or verse, or make visits or hold family celebrations.

Any of these ways of remembering mother, done with honest and earnest purpose, can be an acceptable and happily received tribute. But none of these gifts, however sincerely bestowed and however costly or valuable or imposing, is the one gift that every good and true mother really wants from her child.

Article published in the *Instructor*, May 1956.

What is that gift?

Perhaps the poet said it as impressively and beautifully as it can be said:

TO MY MOTHER

I do not build a monument
Of carved white marble for your sake,
That only those who pass may read
And only they memorial make.
My *life* must be the monument
I consecrate in your behalf;
My charity must carve your name,
My gentleness your epitaph.
Above this record I engrave
No drooping figure;
There must be straight-shouldered courage.
Starry eyes must mark the scroll of destiny.
Any may some fragment of your strength,
By God's great mystery, fall on me;
That through this monument of mine
May shine your immortality.

(Author unknown.)

Truly, the one gift suitable to mother, the one monument or memorial adequate to her blessed memory, is the monument of a life which reflects and represents the virtues and attributes and ambitions she hoped and dreamed and prayed we would have and tried to inspire in us.

It would do all of us well on Mother's Day to honestly consider whether the monument we are building to our mother in our lives is a suitable memorial to her, one of which she and we may be proud. Are we presently possessed of the spirit of faith we felt at her knee? Are we humble before God, steadfast to the ideals she taught us, consistent in the life she led us to live?

As I consider these questions today, I am very grateful to my own mother for the lessons her life has taught me. With my brothers and sisters, I would like my life to be a monument to her honesty and integrity and devotion to the whole truth, under trying conditions.

21

Mother taught honesty by being honest. During the depression, when she was serving as ward Relief Society president, our kitchen would often be filled with vegetables and cans of milk and loaves of bread to be distributed to the needy. It was hard for some of us to understand why in our own difficult circumstances we were never allowed to eat a vegetable or keep a loaf of bread. Sometimes we were sent to the store to buy bread when there were several dozen loaves right there waiting to be distributed. We thought surely just one loaf would not be missed, but we were never permitted to have a taste of it.

Mother was always deeply interested in literature and music and every beautiful thing. She worked far into the night after her multitude of household chores were done and we were safely in our beds, preparing her literary or social science or home art lessons for Relief Society, or her Gospel Doctrine lessons for Sunday School. She always gave her best efforts to an assigned task and tried to teach her children to do the same.

We learned from her that proper performance entails careful and devoted preparation. Often she quoted:

> If you're asked to do a thing
> And mean to do it really,
> Never let it be by halves,
> Do it fully, freely.

We were always proud of Mother's wisdom and teaching ability, and we knew how hard she was willing to work to prepare herself.

To her children, one of the crowning qualities of our mother's life has been her quiet dignity and gentleness under every circumstance. She believed in rules; she demanded discipline and imposed punishment when it was justified. But never can any of us recall her having descended to argument or angry outburst or even to raising her voice. Sometimes, when we disappointed her or failed to live up to her expectations, there was a reprimand, perhaps a tear of sorrow, but never argument or diatribe. She demanded respect.

We learned at our home that mothers can do a lot of things: They can make kites and run down the street with them to the delight of little boys. A mother can make bean bags, dolls out of hollyhocks, and balls out of stockings and string. She can even make a playable violin out of an old cigar box and some piano wire. She can write poems and draw pictures of birds.

She can preserve great quantities of fruit in summertime, over a coal stove in a hot kitchen—sometimes even cutting the wood the boys failed to cut. She can make tempting and satisfying deep-dish meat pies and rhubarb or peach pies that will feed a large family economically.

She can sew and make clothes for all her children. During a fierce thunder and lightning storm she can gather frightened children around the piano and calm them with stories and songs as she plays. She can read many books, accumulate countless clippings, and do it all while the house is kept clean and desirable.

Oh, a monument to a mother *ought* to be impressive!

Though there were many things we didn't have at our house because we couldn't afford them (and Mother would not have what she could not pay for), we never remember any sense of deprivation or poverty. Mother had to be very frugal and thrifty with material things but not with her love. All of us knew that we were loved and wanted, and none of us ever remembers wishing he could change places with anyone. Home meant so much to all of us because we shared things together and took pride and satisfaction in being able to make a contribution to it.

No person of mature judgment would measure the worth of a human soul by the manner of monument raised over its resting place. But no mother—or child—will fully avoid the implications of the poet's words: "Children are what their mothers are."

God grant to all of us that "some fragment" of the strength of our saintly mothers might "fall on us," that on this and every other day we might earnestly endeavor to fashion of our life a monument to mother through which may "shine her immortality."

Choose Your Children's Parents

Last night I read on the editorial page of the *Deseret News* an account of a survey—actually a clinical research inquiry—of a number of men incarcerated in the Utah State Prison as compared with an equal number outside the prison who were of the same general background as to age, intellect, social and economic circumstances, etc. The report reemphasized strongly the vital importance to the well-being of young people of a home where love and interest are shown, where there are fair rules consistently enforced, where there is a religious atmosphere in the home and religious activity outside it, and where parents set the proper affirmative example.

Since I read that article I have been even more grateful for the home I grew up in, humble as it was in terms of material things; for a loving father, who was called home in our infancy; for a wonderful mother and brothers and sisters through whose love, unselfishness, and cooperative effort I came to enjoy some blessings that they did not have themselves.

I am grateful that I know something about some of the problems that exist in the world and that I have the privilege of counseling, weeping, and sympathizing with some of the people who have them.

I am grateful for the kind of mountains that the choir has just sung about (as well as for other mountains), and that

Address given at General Conference, October 1958.

25

God blesses us with strength enough to climb if we are humble enough.

Recently I have been thinking about three great problem areas which actually encompass the whole of human experience, the whole of an individual's life, thinking about them in terms of the Church program and the principles of the gospel. We have a lot of youth problems and we know it— difficulties in many fields of youth behavior and experience. Then there is in our communities, and the nation, a great problem with unhappy adults—broken homes, marriages, and lives; increasing incidence of moral decadence, of alcoholism, increasing prison incarcerations, and so forth. There is a third problem that I am not sure we have thought much about (perhaps in the Church we do not know as much about it as a problem as some do), and that is the needs of the elderly and the aging, many of whom, with advancing age, lose status in the family, community, and business.

Some recent experiences have permitted me the privilege of observing and participating in activities having to do with some of these problems. I have come out of those experiences with increased gratitude to my Heavenly Father that in the graciousness and goodness of his love we have been blessed with the principles, programs, and inspiration which can preserve us from the most serious of these problems, help us overcome them to the measure we find ourselves in them, and lead us, through God's good gifts, to the happiness here and the eternal opportunity hereafter which we are meant to enjoy. There is no occasion today to do more than recognize the existence of the problems and to testify of my deep assurance that through proper parenthood and leadership and instruction, and through a willingness to learn, hearken, and participate, the principles of the gospel and the great programs of the Church will help us avoid or overcome most of the difficulties which beset us.

There is a story in point which I thought of as I read last night. A young man who had lost his father in his earliest years went to an elderly medical man who had been a close friend of his father and asked the doctor what kind of man his father had been. The old doctor answered the question with a question: "Suppose you could have chosen your father —that is, what kind of man he would be—what would your choice have been?"

The young man replied that he would have chosen one who was courageous and forthright and true; a kind, wise, and loving man; a worshiper, worker, and servant of God. He described clearly and forcefully an ideal father, then asked, "Doctor, is that the sort of man my father was?"

Said the doctor, "As your father's friend, let me ask you another question. Is that the sort of man you have chosen to be the father of your own children?" The young man said, "With all my thinking about life and its responsibilities, I confess that I have not thought about this important matter in just that way before. Though I had nothing to do with choosing my own father, I have everything to do with choosing what kind of father my own children shall have. I give you my word that I shall think about and act upon it from now on."

My wonderful young friends, in the Church and out of it, you face real challenges and great pressures, but the objectives and opportunities before you are marvelous. When I look at you, I do not see in you only the leaders of tomorrow; I see what you *now are,* the boy friends and girl friends, the young husbands and wives of today. Stretching ahead before you are important occasions for decision and choice, decisions that will affect your happiness in this world and your eternal future.

Do you make negative judgments about the parents, leaders and teachers you now have? Have you thought enough about what kind of parents, leaders and teachers *you* are going to be? These are not far-off challenges—they are upon you; in less time than you can now conceive, these blessings and burdens will be yours.

A few weeks ago I sat in an auditorium in the East with some of the leading businessmen in America and heard

27

Brother Benson discuss the youth fitness program now underway across the land. As the viewpoints of the Church were so impressively presented, I was again moved with gratitude that through revelation the Lord has blessed us with the principles and the programs which can lead us to effective, participating citizenship in the community, and in the kingdom; which, whatever kind of home we came from, can lead us to be the sort of father or mother we would have been pleased to choose had we the opportunity.

Consider the understanding the Lord has given us as to the nature of this physical body which houses our spirit: "The spirit and the body are the soul of man." (D&C 88:15.)

> For man is spirit. The elements are eternal, and spirit and element, inseparably connected, receive a fulness of joy.
> The elements are the tabernacle of God; yea, man is the tabernacle of God, even temples; and whatsoever temple is defiled, God shall destroy that temple. (D&C 93:33, 35.)

I am grateful to understand that my physical body is an eternal, nonevil component of my eternal soul, and that I have, therefore, a duty to honor and respect and care for it, and to refrain from knowingly imposing upon it any treatment or substance deleterious to it. While I could not choose nor govern the condition of the body into which I came, I have the responsibility to give it the best care I can, and if I do not I am acting in derogation of a great gift of God.

The Lord has blessed us with knowledge that we are under obligation to develop our minds, for "the glory of God is intelligence" (D&C 93:36), and "it is impossible for a man to be saved in ignorance" (D&C 131:6). He has given particular emphasis to spiritual truth, but in addition to charging the early brethren to teach one another the doctrines of the kingdom, he also instructed them to prepare themselves in a wide field of knowledge, including languages, history, and law. In the Church are the principles and programs which can lead us to the possession of minds that are clean and honest, educated, trained, controlled, creative, productive, and useful.

We have received the word of the Lord that "men are, that they might have joy" (2 Nephi 2:25), and we know that there is joy in responsible relationships with our fellowmen. As this is true of other men, it is especially true of our own families. The family, sealed together under the law of God, is the eternal unit, and our own high possibilities in the eternities are contingent upon our relationship with our family, as well as with our Heavenly Father and his other children. Many of the problems that afflict mankind would be avoided or mitigated or overcome if we would learn and act in the light of this truth.

Underlying all that has been revealed to us, the Lord has given us to know that we are his children, that life is purposeful and meaningful, and that we are blessed with the possibility of a high destiny. I thank God that I know these things and I pray that he will bless us to understand that though we may have partaken of some of the problems of the world, though we may have undergone some of the tragedies of the world, there is hope and answer for us in the gospel of Jesus Christ. Though we could not choose or direct in our earliest days the home we grew up in or the parents who bore us, we can do something about the sort of parents we are or will be, and about the home our children will grow up in. We can honor our parents. We can look with appreciation upon those who have lived long on the earth, and who merit our concern and loving attention. We honor lofty principles and honor our rich heritage when we serve and honor them.

I thank the Lord for the good things he has blessed us with, and pray that we may have the wisdom to be steadfast and faithful and to do that which will perpetuate for those who are to come the blessings which the Lord has made available through the principles and programs and inspired leadership of his great Church.

Earn It Anew

My heart is full of gratitude today for many things. I am very grateful for the rain, and for the lovely weather which preceded it, each of which is a blessing suited to our needs. I am very grateful that we may meet in this marvelous old building. I am grateful for the privilege of missionary service on these grounds for the past eight years. One cannot have intimate acquaintance with these buildings day after day and not acquire in his soul an appreciation for them and for those who built them.

These buildings attract others, in addition to us. I remember the guided tour which was joined by a sweet woman from an eastern city. As we left this building she, who had come with some preconceived negative notions about Mormonism but had been touched by what she heard and felt here, turned to her husband and almost reverently and with a tear in her eye said to him, but still with her notions, "George, isn't it marvelous what ignorant people can do?"

Well, it has been a great blessing these years to be able to tell such good people, and many thousands like them, that the people who did the work which we enjoy here today and each day, were not ignorant. They were people of courage and faith and dignity and initiative and integrity, who were always willing to give up conveniences and comforts, but never their convictions; they were not ignorant people.

Address given at General Conference, April 1954.

It has been a great privilege also to know, as we have learned to love these buildings and those who built them, something of other monuments which they left us, not so physically tangible, but infinitely more important. Last night as I walked through these grounds at a late hour—and I make a habit of that, I commend it to you, for these are beautiful and thoughtful and wonderful hours, in the early morning and late evening—I thought of the words reported to be inscribed on the tombstone of Sir Christopher Wren, the great British architect and builder. It is said that there is written on the tomb of this man who built more than fifty churches in London, including St. Paul's, and was one of the great architects of his day, these words: "If you seek his monument, look around you."

I suggest to you that as Latter-day Saints it isn't very difficult to look around us and see the monuments left by those who worked here so well and courageously, and with such integrity, so long ago. May I suggest two or three of these other monuments which they made available to us: The monumental blessing, for instance, of truth and testimony, of spiritual knowledge, of freedom from the sins of the world; the monumental heritage of possibility for personal union with God, for peace in this life, and eternal life in the world to come; the monumental gift of great books of scripture, in which are written not only the lessons of life, but the great revelations of God to men. And with these and all the other monuments, they left us the monument of work, which they were willing and able to perform. Oh, how we need to learn it!

With a knowledge of these monuments they dedicated to us, there comes the sober second thought expressed well by Goethe, the great German poet-philosopher, who said: "What from your fathers' heritage is lent, earn it anew to really possess it," which is to say that while these great blessings of monumental value come to us from our pioneer forebears, they are of such a nature that they may be possessed only by him or her who is willing to earn and merit them.

31

There was the day, and I recall it with pleasure, when a man came here from the government of Israel; in fact, he was a ministerial official of that nation. It happened to be late in the evening, and there weren't many people around, so I had a casual and very pleasant talk with him. He was a jolly fellow, a little corpulent and pleasant and humorous. He asked many questions of interest about us and our faith, and I had the privilege of telling him as best I could of the great truths that had come to us from God through our forebears. He invited conversation about our relationship, him and me, and I told him we were cousins in a real sense, that we both came from the family of Israel, and I identified myself as being of the lineage of Ephraim. He leaned back, startled, and said, "Say again." And so I began to repeat, "Through Abraham, Isaac, Jacob, and through Joseph to Ephraim, came the covenant blessings; many of us are of Ephraim."

"Well," he said, "I came to America to learn about agriculture. I came to Utah to learn about irrigation. I expected to learn many interesting things, but I never expected to find the lost sons of Ephraim."

He went away. He came back in the morning. He said, "Tell me again." So I told him, "From God to Abraham, Isaac, Jacob and through Joseph to Ephraim came the birthright blessings." We talked for some time, identifying his progenitors, his forebears, with ours, and he left figuratively (almost literally) holding his head in his hands with what he had heard. We have heard from him several times since, he bearing testimony in his own way of this, to him, new and marvelous story. I thought how grateful I am for the monumental link left me which connects me with all dispensations past, which tells me who I am, whence I came, and what my destiny might be.

I am grateful for many other monumental truths. If it were feasible, we might show you a file full of letters from people of education, wealth, power, prominence, good character, each of them in his own words reiterating the simple story one of them told as he wrote, "I found in one hour on these grounds among your people more peace and faith and something to hold to than I had ever known before." Well, these are monumental blessings, but they come to us only as we individually earn them, which is the only manner in which we might really possess them.

May I suggest to you, as I conclude, one other item which I think will be of interest. I mentioned the great scriptures, these books of truth and revelation which God has given us. These too must be individually earned to be possessed. It would thrill you, and in a sense make you chagrined, as it has me, to learn the reaction of many great and good people to these scriptures. Let me read you two letters from a certain doctor from Tel Aviv. He has read the Book of Mormon. He said, "The first reading has made this material precious for me in another sense. It deals with many problems occupying me, as every man concerned with his and mankind's destiny." And he writes a little later, "I would like to add that I have been deeply impressed by everything that I have read about you, and particularly as a Hebrew scholar, by the true continuation of the Bible spirit in the Book of Mormon."

I will read one other simple sentence from a lovely woman who picked up a copy of the Book of Mormon and who wrote this: "I am reading with greatest delight the blessed truths contained in that book. I never dreamed that the Book of Mormon was like that; in fact, I thought hard things about it and you, for I received my information from articles in secular magazines. I belong to another denomination, but how I rejoice to know the truth and drink in the precious words of men like Nephi and Mosiah and Alma." My heart rejoices, and I think to myself, how marvelous it is to be able to drink in the precious words of Nephi and Mosiah and Alma, and yet, how many Latter-day Saints have lived and died without ever having known them.

God bless us to appreciate, to understand what the scriptures say. Hear the Lord's word recorded in the Doctrine and Covenants:

> For what doth it profit a man if a gift is bestowed upon him, and he receive not the gift? Behold, he rejoices not in that which is given unto him, neither rejoices in him who is the giver of the gift. (D&C 88:33.)

God help us to appreciate the monuments around us. God bless us that we may have sense enough, faith enough, courage enough, to understand that there are marvelous truths that we might possess, but which we must individually earn anew if we would have them.

Holy Books

At Dachau just outside Munich, Germany, there stands a rather unusual memorial—a kind of monument to man's inhumanity. The concentration camp is maintained about as it was during the tragic and infamous days when scores of thousands of human beings were kenneled and tortured and put to death, then cremated in gas ovens. It is all there still—the blood trench alongside which men were lined up to be shot, the tower upon which they were stood for public torture, some of the miserable barracks in which they were kept like animals in a zoo, and worst of all, the two buildings housing those three terrible gas ovens with the "showers" alongside, out of which came death-dealing gas instead of cleansing water. The showers prepared them for the ovens, the ovens burned them like tinder. It is all too terrible and too tragic and too disquieting to others of the species of those who suffered and of those who caused them to suffer.

The trip to Dachau, with all the tragedy and turmoil and unnerving sense of guilt, is made worthwhile by reminiscences of the heroism that occurred there to balance the hideousness, and by a small pamphlet written by a rare man who survived Dachau. In it is a memorable sentence that one who reads it will not likely forget: *Man cannot trust himself in the hands of man.*

Article published in the *Improvement Era*, November 1968.

35

A generation after Dachau, humankind finds itself in a situation even more threatening than the infamies of World War II. Individuals and nations need answers to the dilemmas of the human predicament. On the one hand, unbelievable advances in human knowledge, inconceivable promises of power and capacity to bless; on the other hand, wars and contentions and slaughterings and threatenings and tensions and conflicts among men who cannot trust themselves in the hands of other men.

Where shall we look for the answers?

Will they be found in the thoughts and solutions offered by the minds of men? Is there a surer source? If so, what is it?

The inmates of Dachau had seen a certain kind of man— man minus a sense of responsibility to conscience, to other men, to God. To such men, the strong were the rulers, the *keepers* of the zoo in which others could be treated like the *occupants* of a zoo. No one can trust himself in the political or personal hands of such men.

Most individuals are more humanely and ethically disposed toward their fellowmen. Humanity struggles to lift itself from its baser ways. Men seek to lift their eyes and to help others to do so.

One aspect of this earnest effort is the flood of books pouring from the presses into the hands of those eager to buy them and gain insight and strength from them. There are books on how to develop the mind and the body and the spirit, how to live with self-forgetfulness or self-esteem, how to win friends, how to wake up the mind or bring it power or bring it peace, how to accept oneself, how to give of oneself, how to believe, how to be happy, how to find security, how to pray, how to love. There are books in number almost beyond comprehension, some of them good and helpful and constructive.

The best of these books either borrow from or allude to or build upon the teachings of other books—a select few mostly contained between two covers and called collectively the Holy Bible. This "divine library" is augmented for us by other sacred books—the Book of Mormon, the Doctrine and Covenants, the Pearl of Great Price. Is it not curious that these few volumes, available to almost everyone, are so seldom read and often so little appreciated? Yet in them are more than the words and thoughts and suggestions of men. In them are the teachings, the truths, of God, the accounts of his dealings with his children and of his compassion and concern and love for them.

What importance have the scriptures for us? How much do we read them? How much do we learn from them? How well do we understand them? Many of us who have them or have access to them do not read them. Others have never learned *how* to read and understand them. Frequently we lack knowledge and appreciation of them. Some know certain verses or stories but do not know the context from which they come or the circumstances under which they were written or the purposes for which they were provided.

Why should we read the scriptures? What do they have for us? How can they help? How can we learn to love and understand them? How did they come to be? How should they be read?

The scriptures were not written especially for scholars and were not meant to be textbooks. They *do* have unrivaled instruction and insight to offer in philosophy, ethics, and human relations; they have wonderful poetry and marvelous history and significant theology and the most sententious proverbs. Yet the primary purpose of the scriptures is not in any of these. They were written for common people, for their spiritual guidance. Their message is of God and his relationship with his children. They are religious books presenting the faith, the aspirations, and the experiences of God's children through the centuries. They are important for their message of God's love and concern and compassion for his people. They hold God and man in "one thought at one time, at all times." They teach of God's involvement in the human situation and of man's meaning in the light of God's relationship with him. God and man together is the focus of the scriptural objective.

President Joseph F. Smith gave us pure insight into the purpose and product of personal acquaintance with the scriptures:

> That which characterizes above all else the inspiration and divinity of the Scriptures is the spirit in which they are written and the spiritual wealth they convey to those who faithfully and conscientiously read them. Our attitude, therefore, toward the Scriptures should be in harmony with the purposes for which they are written.
>
> They are intended to enlarge man's spiritual endowments and to reveal and intensify the bond of relationship between him and his God. The Bible, as all other books of Holy Writ, to be appreciated must be studied by those spiritually inclined and who are in quest of spiritual truths. (*Juvenile Instructor,* April 1912, p. 204.)

The true blessing of the scriptures lies in bringing their "spiritual wealth," in enlarging our "spiritual endowments," and in their revelation and intensifying of the "bond of relationship between [us and our] God." To this President Brigham Young added an important dimension:

> On reading carefully the Old and New Testaments we can discover that the majority of the revelations given to mankind anciently were in regard to their daily duties; we follow in the same path. The revelations contained in the Bible and the Book of Mormon are ensamples to us, and the Book of Doctrine and Covenants contains direct revelation to this Church; they are a guide to us, and we do not wish to do them away; we do not wish them to become obsolete and to set them aside. We wish to continue in the revelations of the Lord Jesus Christ day by day, and to have His Spirit with us continually. If we can do this, we shall no more walk in darkness, but we shall walk in the light of life. (*Journal of Discourses,* 10:284.)

When Christ answered the cynical question of the Sadducees concerning marriage in the resurrection—a resurrection in which they professed no belief—he said to them that which has great meaning for all men: "Ye do err, not knowing the scriptures." (Matthew 22:29.)

All of us err, not knowing the scriptures. The writings of the prophets have great relevance to us and our time. They were written under other circumstances in other times, but every era, every nation, every generation, and every man is included in the scriptures. Thus, every question, counsel, admonition, instruction, commandment, and promise may have importance for modern man—to each and every one of us. God asked Adam, "Where art thou?" (Genesis 3:9.) So does he ask us today where we are in our lives and relationships.

In the scriptures are counsels for our every problem, answers to our every need. Across the barriers of many ages and many translations comes the message of current meaning to contemporary man.

In the scriptures the truth is taught about God and Christ and man and his relationship with the Father and the Son. Learning these truths can be and is meant to be a fascinating adventure. Nothing in this world could be more precious than to have a personal testimony of Almighty God, of his holy Son, and of the restoration and leadership of his gospel plan by holy prophets chosen under his inspiration and leading under his guidance. Read the words attributed to Joseph Smith, written in 1832 and recorded in *Documentary History of the Church,* volume 1, pages 282-284:

> Search the Scriptures—search the revelations which we publish, and ask your Heavenly Father, in the name of his Son Jesus Christ, to manifest the truth unto you. . . . You will then know for yourselves and not for another. You will not then be dependent on man for the knowledge of God; nor will there be any room for speculation. . . . Wherefore, we again say, search the revelations of God; study the prophecies, and rejoice that God grants unto the world Seers and Prophets. . . . And, fellow sojourners upon earth, it is your privilege to purify yourselves and come up to the same glory and see for yourselves, and know for yourselves. Ask, and it shall be given you; seek, and ye shall find; knock, and it shall be opened unto you.

As to the Lord Jesus Christ, Peter taught the men of Israel that "all the prophets from Samuel and those that follow after, as many as have spoken," had written of the coming of the Christ and had looked forward to his advent. Thus in the beautiful prophetic visions of Isaiah and the Psalms and Job and throughout the Old Testament was the glory of his mission foreknown and faithfully foretold. Jacob in the Book of Mormon added his testimony that "all the holy prophets which were before us. . . . believed in Christ and worshiped the Father in his name." (Jacob 4:4-5.)

One of the most powerful scriptural testimonies of Christ is the account of the Lord's angel directing Philip to travel from Jerusalem unto Gaza, in obedience to which he came into the company of the Ethiopian eunuch who was reading Isaiah the prophet. Under the inspiration of the Spirit, Philip approached him and asked him if he understood what he read. The man invited Philip's guidance in giving him the meaning of the passage: "He is brought as a lamb to the slaughter, and as a sheep before her shearers is dumb, so he openeth not his mouth." (Isaiah 53:7; see also Acts 8:32.) "Then Philip opened his mouth, and began at the same scripture, and preached unto him Jesus." (Acts 8:35.) The result of this great experience was the baptism of the eunuch by Philip, and the redirection of a life.

Paul taught Timothy that the scriptures are "able to make thee wise unto salvation through faith which is in Christ Jesus." (2 Timothy 3:15.)

In the scriptures we are taught that man was in the beginning with God, and can, through the atonement of Christ and through his own faith, obedience, love, and righteous endurance, be with him again. We learn that the earth was created for man, and that he was put here to choose whether he will "subject himself to the devil" or "yield to the enticings of the Spirit."

Life is meaningful because it is eternal. Man is God's child and has within him embryonically the qualities of his

Father. Christ is the divine Savior. God is the father of the spirits of all men, our eternal Heavenly Father. God's plan for his children is revealed as a "plan of redemption," a "plan of mercy," a "plan of happiness." His children, eternal persons, are blessed with mortal life and agency therein and a condition of opposition in which choices are made, with "all to win or all to lose." A Savior was commissioned and prophets called to teach us through love and to die for us. Man, blessed with divine heritage, granted a period of development in the stream of mortal experience, has infinite possibilities and the ultimate chance, if he will, to live with God, cooperating with him in his great creative work. This, through search and service and reverence, a man may learn and is here on earth to learn. The scriptures and the prophets are his guide to knowledge, inspiration and reproof.

The theology of the scriptures is blended with the great religious lessons that lead to feeling and doing and living. Man's love for and relationship to God is wedded to man's concern for and brotherhood to all men. Spirituality and morality meet in their message. They are written not alone to teach man what is true, but how to live, and to help gain the spiritual witness to know for himself what is true and to live as he should live.

For those who have read in times past and remember with joy but have kept no current acquaintance with the sacred works, the question of Alma to his people is supremely important. Reminding them of the goodness of the Lord to their fathers and to them, and of the feeling and faith that had come to them through the marvelous forgiveness of God, he asked them, as it is recorded in Alma 5:26, *"Can ye feel so now?"*

We need to keep current and to keep concerned and to keep qualified in the things of God. To read of his relationship with people in other times and other places is to learn principles and lessons that are appropriate and can be applied to us and our daily experience. To hear the assurances of his love and his mercy to wavering, wayward children long ago strengthens us in our knowledge that he loves and wants us to enjoy his blessings in our time and in our special circumstances. We need again the strength of his commandments and to feel in ourselves the capacity to obey, to meet his demands, to do his will. This is what we need, what in our quieter moments we know we want, and what we must have if we are to truly be his sons and daughters and to enjoy his eternal companionship and counsel as we labor with him in accomplishing his creative work.

Our study of the gospel and of the scriptures when we were "young," when we were on a mission, five years ago, or even a year ago, is not enough. There is, as someone has said, "something in the air." There is a living, revealing, communicating God. There is a living prophet. Life is full of change and experiences and adventures. Every day brings its relentless demands and its limitless opportunities. We have lived a little longer, thought more, wept in desperation or sorrow or apprehension, prayed earnestly, learned to love more deeply. We need the current companionship of the sweetest and most gracious and godly One who ever lived. We need the assurance that comes with the reading anew of the problems he faced, the tragedies he endured, the patience and forgiveness and love he manifested in times of trial. We need to think again of his triumph and his purposes for us. We need refreshment in the knowledge of the goodness of God and of his matchless power. We need an increase in our faith, in our courage to repent, our capacity to obey, and our sensitivity to the Spirit.

These and manifold blessings more we may gain as we turn again to the scriptures and turn from them with a greater light and a greater sense of responsibility and capacity to share the message of the plan of happiness.

Men can trust themselves in the hands of God, and to the leadership of men who serve as God's appointed agents, who teach and lead and testify under the motivations of the Almighty. Our need is to know the will of God, what he has done, what he wants. In this knowledge, and not in the opinions of men, is our safe and sure way.

In the visions of Lehi and Nephi, those who reached the tree of the love of God and tasted the fruit, having traveled through many hours of darkness, appreciated the sweet blessing and sought immediately to share it with God's other loved children. This is the spirit of the scriptures and the gospel. This is the challenge and possibility of every man who lives as they lived of old, imperfectly, to be sure, and struggling to keep the Spirit, but able through consistent attendance to the word of God in the scriptures, and to the application of the timeless truths therein, to find the direction and the strength and the faith to accomplish God's purposes for him.

Relief Society Mother

A child's kiss
Set on thy sighing lips shall make thee glad;
A poor man served by thee shall make thee rich;
A sick man helped by thee shall make thee strong;
Thou shalt be served thyself by every sense
Of service which thou renderest.

(Elizabeth Barrett Browning.)

Happy he
With such a Mother! Faith in womankind
Beats with his blood, and trust in all things high
Comes easy to him; and though he trip and fall,
He shall not blind his soul with clay.
(Happy he with such a Mother!)

(Tennyson.)

It is not always possible to look into our lives and specifically identify and credit, as to origin, lessons learned and influences felt and inspiration received from individuals and incidents and institutions. Perhaps many of us acknowledge gratefully the effect and impact in our lives of some fine teacher or friend or leader, without being able to recall any specific lesson or idea that he or she taught us. Some of us remember some particular class we participated in for a period, out of which we came humbler, wiser, more dedicated individuals—without recalling a single specific example of

Article published in the *Relief Society Magazine*, September 1955.

the lessons or experiences which so affected us. Yet most (if not all) of us recognize the great influential effect in our lives of certain people and experiences and activities and organizations. So it is with my life and the influence of Relief Society in my mother's home: some few specific aspects of its strength I can now clearly see and remember; but this great auxiliary organization had a wider and more important meaning in our home than any certain set of lessons or experiences would seem adequate to indicate. This has been true, I am sure (and is today and will always be), in countless other homes where the wonderful influence of this prophetically established organization has been felt.

Some time ago I visited my mother and found her chuckling over an entry she was reading from the minutes of a Relief Society meeting held June 11, 1887. Having been involved in Relief Society work all the adult years of her life, as a member, literary and social science class leader, ward president for six depression years, stake board member, stake president for ten years, and, now again, as a faithful member, Mother has maintained a lively interest in the organization and all its activities. The entry she was reading in the 1887 minute book follows:

> Sister Z. Smith said they were choice spirits that came to these meetings to be fed and urged all the sisters to arise to their feet and they would obtain a blessing.
>
> Sister Watmough advised the sisters to live nearer the Lord and thereby regain His presence. She said when the earth's foundations were laid "the sons of God shouted for joy," but no mention was made of the sisters being there. "Let us do our duty and get along the side of the sons," she said.
>
> Sister Stevenson arose to correct the quotation referred to by Sister Watmough. She said: " 'The morning stars sang and the sons of God shouted for joy.' Sisters, *we* were the morning stars and *we were there* when the foundations of the earth were laid."

This priceless and very humorous exchange might well be taken as indicative of the understanding and faith the wonderful women of the Relief Society have always had in the Church and gospel of Jesus Christ. The faithful women of the Church know that while the priesthood is conferred upon the men, the highest blessings of the priesthood can only be shared by man and woman together: "Neither is the man without the woman, neither the woman without the man, in the Lord." (1 Corinthians 11:11.) The woman's place in the Church is by the side of her husband, neither superior to him nor subservient to him. She might well be thought to be the "morning star" in the lives of her husband and family.

What an incalculable boon it would be to the full realization of the Lord's purposes for the Church and its people if every mother in the Church would understand and accept the responsibility of gaining a personal knowledge of the principles of the gospel, and a personal testimony of their truthfulness and divine origin, and then set about prayerfully and faithfully to live them and teach them to her children. It was the Prophet Joseph who said: "The Ladies' Relief Society is not only to relieve the poor, but to save souls." (*Documentary History of the Church*, Vol. V, p. 25.) I am grateful beyond expression that my mother had the wisdom and inspiration to know that her own dedication to learning and living the gospel were vital to the faith of her children. The basic Relief Society objectives of developing faith, of studying and teaching the gospel, of participating in the full program of the Church were implicit in her home. Widowed early in life, with six minor children, ill herself, she found strength and courage in her faith in God and his revealed truths, and reared her family in the light of them. When outside influences and temptations beset some of us, her firmness and faith and high expectations for us helped to combat them; when some of us sometimes fell short of what we ought to have been, her calm courage and confidence in us helped to regain the ground.

While I remember Mother studying the gospel and preparing to teach its principles in her Relief Society and MIA classes, I do not now recall any specific occasions when we discussed them (though I am sure we did in our home evenings). I do not remember ever hearing, for instance, a specific *discussion* on the principle of faith at home, but I will never forget the *lessons* of faith I learned there. I could not have been more than three or four when my sainted father came back to visit Mother and me as I slept in my little bed alongside hers. It was a time of deep difficulty and he had come to give encouragement and love. We talked the next morning of his visit, and there was no question in either mind that he had been there; each of us saw him and heard him and remembered what he said. Probably I was not yet five when a serious illness brought us to Mother's bedside in the early morning hours. The first order of activity was to kneel there and pray to our Heavenly Father; the second was to run for our neighbor, Brother Kotter, to come to administer to her; the third was to discuss whether a doctor should be called.

My first lesson in repentance and forgiveness I learned on Mother's lap, sobbing out a confession of some childish misdeed, observing her sorrow and disappointment, and feeling the warmth of her love and the gentleness of her heart in her pardon.

Among other truths we learned from our mother was a firsthand lesson on honoring our parents. Mother's own pioneer mother came to live in our home the last years of her life. There was some talk from others outside the home about civic or other welfare assistance, and very little personal concern from some who should have been concerned. There was sometimes foolish (and now deeply lamented) youthful intolerance of Grandmother's problems and difficulties. But none of this came from Mother, the one who bore most of the burden. She truly honored her mother in health and in sickness, in happiness and in very trying circumstances. This lesson I'm sure I shall not forget nor cease being grateful for. As to obedience to the Lord's commandments, as to Church activity, as to courage, to us our mother's own life has always been the most impressive lesson available.

And how did the Relief Society program help in our home? The Relief Society would have all of its members "care for the poor, the sick, and the unfortunate," and "minister where death reigns." Just how important would it be to our Father in heaven and to our brother men to have this ideal realized in the lives of his children? I'm sure that countless homes of Relief Society workers reflect my own appreciation for learning this lesson. I could not number the hours nor occasions of friendship and loving sympathy given the ill, the sorrowing, the needy or fearful, the bereaved. Nor could I put a price on the worth of observing, as a youth, the activation of this ideal. My first remembered lesson in unselfishness came with my weekly commission to carry a plate of warm dinner from our Sunday table up to old Sister Olsen on the corner, a plate usually prepared before our own meal was undertaken. Awareness that even the humblest and most modest of homes and individuals have something very vital to share with others came as, in her Relief Society and other Church work, Mother daily gave freely of her love, faith, deep sympathy and understanding, of her encouragement and kindness, and of her meager material supply.

One of the goals and objectives of the Relief Society organization is to "foster love for religion, education, culture, and refinement" in the lives of its members and all whom it touches. How wonderfully important this ideal should be in every LDS home! Every complete life needs the direction and inspiration of religious truth, needs to be acquainted with the working areas of civics and political thought, needs the soul-lifting touch of wonderful literature and music. How grateful I am for the Relief Society work my mother did in teaching literature and social science! I first heard of Longfellow and Hawthorne, of Shelley, Keats, Byron, and Shakespeare through her studies. My first acquaintance with the names of Sir Walter Scott, of Lewis and Clark, of Sacajawea, came around the table as she talked of her lesson work. My first efforts to write poetry were based on her lovely poems, stimulated by her Relief Society labors. (As a little boy I once insulted a less literary minded four-year-old playmate by calling him "James Whitcomb Riley," a name I'd learned from a Relief Society lesson but which he thought was an epithet!)

The Lord has told us that the "fulness of the earth" (all those things which he has provided for our "benefit and use") is given us "both . . . . to strengthen the body and to *enliven the soul*." (D&C 59:16, 18-19.) No life is really full which gives entire emphasis to material things and ignores the beautiful and cultural and inspirational in the world. No home meets its full opportunity which fails to awaken its inhabitants to an appreciation of these things; and it would seem to me that a mother does not meet the full possibilities of her parenthood who makes no effort to open the lives of her children to an enjoyment of them. Possibly no organization in the Church is more awake to its responsibilities in the realm of the beautiful and cultural than the Relief Society.

Some of the earliest and clearest memories of my youth are of the (to me, then) impossibly intricate quilts taking form on the quilting frames in our front room, with the ladies chatting happily as they painstakingly stitched the patterns. I remember, too, the rugs that were sewed and woven, the old phonograph records that were heated and softened and molded into trays and dishes, the cloth and paper and wire flowers that were fashioned, the piano-bench cover and the chair seats that were sewed or done in needlepoint, the vases that were made out of bottles covered with numerous bits of the lining of Christmas card envelopes and shellacked. These early lessons in beauty included, too, the musical duets and choruses being practiced around our piano, and the sight and smell of bread and cookies and pies and cakes and chili made for the ward dinners and bazaars, where we each proudly identified our own mother's pies and her aprons and handiwork as they hung on display.

Would any mother be unaware of the importance of these activities in building a love of beauty and creativeness in the lives of her children? The poet Saadi said:

> If of thy mortal goods thou art bereft,
> And of thy meager store

> Two loaves alone to thee are left,
> Sell one, and with the dole
> Buy hyacinths to feed thy soul.

God's gifts to man, he said, are to "strengthen the body and to enliven the soul."

A member of the Relief Society fully meeting the challenge of the organization's objectives would be diligently engaged in seeking "to assist in correcting the morals and strengthening the virtues of community life." She would be studying the story of her country's and community's institutions and would insist upon being a participating citizen, and urge her children to do likewise. She would be interested in all candidates for office, and might become one herself. The effect of consistent attention to the Relief Society social science lessons over the past years would be to supply a remarkable education in the basic documents and institutions of our country and our society. (The practical effect of Relief Society's stimulus to civic responsibility was to move me, at the age of eight, to leave a ladies' political caucus in our front room and go to a typewriter to prepare a personal ballot on which I indicated my preference for one of the then candidates for the presidency of our country!)

Does one really wonder how much the attitude of a parent toward mankind influences a child in his later relationships? One basic Relief Society objective is "to manifest benevolence, irrespective of creed or nationality." I will not forget an experience of a few years ago when I tried, unsuccessfully, to find public accommodations in our city for three fine, clean, educated Negro boys who were visitors to Temple Square as members of a college choir. All efforts having failed, I called my mother and found, as I expected, no hesitancy in her at all as she offered her home for the use of the boys during their stay, and came herself to share our tiny apartment while they lived in her home. The young men discovered a benevolence and a Christian kindness in her act which made them truly love her and which stimulated in them, as it has done in me, a greater desire to be a brother to all men.

Our home was a very average and humble one—no one us would ever think to suggest otherwise—and we were all average children. But our home (like countless other Latter-day Saint homes) and our lives (like the lives of countless other Latter-day Saint children) were greatly blessed and affected by the influence of the wonderful program of the Relief Society.

What a blessing would come to the Lord's children and his Church if every Latter-day Saint woman were to carry into her home and make available to her family the religious, educational, cultural, social, and humanitarian program of this inspired organization, the Relief Society of The Church of Jesus Christ of Latter-day Saints!

Happy the home and fortunate the child . . . with such a mother!

II.
Give
Concern

The individual is the focal point of all the program and performance of the Church—not the program itself, not the statistics. Not institutional expansion but individual exaltation is the purpose of it all.

Person to Person

Three recent experiences form the core of my message this morning. I would like to relate them briefly.

In the northwestern area of the United States an alert young adult, who is actively involved in his own church, attended an open house at a new Mormon Church structure with a friend. He was respectfully responsive as he viewed the lovely chapel where our people worship, and then became increasingly interested as he was conducted through the rest of the building. He saw the cultural hall where drama and music and recreational dancing and sports activities are enjoyed; he saw the Scout room and the Junior Sunday School, the classrooms where we learn and teach. He was shown photographs of missionaries at their work across the world, of a baptism, of a family home evening where parents and children were pictured in counsel, at prayer, and at play. He listened to the principles of temple marriage—this uniting of a couple and a family for time and eternity. He heard about the priesthood and its importance as a man presides in love as the head of his home, and teaches and blesses his family.

Finally, he stopped at the lovely Relief Society room where he heard the story of the honored role of women in their homes and in the Church and where he heard one of the ladies who was explaining the program that evening refer to another

Address given at General Conference, October 1970.

55

as "sister." He inquired about this and was told that in the Church a woman is often called "sister" as a man is called "brother."

The visitor shook his head in wonderment and said, "Every woman a sister, every man a priest, and every home a sanctuary in itself."

Last week a wonderful young lady just beginning her university training talked with me about her experience as a youth representative on governmental agencies studying problems of young people who have been involved with drugs. Earnestly and often tearfully she related the feelings she had had as she learned about the breadth of this problem in various cities across America, and as she had discussed it not only in the council room with experts from various disciplines but on the streets, in the communes, in custodial and treatment centers, and in many personal conversations with disaffected young people. She repeated some of what she had heard from these alienated and confused and fearful youngsters, of heartbreaking scenes and troubles. "And what about you?" I asked her. "What has this done to you? What did you have to say to them?"

Through the tears and the sweet compassion and concern came answers I can only abstract this morning. "I've never been so grateful," she said. "I found myself talking about the things I've been learning all my life—the importance of faith in God, of genuine concern for others; of commitment to Christ; the need for goals, for work, for prayer; the significance of a self-image based on self-discipline, responsible relationships, worthwhile accomplishments, rather than on the temporary, the trivial, the tainted."

Many of them, she said, were critical of their parents and the older generation, and I found myself wondering what their descendants would have to thank some of them for.

The third incident involved two young men, one a young American born in Mexico who had started ninth grade at the age of nineteen while still a migrant farm worker, the other a part-Indian, born in a small village near the reservation where many of his relatives lived. Both of them are handsome, articulate, exuding strength and sincerity and a sense of urgency. Each is pursuing advanced university training, each is working to serve the special needs of those with whom he shares proud heritage.

The two were interviewed separately by a civic committee seeking help from them in understanding the problems of their people and offering possible solutions. Each answered searching questions knowledgeably, effectively, earnestly. When asked what could be done to help, each responded repeatedly and firmly that what his people need is not handouts but *opportunities,* equal opportunities in order that through their own efforts they can reach the goal. They will do the rest themselves. Both pointed to faith in God and a religious commitment as basic needs of their people, and each explained that active involvement in The Church of Jesus Christ of Latter-day Saints is the key to his own growth and development. How had this blessing come about?

To the young Mexican-American, it was through a school administrator in a small LDS community in Nevada where the verbal answers concerning salvation and redemption through Christ had been personalized into the *experience* of kindness and concern and contagious love. There the young man had found not only the answers which gave meaning to life, but direction and inspiration and purpose in living it. The love he found came not chiefly from books or sermons or lessons, but from *persons* in a community of saints who were able and willing to give it.

For the part-Indian, it had been a man living next door, a Mormon bishop whose interest and kindness had opened his heart and his home to this youngster. There he found acceptance and affection and unconditional love. Theological answers the little boy was not prepared to understand; loving concern he could readily comprehend. Through the life of a good man he learned to care about and to know Christ.

To summarize these three incidents, then, the man who visited the church building in the northwest only dimly understood on first contact much of what he saw, but he had caught a glimpse of what can be.

The lovely girl to whom I listened had found many who had no consciousness at all of being children of God, who were frantically trying to arrange, in the words of a wise observer, "some acceptable horizontal relationship with their social environment," instead of seeking to establish a "supremely important vertical relationship with God." She learned again the importance of the principles of Christ.

The two young men had seen those principles applied and had accepted them.

There are many strong efforts in the Church to bring the principles of the gospel of Jesus Christ and the full impact of his Church into the lives of its members and all who will participate. A number of these have gained wide attention and respect: the youth and welfare programs, the family home evening, military relations activities, Indian placement. In educational effort, missionary work, genealogical undertakings, home teaching, student wards and stakes, and other correlated efforts, the Church is effectively serving the Lord's children.

All of these are praiseworthy endeavors, but we are clearly aware that it is not the programs of the Church themselves that save; yet it is often *through* the programs that the love and graciousness of God are expressed and communicated.

As I think of the wide efforts of our people in these various ways, three other related words come to mind of which, with their meanings, we must continually remind ourselves. If we had a giant chalkboard upon which I could write, I would like to print in large letters three words: OBJECTIVES. PRINCIPLES. SPIRIT. I will comment briefly about them.

Objectives

Recently we have been discussing throughout the stakes of the Church the great effort currently being made to keep closely in touch with our young men in the military forces, to prepare them for the experiences they face in military service away from home. Always as we discuss the operation and mechanics of this important activity, we are asking ourselves the meaning of it, the purpose and goal for which it has been established.

The answer is in the boy sitting against the bulkhead of the Navy ship reading a letter from his bishop or from his quorum at home. It is in the young man wading through the red dust of Takhli or Nakhon Phanom or the heat or rain of the Delta to get to his group meeting with three or four or a dozen other members of the Church, to partake of the sacrament of the Lord's Supper and to participate in the worship service that will strengthen him against envelopment by the hollow world around him.

In the Church's educational effort, the objective is the young man or woman surrounded by issues and pressures and voices of unwisdom, needing the stabilizing strength of the Lord and the companionship of others who know the way.

In the priesthood quorums, the objective is those who are accounted for, and the prodigal; in the auxiliaries, every available individual. What was quoted this morning? The work and glory of God is to bring to pass the immortality and eternal life of man.

In every effort of the Church, the purpose is to tie in God's children to his community and kingdom; to bless the individual with a knowledge of his origins and heritage, a sense of his purpose and a plan to fulfill it, and a vision of his eternal potential. It is to strengthen and qualify God's children in the application of the eternal principles we have been discussing here; to learn and to serve, to grow and to give. It is to help him face the burning, urgent problems of the moment, grateful for his relationship with God and for the great marvel of being alive to the richness of life; to revere God who expects and demands something important of him.

The objective of it all then is not counting the sheep, but feeding them; not the proliferation of buildings or units or organizations or statistics, but the blessing of the individual child of God.

We know Christ had a great interest in human beings of every description, and great love for them. He companied with little children, sought out the sinner; he summoned men to follow him from the fishing boat and the counting table. So conscious was he of individuals that in the midst of the multitude he felt the woman's touch of his robe. He memorialized in a magnificent parable the selfless consideration of a despised Samaritan toward another human being in need. He enfolded the ninety and nine and went seeking the lost one. Our purpose is to follow him.

Principles

And what of principles?

What are the principles through which we can help God's children to realize his purposes for them? We can start—and almost end—with love. "God so loved the world, that he gave his only begotten Son, that whosoever believeth in him should not perish, but have everlasting life." (John 3:16.) Christ so loved God and God's other children that he willingly undertook his pivotal part in the great plan of salvation, knowing what it meant, what it was going to cost. Another special son, brilliant (the scriptures call him "an authority in the presence of God"), but lacking love except for self, disdained the Father's plan and rebelled against it. He had strong opinions of his own; he contrived some rules of his own, seemed to feel his Father's way inefficient and ineffective. He rebelled, and misled and led away a multitude of his Father's children. Christ loved his Father and desired to do his Father's will. He used his agency to willingly accept the responsibility to open the door to salvation and to eternal life to every individual child of God who would give his heart to God and manifest his acceptance of the gift and his love of the giver by obeying his commandments.

Tillich has spoken of God's love as "ultimate concern"— that is, that God cares about us as much as can be. We are here to learn to care that much about each other.

I often think of the young bishop who, against pressures and problems and at considerable inconvenience, traveled to another city to visit a bereaved widow on the eve of her husband's funeral. The couple had long since moved from the bishop's area, but he had made the effort to be with his good, wonderful old friends at this tender time. He found the elderly lady standing alone beside the body of her beloved of more than half a century. As he comforted her, she said through her tears, "Oh bishop, I knew *you* would come."

Every child of God needs and wants love.

The principle of agency must be mentioned, too, of course, for not even through love can one against his will be conveyed to useful, constructive living or to eternal creative life. Each must individually choose that destination and qualify for it.

Spirit

The third word is *spirit*. In what spirit must we act to help our brother achieve God's purposes for him? Paul, who knew remorse as perhaps few men have, said to the Galatians:

> Brethren, if a man be overtaken in a fault, ye which are spiritual, restore such an one in the spirit of meekness; considering thyself, lest thou also be tempted. Bear ye one another's burdens, and so fulfil the law of Christ. For if a man think himself to be something, when he is nothing, he deceiveth himself. (Galatians 6:1-3.)

Alma, who also knew error and remorse, prayed for the apostate Zoramites: "Behold, O Lord, their souls are precious, and many of them are our brethren; therefore, give

61

unto us, O Lord, power and wisdom that we may bring these, our brethren, again unto thee." (Alma 31:35.)

The programs of the Church are important—but they are not ends in themselves. They permit organized efforts to be made to reach and bless the individual. They are designed to help God's children to achieve the purposes of the Lord for them, to operate in the principle of real love, to be implemented in the spirit of compassion and contrition. They are to help us bear one another's burdens and thus fulfil the law of Christ.

One of the major problems of our time is loneliness—the insecurity and anxiety that come with separation from God, and from one's fellowmen, and from a sense of alienation from self. The source of reconciliation and wholeness is Jesus Christ. The function of the true Church of Christ is to provide for the individual that concerned, loving, accepting, forgiving community, animated by the Spirit of Christ, in which the individual can find a place, establish true friendships, and gain confidence in God's presence.

Through it every woman will have opportunity ultimately to become what the most fortunate of women are blessed to be in this world—the heart of a loving home. Every man may be a true priest of God in his own home. And every home may be a true sanctuary where the love of God may dwell and where the Spirit of God is.

It is important to learn and apply the programs of the Church—they are great and wonderful and inspired and effective—but the only way this can truly be achieved is with a constant understanding of the objectives for which a program exists, of the principles which apply, and of the Spirit which must be present in those who are called to serve and lead.

In our Father's house are many mansions, and a place for each of his children who will qualify. Our assignment is to accept God's gift and know that we are accepted, and to seek to share the warmth of his love and the power of his example with all who will heed his call.

Souls in Jeopardy

Yesterday President Romney referred to chapter 27 of 3 Nephi in recalling the Lord's admonition to name his Church after him. Subsequently, in that same marvelous chapter Christ defined his gospel in some beautiful and, to me, eternally significant words: "Behold, I have given unto you my gospel, and this is the gospel which I have given unto you— that I came into the world to do the will of my Father, because my Father sent me." (3 Nephi 27:13.)

It is my earnest conviction that we came here for the same reason. Christ expresses his understanding of the will of his Father and his own commission in these words which follow:

> And my Father sent me that I might be lifted up upon the cross; and after that I had been lifted up upon the cross, that I might draw all men unto me, that as I have been lifted up by men even so should men be lifted up by the Father, to stand before me, to be judged of their works, whether they be good or whether they be evil—and for this cause have I been lifted up. (3 Nephi 27:14, 15.)

And then the Master taught what we know to be the first principles and ordinances of the gospel, concluding as he had begun, "Verily, verily, I say unto you, this is my gospel." (3 Nephi 27:21.) Then he added: "Therefore, what manner of

Address given at General Conference, October 1972.

men ought ye to be? Verily I say unto you, even as I am." (3 Nephi 27:27.)

Christ's commission was clear, and it seems to me that through him our commission becomes clear, that we are so to live that through him and his love we may be lifted up by the Father to enjoy the consequences of our convictions and our decisions.

We are here to love God and to keep his commandments, to live with an integrity that will merit our own self-respect and the respect of our loved ones, and make us worthy for the companionship of the Spirit. We are here to love and serve our fellowmen, to reflect in our own lives daily our true convictions as to the priceless value of the individual child of God, to live with joy in a way worthy of the sons of God, to become the manner of men he is.

He taught us very clearly the worth of souls and that they are very great in the sight of God. The lost sheep should have an anxious shepherd seeking him. The lost coin must be searched for. The prodigal who comes to himself and turns homeward will find his Father running to meet him. Thus taught the Lord.

Perhaps not all of us understand and apply this principle effectively, but there are those who do. Recently a stake president told of his visit, with others, to a Junior Sunday School class. When the visitors entered, they were made welcome, and the teacher, seeking to impress the significance of the experience for the youngsters, said to a little child on the front row, "How many important people are here today?" The child rose and began counting out loud, reaching a total of seventeen, including every person in the room! There were seventeen very important persons there that day, children and visitors!

That is how Christ feels, and so should we.

We are all aware that many valuable souls are in jeopardy these days. Many sheep are wandering, many coins are being dropped, many young prodigals have left home and are wasting their inheritance. In substantially every community across the earth, there are those who are cynically trading in filth, mining gold from dirt. They press pornography and drugs and destructive behavior. They seek to beguile unstable souls, as the scriptures warn.

> For when they speak great swelling words of vanity, they allure through the lusts of the flesh, through much wantonness, those that were clean escaped from them who live in error. While they promise them liberty, they themselves are the servants of corruption. (2 Peter 2:18-19.)

Some other adults are not wise or sensitive to the needs of the young, or are guilty of cowardice masquerading as enlightenment and liberalism, or are indifferent.

Unfortunately, too many young people surrender to the enticements and arguments, often, perhaps, because they never get a chance to see or experience the happier, purposeful, more excellent way. Some have no experience with a loving home, or concerned, loving parents, or a unified, happy family. Not knowing, or choosing immaturely against knowledge, they make bad decisions, and commit themselves to courses that are destructive.

The marvel to me is how many choice young people see through the mists and choose a wiser way. Some of them do this even though they have not had the benefit of a good home and family and parents who care and try. Somehow they are wise enough to take a stand against the crowd or the current, even when the source of the pressure seems respectable and when those who should care seem not to care.

There are many great young people. One who comes to mind was a well-dressed, good-looking young man, sharp, well-spoken and contemporary in every constructive way, but he was obviously deeply distressed as he rose to offer a greeting in behalf of the university student body of which he was president. His audience was made up of regents and

trustees of institutions of higher education meeting in conference at his school. The group had listened to a series of
speeches from educators noting with approval the abandon-
ment on college and university campuses of the doctrine of
in loco parentis, a term which means, as you may know,
"standing in the place of a parent." The schools, the speakers
said, no longer accept the responsibility of standing in the
place of a parent to the students who attend them. Knowledge, intellect, reason—these are the goods with which these
institutions deal; the private life of the individual is not their
proper concern.

The young student president said what many of us were
thinking: "I've listened to your announcement of the aban-
donment of the principle of *in loco parentis,* and I feel there
is something you should know. If in fact the school is no longer
interested in or willing to fill that role, if it doesn't care
about us as persons, as good parents would care, that leaves
a great many of us with no parents at all anywhere."

No further explanation was made, and none was needed.

As pressures in our communities have intensified for
the young, so life on many college campuses has undergone
a great transformation in the last decade, not so much in
the classroom or curriculum as in the nature of student life out
of class. While a few activists have had the chief attention,
every student in the affected schools has been influenced by
the breakdown of the rules that once governed the lives of
undergraduates. Only a few years ago, most colleges made a
vigorous effort to enforce regulations governing dormitory
standards and hours, student dress, sexual behavior, drinking
and chaperonage. Now in many institutions all of this has
changed. Revolutionary and rebellious behavior seems to have
toned down, but many rules formerly enforced have all but
disappeared.

What is likely to happen to inexperienced young persons
dropped into such a situation in the school or community?

There is a story which may offer significant insight. Outside Chattanooga, Tennessee, is a place known as Missionary Ridge. During the Civil War a numerically superior Southern force was dug in on the Ridge protecting it against Northern attack. The defenders were well fortified and strongly entrenched, holding strategic positions which would seem to make them invulnerable. Yet the hill was lost. Why? The soldiers on Missionary Ridge were so isolated from each other that they had lost touch with each other. They could not hear their leaders through the din. Plainly visible to them were the large numbers of the enemy coming up the hill to attack them. Feeling alone and frightened, a few individual defenders panicked and surrendered, and were soon joined by large numbers of their fellows. The battle was lost. They were not cowards; they thought they were alone.

How very parallel are some of the scenes of conflict we see going on around us! God's choice young sons and daughters are being subjected to the new social arrangements and pressures currently in vogue. Many are cut off from any supportive roots. They feel alone, abandoned, unloved. Some panic and surrender to the advancing enemy. They sin, and then let their sins become habits. What if they have no place to turn to for refuge, for strength, encouragement, instruction? What if they have no parents to whom they feel they can go for reassurance, forgiveness, unconditional love?

Oh, the implications are so clear for those of us who have been granted stewardship among the children of God—for parents, teachers and leaders, neighbors, concerned adults, advisors, home teachers!

Of late I have found myself thanking God more fervently than ever before for the gospel and the Church. I thank him for people and for programs which reach out to support parents and to bless young men and women like my choice young friend who felt that he had no parents any place. No young person who is truly involved in the warmth of the kingdom need ever feel that he has no place to go and no one who is genuinely concerned about him. No one of them should ever fall for the false proposition that a human being can have his mind unbraided from his heart, sinews, and spirit, the rest of him conveniently stored away while the mind is disciplined and filled like a silo with grains of knowledge, and then the whole braided together again with the expectation that the individual will now function in the moral, ethical, spiritually strong way we would like in our teacher or doctor or carpenter or lawyer or banker or son-in-law. None should be surrendered ever, unsupported, to circumstances which will certainly make much more difficult for them the enjoyment of those blessings that make life worth while— and I speak of good conscience, wholesome marriage and family and other human relationships, and the confidence we are entitled to have in the presence of God. "Character is higher than intellect," wrote Emerson. "Men must be fit to live as well as to think."

Of course, every young person must make his own decision and give his own answer. He must try to see the long view, and it is our responsibility to help him to see the moral hazards in the course that starts out to be fun and turns out to be artfully camouflaged trouble. "The way in is easy, the way out is hard," someone has said. The world is full of booby traps and pitfalls, with signs pointing to them which read, *This Way To The Fun House.* To meet the tests of the times, the young person must think, put down roots, establish wise loyalties, learn and actively appreciate his heritage, and know that he is ultimately responsible for his decisions.

My spirit today is one of gratitude, but not one of self-congratulation. How well are we doing with what we have, with what we know? I am only hours away from a sobering interview with another beautiful young person who has apparently experienced failure of relationship at every level— with family, friends, leaders, teachers—even with God, she felt. She seemed so alone in the presence of great pressures that she surrendered to the enemy for a time. Now she has some help. She has learned that Christ the Lord has the answer; she will be liberated because she is looking to him who is strengthening her in this and all things.

How tragic it would be if such a beautiful spirit were lost because one of us, one of God's stewards, fails in an assignment or relationship. Recently I recalled for a wonderful group of great young Latter-day Saints the thrilling story of Gideon of old, humble in the face of a seemingly insuperable challenge, but called of God, who through his resourcefulness and the strength of the Almighty, won a battle. His rallying cry is remembered: *"The sword of the Lord and of Gideon."* One other line from that marvelous story is so important that I call it to your attention: "They stood every man in his place round about the camp." (See Judges 7.) The battle was won.

Asa, king of Judah, commissioned of God to the conflict, facing an enemy army of more than a million soldiers, gave us the key. He said, "We rest on thee, and in thy name we go." (2 Chronicles 14:11.)

I thank God for the multitude of marvelous young people I know. I pray for them and invoke God's Spirit to be with them, and as plainly as I know how, and as earnestly, invoke God's Spirit to be upon us, the stewards. Let me repeat that beautiful line from a hymn, "How Firm a Foundation":

> The soul that on Jesus hath leaned for repose,
> I will not, I cannot, desert to his foes;
> That soul, though all hell should endeavor to shake,
> I'll never, no never, no never forsake!

The Apples in a Seed

During these conference sessions I have been thinking of you—you and your counterparts all over the Church, all over the world—you who do so much of the meaningful work of the Church in your own area and sector. I am sure that you, like I, will go home with the desire and determination, born of appreciation, to apply and make use of what has been said here.

Perhaps you will go home strengthened in two pivotal principles around which our efforts revolve. The first is provocatively expressed in a few words shared with me by a choice friend some time ago. I suspect you will remember them as I have. He said: "You can count the seeds in an apple, but can you count the apples in a seed?"

"The worth of souls is great in the sight of God." The worth of the individual soul is great in the sight of God, and in the lives of those who love God and seek to express this love through affectionate service to his children.

In order that we might cooperate with our Heavenly Father in his stated purpose to "bring to pass the immortality and eternal life of man," we have been blessed with the gospel, the Church, and the priesthood.

The gospel is God's plan for the exalting of man to an eternal creative opportunity with his Father through giving

Address given at General Conference, April 1966.

70

him a vision of his great origins and heritage, his purposes and responsibilities, and his inspiring potential.

The Church is the institutional embodiment of the gospel, the organization through which one may experience and express the great principles of God's plan.

The priesthood is the power by which God and his sons move in spiritual leadership. And all of these—gospel, Church, priesthood—are designed to bless man and bring about God's purposes for him.

The earth itself was prepared for man. "Behold, the Lord hath created the earth that it should be inhabited; and he hath created his children that they should possess it." (1 Nephi 17:36.)

The individual, then, is the focal point of all the program and performance of the Church—not the program itself, not the statistics. Not institutional expansion but individual exaltation is the purpose of it all.

The implications of the thought are clear: "You can count the seeds in an apple, but can you count the apples in a seed?" Every choice child of God is a link in a chain stretching from the past to the future. In the choice young people of the Church are the seeds of the future.

Do you know four lines that mean much to me?

> Nobody knows what a boy is worth,
>   We'll have to wait and see;
> But every man in a noble place
>   A boy once used to be.

Each boy and girl, and every adult also, is infinitely valuable. None is to be rejected, none written off, none neglected or left without the conscious concern of devoted brothers and sisters in the kingdom of God.

This leads, then, to the second basic conviction of which I have been thinking: Each of us has a solemn and significant responsibility to others of God's children, and the capacity to wholesomely and favorably influence them for good if we will. We are brothers to all men, and we have a special responsibility to those of our own household and to those in whose lives we may, by reason of our Church membership and by reason of responsibilities assigned us in the various organizations and programs of the Church, exert some important influence through love.

The organization of the Church is meant to make available to every individual, old and young, at every stage in his life, strong supportive friendships and leadership. From babyhood through the whole of life, every individual should have available always the friendship and sincere concern of a bishop and his counselors, of priesthood and auxiliary organization leaders and workers, of interested and loving family and friends and neighbors, relating under the special motivation and inspiration of the Lord through his Church. Every individual all of his life should be blessed in the Church by a program that involves the consistent concern of teachers—home teachers they are now called—who are assigned to a special relationship of interest and helpfulness.

In preparation for the imminent organization of the Church in 1830, the Lord revealed through the Prophet Joseph that his representatives holding the priesthood were to visit the homes of the members of the Church,

> exhorting them to pray vocally and in secret and attend to all family duties . . . to watch over the church always, and be with and strengthen them; and see that there is no iniquity in the church, neither hardness with each other, neither lying, backbiting, nor evil speaking; and see that the church meet together often, and also see that all the members do their duty. They are . . . to warn, expound, exhort, and teach, and invite all to come unto Christ. (D&C 20:51-59.)

As in the ancient Church, the members of the Church are to be

> remembered and nourished by the good word of God, to keep them in the right way, to keep them continually watchful unto

prayer, relying alone upon the merits of Christ, who was the author and the finisher of their faith. And [to] meet together oft, to fast and to pray, and to speak one with another concerning the welfare of their souls. (Moroni 6:4-5.)

To every person thus blessed by office or assignment or membership in the Church with the special responsibility of stewardship and concern in the lives of others, the Lord said:

Therefore, let every man stand in his own office, and labor in his own calling; and let not the head say unto the feet it hath no need of the feet; for without the feet how shall the body be able to stand? Also the body hath need of every member, that all may be edified together, that the system may be kept perfect." (D&C 84:109-110.)

Let me spend a few minutes illustrating the great importance of our responsibilities to each other under these sacred assignments from the Lord to be stewards in his kingdom.

In one of the stakes of the Church in another land, a lovely young lady left her home to live in another city where she had found employment. She was away from family and established friends and from the Church and its warm involvements. She didn't take occasion to look up the Church organization in the city to which she went, finding it easy for a time to avoid the customary associations of her Church membership. She formed other associations in the new city, and they were not the kind she had had at home. Gradually she began to become involved in another kind of attitude and another kind of behavior. She had not made serious mistakes, but had begun a way of living that would not have pleased her parents and that was not in the manner of her former life.

There came a night when, dressed in clothing which she might previously have been embarrassed to wear in public, perhaps harboring in her mind anticipations of conduct that she would not have even considered before, she waited for the arrival of some of her new friends. It was a critical hour in her life and a critical night in her life and she knew it. When she answered the knock at the door, she was surprised to find not those whom she was anticipating, but rather three adults whom she did not know. They identified themselves as the bishop and his counselor and the president of the Young Woman's Mutual Improvement Association. The bishop had received a letter from the bishop of the girl's home ward notifying him of the address and circumstances of his ward member in the new city. The bishop and his associates were calling to express their friendship and concern and to invite the young lady to the activities and associations of the Church in this town.

As she talked with them, she became embarrassed at her clothing, chagrined at the activities of the recent past and the anticipations of the evening. She wept and rejoiced and responded gratefully to the friendship of this bishop and his fellow workers. The anticipated events of the evening never transpired. She formed the warm and wonderful friendships she needed with people of quality and devotion. She became active in the Church and went on to her happy and wholesome opportunities.

In another city, long enough ago that the story can now be told without likelihood of the recognition of the individuals involved, I heard another and different story.

Let's use the name Donna to designate another sweet young lady who left her home for a nearby bigger city for employment. She had a great desire to attend a Church university and needed funds to help her achieve her ambition. She failed to find work in the big city and as time went by become more and more discouraged. Then, through a series of incidents Donna came into the influence of an unscrupulous and designing person who took advantage of her loneliness and youthfulness and the discouragement of her inability to find work to lead her into an immoral experience.

The experience was horrifying to Donna, and she returned home with a broken heart to tell her mother and after a time her bishop of the tragedy.

There was counsel and compassion, admonition and direction and prayer and blessing. Donna went back home to make her adjustments and to begin to learn the sorrow of remorse of conscience and the blessing of gratitude for the graciousness and goodness and mercy of God. Then one day she had to counsel again with the bishop, to report to him that through this one fragmentary tragic experience it was now apparent that she was with child. Now a different situation existed, and there was additional counsel and an effort to meet this new situation. There was consideration of the Relief Society Social Service program, which provides for such situations; other possibilities were discussed, but the decision was finally made by Donna that she would remain at home in her small town to wait her time. Some efforts were made at dissuasion, in view of the problems this course involved, but Donna decided that under the special circumstances of her widowed mother's illness, and otherwise, she would remain there.

Donna stood up in the next fast and testimony meeting and explained her condition. She acknowledged her fault and asked forgiveness of her people. She said to them, "I would like to walk the streets of this town knowing that you know and that you have compassion on me and forgive me. But if you cannot forgive me," she said, "please don't blame my mother—the Lord knows she taught me anything but this —and please don't hold it against the baby. It isn't the baby's fault." She bore testimony of appreciation for her bitterly won but dearly treasured personal knowledge of the importance of the saving mission of Jesus Christ, and then she sat down.

The man who told me the story reported the reaction of the congregation to this experience. There were many tearful eyes and many humble hearts. "There were no stone throwers there," he said. "We were full of compassion and love, and I found myself wishing that the bishop would close the meeting and let us leave with this sense of appreciation and concern and gratitude to God."

The bishop did rise, but he didn't close the meeting. Instead he said, "Brothers and sisters, Donna's story has saddened and touched us all. She has courageously and humbly accepted full responsibility for her sorrowful situation. She has, in effect, put a list of sinners on the wall of the chapel with only her name on the list. I cannot in honesty leave it there alone. At least one other name must be written—the name of one who is in part responsible for this misfortune, though he was far away when the incident occurred. The name is a familiar one to you. It is the name of your bishop. You see," he said, "had I fully performed the duties of my calling and accepted the opportunities of my leadership, perhaps I could have prevented this tragedy."

The bishop then told of his conversation with Donna and her mother before her departure for the big city. He said that he had talked with some of his associates. He had talked with his wife, expressing concern for Donna's well-being. He worried about her lack of experience and her loneliness. He had talked, he said, with the Lord about these things also.

"But then," he said, "I did nothing. I didn't write a note to the bishop or to the brethren in Salt Lake. I didn't pick up the telephone. I didn't drive a few miles to the big city. I just hoped and prayed that Donna would be all right down there all alone. I don't know what I might have done, but I have the feeling that had I been the kind of bishop I might have been, this might have been prevented.

"My brothers and sisters," he said, "I don't know how long I am going to be bishop of this ward. But as long as I am, if there is anything I can do about it, this won't happen again to one of mine."

The bishop sat down in tears. His counselor stood up and said, "I love the bishop. He is one of the best and most conscientious human beings I have ever known. I cannot leave his name there on the list without adding my own. You see," he said, "the bishop did talk with his associates. He talked with *me* about this matter. I think that he thought that because I travel occasionally in my business through the big city that I might find a way to check on Donna. I might have done," he said, "but I was hurrying to this meeting or that assignment and I didn't take the time. I too talked with others. I mentioned my concern to my wife. I am almost ashamed to tell you I talked to the Lord and asked him to help Donna. And then I did nothing. I don't know what might have happened had I done what I thought to do, but I have the feeling that I might have prevented this misfortune.

"Brothers and sisters," he said, "I don't know how long I will be serving in this bishopric, but I want to tell you that as long as I am, if there is anything I can do about it, this will not happen again to one of mine."

The ladies' president of the MIA stood up and told a similar story. The bishop's counselor in charge of this auxiliary organization had talked with her. She had had some moments of thought and concern, and had done nothing. She added her name to the list.

The last witness was an older man who stood and added two names to the list—his own and that of his companion ward teacher. He noted that they were assigned to the home where Donna and her mother lived, and that they had failed in some visits and made no effective effort to be the kind of teachers that the revelations of God had contemplated.

"I don't know," he said, "how long I will be a ward teacher, but as long as I am, I will not miss another home another month and I will try to be the kind of teacher that the Lord seemed to have in mind."

The meeting ended, and the wonderful man who shared this great experience with me said, "Brother Hanks, I think we could not have more clearly understood the importance of the offices and officers and organization in the Church if the Lord himself had come down to teach us. I think that if Paul had come to repeat his instructions to the Corinthians that 'the eye cannot say unto the hand, I have no need of thee; nor again the head to the feet, I have no need you. Nay

. . . . the members should have the same care one for another. And whether one member suffer, all the members suffer with it; or one member be honoured, all the members rejoice with it' (1 Corinthians 12:21, 22, 25, 26), we could not have understood the point more clearly."

A number of years ago, Brother Joseph Anderson and I had the privilege of driving with President J. Reuben Clark to a solemn assembly in St. George. On the way I related to him this story, then recently having happened. He thought a long time and had a tear in his eye as he said, "Brother Hanks, that is the most significant story I ever heard to illustrate the great importance of our filling our individual obligations in the Church. When you have thought about it long enough, pass it on to others."

I have thought about it long and often. I believe it illustrates powerfully and humblingly the purposes of the Lord in establishing his kingdom and permitting us the blessing of individual service therein. I now share it with you and pray God to bless us all to understand its implications and to act on them.

Individual Impact

When the apostle Paul wrote to the Corinthian Saints, he spoke of a Spirit through which the things of God may be known. In a modern time, when God revealed his will to his choice servant Joseph Smith, there was spoken of a Spirit through which they who listen and he who speaks may find communion and be mutually edified. For that Spirit I earnestly pray.

In the great land in which I am privileged to work in the missionary cause with many of your choice sons and daughters, a clergyman recently issued a statement urging his people not to listen to the representatives of The Church of Jesus Christ of Latter-day Saints as they seek to converse with them. He urged the people not to "surrender the substance for the shadow." This latter admonition is interesting and should receive the most serious consideration. All through this conference, as testimony and witness have been borne as to God and Christ and the relationship of man to them, as to the eternal nature of life, the reality of the resurrection, the profound importance and absolute validity of the restoration, I have been thinking, "Where is the substance? Where is the shadow?"

This inquiry would be valid and of great interest in every aspect of religious faith and practice. Comparisons of the

Address given at General Conference, October 1962.

revealed word of God and the Church established on the earth by Christ and his apostles with presently existing churches and their creeds and organizations and practices would be interesting. I commend to you this experience. For today, let me center attention on one theme to which the clergyman's suggestion is pertinent.

It has been my blessing for many years to work among the young and among those who work with the young. Recently it has been my special privilege to labor with several hundred choice young men and women, serving as missionaries in a foreign land. I believe I know better today than I have ever known in my life how substantial and remarkable and marvelous are the blessings of God to this Church in these days. He has blessed us with substance in a day when mists of darkness shadow the land. Ours is a family-centered religion; our families are religion-centered, and the gospel as we understand it affects the total personality and all of the aspects of the life of the individual child of God. What do the young people need? What can we offer them of real substance which will help them to avoid the shadows of falsehood and failure and sin and sorrow?

There are some suggestions I'd like to make, not to the young and not especially or at least uniquely to their parents, but to all of us, including parents, who deal with and influence or have great potential to influence and bless the young.

I am sure that we are united, you and I and all people of goodwill and honest intent throughout the world, as to the objectives we may desire for the young. I don't know a single parent or other honorable human being who does not want for the young a decent, constructive, contributing, happy life. Many of us would like to help youth, though many give only lip service to their need for help. What would we want for them? Oh, I'd like my son to win an Olympic event. This would delight me, please me greatly, make me proud. I'd like my little boy to be a fine surgeon or lawyer or salesman, or whatever he chooses to be. But if he were to succeed at some significant service and fail to be an honest, ethical, moral, spiritually perceptive man, I would be a failure in my own eyes, and certainly a sad father. What good people really want for youngsters is constructive, happy, participating lives.

It would seem likely that we are united also in our estimate of their value as individual children of God. They are infinitely valuable.

Bishop Simpson's allusion to the Second World War brought to my mind a story which impresses me greatly as to the significance of one individual and the impact of one life in the lives of others.

The first great B-29 strike on those who were then our enemy, flown from a land base, was led by an airplane named "City of Los Angeles." (There had been previous strikes from carriers, but this was our first flown from our own airfields recovered from the enemy. It was meant to inform him that the war was now to be carried to his own homeland, and it was a very important mission.) Aboard the aircraft were twelve men, eleven regular crewmen and a colonel flying as squadron commander for the mission. They were to reach a rendezvous point fifty to seventy-five miles off the mainland of the enemy, then assume regular fighting formation and fly in on target, which was a complex of high-octane gasoline plants feeding the enemy war potential.

Rendezvous point was reached as scheduled, and Colonel Sprouse ordered the dropping of the phosphorous bomb which was to mark the point. Sergeant "Red" Irwin skidded the bomb down the chute as ordered. The act was loaded with death. The flap at the end of the bomb chute had somehow become stuck. When the bomb struck it, it exploded prematurely and burst back into the cabin of the airplane and into the face and chest of Sergeant Irwin. Dropping to the deck, it began swiftly to burn its way through the thin metal flooring separating it from the incendiary bombs stored in the bomb bay below. In moments the "City of Los Angeles" and its crew would be blown to bits far out over the ocean in enemy territory.

Sergeant Irwin, tragically wounded, got to his knees, picked up the bomb in his bare hands, cradled it in his arms, and staggered up the passageway. Crashing into the navigator's table, he had to stop and unlatch it with fingers that left burn marks in the hardwood. By now the aircraft was filled with acrid fumes, blinding the pilot, and was wallowing less than three hundred feet above the water. Irwin staggered into the pilot's compartment shouting, "Window, window." He could not see that it was already open, and his fumbling fingers left burn marks on the metal. He threw the bomb out of the window and collapsed to the deck. Two hours later, Colonel Sprouse having ordered the "City of Los Angeles" back to base in the slim hope that Irwin's life might be saved, they reached Iwo Jima. Irwin's flesh was still smoking with imbedded phosphorous when he was removed from the plane by comrades who had to avert their faces from his tragic wounds.

Sergeant Irwin lived to receive his nation's highest honor for extreme bravery and to survive nearly fifty plastic surgery operations which restored him to a somewhat normal life. He lived to marry and to become a father. And with him there lived eleven other men who, but for his almost unbelievable courage, would be dead. Eleven men, spared to their lives and work and families through the decision and courageous act of one man! When Sergeant Irwin picked up that bomb, he knew that it was burning at 1,300 degrees Fahrenheit, 1,088 degrees hotter than boiling water!

This dramatic story came out of a war, but its implications are applicable to each of us, to our families, communities, nations. How many young people are there in your home or neighborhood, choice young children of God, who are wanting for lack of someone who has the courage and concern to interest himself or herself in their welfare? The prime responsibility, of course, is in the home, and we are as a Church and people anxiously interested in strengthening our homes and families. But we are aware that there are literally millions of youngsters who are not receiving in their homes the care they desperately need. They are the legitimate concern of all of us.

What can we do for them?

I offer these quick suggestions in headlines only. The rest of the story each of us may fashion as we will. I believe them to be the substance of youthful success and joy.

1.   Be concerned with their welfare. Recognize their worth and our potential to bless them and influence them and help them and lift them.

2.   Understand that they are different. They are not all out of one mold. They are at varying levels of spiritual and social and intellectual maturity, even though they may be the same age. They must be accepted and dealt with as individuals, as they are, and in terms of what they can be, and helped to become the best that they can be.

3.   They need to be taught. They need instruction. Someone has said that we habitually overestimate their experience and underestimate their intelligence. We expect them to act like little adults, and yet we fail to take time and interest to teach them.

At a meeting in England a few weeks ago a little girl, perhaps younger than four years of age, walked into a hall where a film and lecture were to be presented. I watched her as she stepped daintily over a moving picture projector cord. A man standing near the machine to protect it from accidental damage said to her, "Sweetheart, hurry and sit down. We're going to start." She *sat* down, right there in the middle of the aisle, smiling sweetly at those around her. He picked her up and explained that he had wanted her to sit up in front on a chair and escorted her there.

Now, as the father of five children I am not blind to reality. I know that they don't always do what we tell them, but if we have a proper appreciation of their value and of our ability to influence them, if we will accept them as they are and teach them in a spirit of love, wonderful blessings will come to them and to us.

4.   We must really love them. We can afford to make the mistakes of the inexpert if we sincerely love them.

5.   They need discipline. They need to realize that there are rules, wise and fair rules, which apply to them, lack of conformity to which brings a penalty.

You will remember the wonderful counsel given by the Lord to Joseph Smith in response to his anguished cry from the dungeon at Liberty, Missouri, where he had been cruelly confined for months, away from his friends and loved ones. The spirit of the priesthood was movingly explained and direction given as to how it must be used. Included was this remarkable statement: "Reproving betimes with sharpness, when moved upon by the Holy Ghost; and then showing forth afterwards an increase of love toward him whom thou hast reproved, lest he esteem thee to be his enemy." (D&C 121:43.)

Young people need discipline, administered in love.

In the great state of Vermont a time ago I faced an unruly crowd of choice teenagers brought from all regions in the state. They had listened to good music, had heard the mayors and the governor, and had responded to every effort with contempt and discourtesy. The person who introduced me was quite apologetic. I think he wished that I would disappear, so embarrassing had been the behavior of the young people to that moment. I stood up and said something I hadn't ever said before to a group of teens:

> I'm sorry that most of you didn't hear the great talk that your governor just delivered. It was a wonderful talk, and you would have profited from hearing it, but you weren't listening. Let me repeat the theme of what your governor said. He talked about "Vermont's Chief Asset, Her Teenagers." I'd like to tell you the truth. I'd like to tell you that I've been all over America commending your generation and expressing confidence

in you, and tonight you have made me wonder. For the first time, you've really made me wonder. I'd just like to tell you that if your behavior tonight is typical, if you've been acting as you really are, and if you are Vermont's chief asset, the Lord help Vermont!

Well, they listened. I spent the next forty-five minutes showing forth an increase of love toward them, talking to the theme of "Moral Courage." I did my best to recover from what might be thought a very strange way to approach a group of young people. They didn't move a muscle. They listened, and their response was wonderful.

When the meeting was over, I walked out of the building and was stopped on the path outside by a rather grim-looking group of handsome, rugged young men. One of them stepped forward and said, "Mr. Hanks, we were very grateful for your talk on moral courage. We learned a lot. But we'd like you to know that what you *did* here tonight was lots more important than anything you *said,* and we're never going to forget it."

Young people need to be disciplined in love.

6. They need wholesome participation with others.

7. Young people need to be encouraged to stretch, to develop their creative capacities.

8. They need to be taught and given experience in the great religious truths. Would you bless youth? Teach them the truth about God and Christ and themselves. Teach them that they have a special responsibility toward God and all their fellowmen, his children. Teach them to be compassionate and considerate and kind, which they can best be when they know God as their true Father in whose image and likeness they are created; when they know Christ as their living Savior; when they recognize themselves as choice, responsible children of God, brothers to all men. Lead them to religious search and service and reverence. Help them to learn the truth.

9. Be an example to them of what you'd like them to be.

I testify that God lives, that we are his children, and that we can bless each other and our choice young brothers and sisters if we will.

The Listening Ear

Individuals who are blessed with someone to whom they can confidently and comfortably talk and who will listen to them are fortunate indeed. Most persons in the Church have had the experience of working with individuals whose minds are made up, who seem to have great confidence in themselves and little or none in others, or at least seem uninterested in anything they have to say. If they listen at all, it is defensively, with "the curtain down," perhaps cynically or doubtingly or with seeming willingness to question motives or purposes. Others clearly do not intend to be reached.

We ourselves might have responded in some of these ways to others who were trying to reach us. We have not had time. It was someone else's assignment to listen to them. Perhaps we have made up our minds about individuals with whom we work and serve and have typed them so that we don't really listen to what they have to say.

I remember with interest the new stake mission president in a small town with few nonmembers. He was humbly and earnestly pleading with the priesthood leaders of the stake to support him and his fellow workers in their difficult new assignment. "Over the years," he said, "I have exercised the luxury of making up my mind about substantially every nonmember in this community. I suspect many of you have done the same. As stake mission president I now have the

---

Article published in the *Improvement Era*, March 1969.

interesting opportunity to unmake my mind and start with a fresh, wholesome, optimistic attitude toward all of them. I earnestly plead with you to do the same."

Since real listening can be an exhausting experience, we may not be able to physically, emotionally, and intellectually receive and react to all that may be said to us, so we set up screens to protect ourselves. However, we may often end up using those screens to screen out what we don't want to hear.

In an authoritarian church it is easy for a leader on any level to stop listening, to become accustomed to engaging in one-way communication. The bishopric of a ward does not operate on a consensus or majority rule basis, so on occasion the bishop might be inclined not to seek the counsel of his counselors, or to listen to it impatiently or without interest or respect. But decision-makers need counselors. There is safety in counsel. We have seen and experienced sorrow and tragedy and serious error because good men—even great men—would not seek or accept counsel, or received it from questionable or self-seeking sources, or were not given information because subordinates lacked the courage to speak.

I shall never forget and have often repeated the words of President David O. McKay as he gave me a blessing. "Let your voice be heard," he said. "Speak prayerfully, honestly, courageously. But let your voice be heard."

Is this not wise instruction for all who are called to assist or counsel? And is it not wise for leaders to make certain that opportunity is provided for this to happen? Decision-makers at every level need the experience, the information, the wisdom, the inspiration of their associates who have been called to counsel, in order that judgment may be exercised with all available facts and understanding at hand. Since we are seldom more effective than our information, we need to be aware of facts and feelings—and this involves listening.

The leader's success in his decision-making assignment will be materially affected, if not conclusively determined, by his capacity and willingness to create a climate that will free individuals to talk with him without the fear of being too quickly categorized, rejected, or reproved.

Listening is tied in part to loving. If we are basically heedless of some people, we are apt to be heedless of their words. Then they will suffer and the work may suffer through loss of strength that could be important.

What is listening? It is much more than the mechanical act of hearing. Listening is the giving of close attention for the purpose of gaining information, understanding. One of our Church manuals has this statement:

> One of the great facilities of communication is the ability to listen with understanding. Most of us feel we are good listeners just because we have the self-restraint to be quiet while another is talking. However, there is a big difference between letting the decibels pound on the ear drums and listening with understanding. To listen with understanding is to view the issue and feel as the speaker does about it. It is to stand in the other man's shoes and see it as he does.

Listening is active. A good listener is involved, interested, concerned.

To whom shall we listen? To our Heavenly Father, of course, and to his Holy Son, and to the Spirit. How significant it is that the Father, in introducing his Son on sacred occasions, said, "Hear him!" How tragic the consequence would have been if those so majestically admonished had not listened, perhaps through indifference or arrogance or unbelief or prejudice—the attitude of a closed mind. The invitation to hear him is, of course, to all men, and so is the responsibility to decide whether we shall listen.

The Lord may speak to us by his voice, as he did to Joseph; or his voice may come into our mind, as it did to Enos; or he may speak to us by his messengers, the prophets, and others who are commissioned to speak for him.

He may speak as he did to Elijah, who did not find the Lord in the wind or the earthquake or the fire but who listened to the still, small voice.

He speaks to us through the scriptures, admonishing us, as he did the Prophet and Oliver and David, to read the scriptures to one another: "Wherefore, you can testify that you have heard my voice, and know my words." (D&C 18:36.) For the word of the Lord, we need a listening ear, an open heart, a contrite spirit.

There are others to whom we should listen.

Husbands and wives should listen to each other, and to their children. Children should listen to their parents.

We should listen to those whom we serve, to those with whom we serve, and to those under whose direction we serve.

We need to listen to speakers and teachers, to counselors and leaders, to those who really love us. On occasion we need to hear the voice of someone who disagrees with us, or who disputes the passage with us, or who has another view of the path to the same objective.

How shall we listen? As to how we should listen, perhaps King Benjamin said it most effectively:

> My brethren, all ye that have assembled yourselves together, . . . I have not commanded you to come up hither to trifle with the words which I shall speak, but that you should hearken unto me, and open your ears that ye may hear, and your hearts that ye may understand, and your minds that the mysteries of God may be unfolded to your view. (Mosiah 2:9.)

James Stevens wrote, "I have learned that the head does not hear anything until the heart has listened, and what the heart knows today the head will understand tomorrow."

Listen with the heart. Practice empathy. Put yourself in the other person's place and try to hear his problems in your heart.

Listen with patience. Others deserve unhurried time. Even five minutes can be made unhurried if the attitude is right.

Listen to learn, to weigh, to consider. The scriptures say: "He that answereth a matter before he heareth it, it is folly and shame unto him." (Proverbs 18:13.)

Listen creatively, with curiosity.

Listen with compassion and with depth. Create a climate in which others may confidently speak, an atmosphere of candor, consideration, and kindness that permits and encourages another to say those significant words, "I need help."

Listen with courtesy and intensity.

Listen to help, to comfort, to bless.

Listen attentively to speakers and teachers. An expectant, cooperative, responsive listener induces an ordinary speaker to communicate with improved effectiveness. We listen to a thousand times more words than we read, and we spend almost as much time listening as the combined time we spend in reading, writing, or speaking. The average speaking pace is about 125 to 150 words a minute. Hearing words at this speed, however, consumes only 10 percent of the brain's thinking power. A good listener has 90 percent of his listening ability, then, to contribute something mentally to what is being said, or to review or anticipate and thus get the benefit of the message.

Listen with a pencil and note pad in hand. Someone has said that the palest ink is better than the best memory.

Note-taking, though it can be too voluminous, is frequently helpful not alone in remembering at a later time what has been said, but also in evaluating and understanding what is being said. In addition, it helps us to concentrate and apply the message.

One important need for a listener is to recognize that he sometimes reacts emotionally to certain words or concepts that might block effective listening. Each listener should be aware of such words and learn to react properly to them.

When should we listen? The time to listen is when someone needs to be heard. The time to deal with a person with a problem is when he has the problem. The time to nurse one is when he is ill. The time to listen is the time when our interest and love are vital to the one who seeks our ear and our heart and our help.

The capacity to listen is important. A great amount of time is spent in teaching us to read, to write, and to speak. How much time has been spent in preparing us to listen? Much can be done to help us learn to listen, to help us overcome such bad habits as feigning attention while our thoughts are elsewhere—a strange form of self-deceit; allowing external distractions to lead our mind from the situation at hand; ceasing to listen when something difficult to understand is said; the premature dismissal of subjects as uninteresting and thus the closing of our minds to vast areas of important human knowledge; letting criticism of delivery or physical appearance or language interfere with significant information or inspiration.

We have been talking of two major aspects of listening: (1) listening that brings benefits to us, and (2) listening with a desire to understand and benefit others. The first is indispensable to our own successful service and salvation, the second to the well-being and happiness of others.

The results of good listening are reflected in man's total behavior. He is the sum of his listening habits; to whom and how and where and when he has listened are plainly manifested in the way he acts, the things he says, the way he speaks, the manner in which he treats others who may not be important in affecting his destiny. A man's learning experience can be rich and fruitful, his interests in the problems of fellowmen wide; and if he has listened well and if he is listening, he will do something about them.

Every human being is trying to say something to others, trying to cry out, "I am alive. Notice me! Speak to me! Listen to me! Confirm for me that I am important, that I matter!"

As we learn to listen to the Lord with understanding, learning to appreciate his point of view, we should also be emulating with our fellowmen the marvelous quality of his great listening mind and heart. We know that he listens, and we love him. It should be more possible for us, then, to listen to each other and to other men. We are here to learn to love as we are loved.

In the Book of Mormon is recorded the solemn warning of Jacob of old: "And wo unto the deaf that will not hear; for they shall perish." (2 Nephi 9:31.)

Amulek, son of Giddonah, bore a sorrowful testimony of a dark period in his life before he opened his ears to the Lord: "I did harden my heart, for I was called many times and I would not hear; therefore I knew concerning these things, yet I would not know." (Alma 10:6.)

From the scriptures anciently comes the divine invitation to us and to all men: "Incline your ear, and come unto me: hear, and your soul shall live." (Isaiah 55:3.) God bless us with a listening ear.

The Importance of One

I sat thinking a moment ago of my sainted father who left his little family and departed this earth more than thirty-five years ago, how he went into the missionary field at the call of the Lord through the Brethren, in his late teens, carrying copies of the Book of Mormon with testimony and conviction, expressing his deepest assurance of the validity of the work he represented and yet without adequate knowledge, perhaps because he was but a boy and because much knowledge now available was not had, to defend his viewpoint in the eyes of the world. He had only his testimony, his faith, and the Book.

As President Smith spoke, I marveled that we have lived long enough and that we live in a time, you and I, when the wise men, the honest men of the world, are coming to understand some of the things the Lord has taught us through all the years since the establishment of the Church.

As President Smith referred to the age of eight and his faith that a youngster at that age can know, I thought of my little children and then of a book published recently, written by two child psychologists who comment on the age "eight" in the lives of the young. They say that at the age of eight it frequently happens that much that was not comprehended previously is easily understood; that at that age the child's understanding almost seems to take on a new dimension.

Address given at General Conference, October 1959.

It is remarkable that qualified and earnest seekers after truth should discover that at age eight a new dimension enters into the life of the child. The Lord assured us of this when he talked of the age of accountability long ago.

A thoughtful friend phoned this morning to tell me of a book he had just received—I had not seen a copy nor is it available in our bookstores yet—a book called, *I Found God in Soviet Russia,* in which a man tells of his own experiences as a prisoner in a concentration camp in Siberia.

He talks of the religious faith that permitted people to endure and survive. He mentions in at least four different places, and this would perhaps be a satisfying if sorrowful and surprising thing for us to know, that in a concentration camp in Siberia there is a little band of members of The Church of Jesus Christ of Latter-day Saints, meeting faithfully and loyally, unwilling to deny or let rest or become indifferent to their responsibilities even though to be a member of the Church makes them liable to life imprisonment according to the book.

The book notes that these Mormons insisted on coming together in the name of the Lord—that when they had a few minutes they met to worship God in their own way.

When I think how the Lord must love and look with compassion upon such individuals, when out of my own experience as a parent I can see how much I love my little ones, I can understand (at least within my limitations) what the Lord meant when he talked about the worth of souls in his sight. And I believe I may understand it more impressively and movingly today than I have ever understood it before.

May I read you some words with which all are familiar and read them in context of what has been said? "Remember the worth of souls is great in the sight of God; for behold, the Lord your Redeemer suffered death in the flesh; wherefore he suffered the pain of all men, that all men might repent and come unto him." (D&C 18:10-11.)

There follows the great statement of the joy of the Lord in the soul that repenteth, and this: "And if it so be that you should labor all your days in crying repentance unto this people, and bring, save it be one soul unto me, how great shall be your joy with him in the kingdom of my Father!"

And then the marvelous statement that "if your joy will be great with one soul . . . how great will be your joy if you should bring many souls unto me!" (D&C 18:15-16.)

I have in mind to express my testimony about the importance of the one, to add my humble witness to the charge that has been given each teacher and parent, every youth-influencing Latter-day Saint, to be concerned about the one individual child of God.

As I drove toward Brigham Young University the other morning, I heard a statement from the Talmud, or so it was quoted: "To save one life is like saving a whole nation." And I began to think of other statements, including the one from the eighteenth section of the Doctrine and Covenants, to which we have alluded. I thought of the statement of Oliver Wendell Holmes, who said, "Every individual is an omnibus." Do you see the significance and implication of this?

As we have the marvelous blessing of setting missionaries apart, I can seldom refrain from thinking (and occasionally say it) that in each of them, as in each of us, is wrapped up a heritage and a promise, for each is a distillation of much that has gone before, and beyond all that is represented in the individual now and of the past, there is also the future, because in each of us are the seeds of the future; in each of us there is, in fact, the capacity and possibility of becoming many.

Could I tell you one story which bears repetition—and I have had the blessing of repeating it in some of the stakes of the Church. It is the most significant single experience I have ever had, personally, about the importance of one. It happened long enough ago that I think the individual involved would not be conscious of our noting him, though I see no harm if he is.

A man walked into these grounds and into an office in the Bureau of Information one day long ago. He interrupted a conversation which was private and serious, and did it without apology. He was quite an elderly man; he was not what you would call an attractive human being. He was unkempt, unshaven; he reeked of alcohol and tobacco.

He walked over to the desk where I sat, pointed his hand in the direction of the temple, and said, "How do you get in there?" I assumed that he was a tourist, one of the infrequent but occasional few who do not understand the purpose and the reason of temple-going and who have become affronted because they are not taken into the temple, and perhaps had come to complain.

I told him as best I could, or began to, the story of the temple, but had proceeded only a little distance when he interrupted. He waved me away and said, "Oh, you don't have to tell me all that. I know that. I am a Mormon."

"Well," I said, "if you are a member of the Church, and you know all of this, what is it you want from me?" He said, "Frankly, nothing. There isn't anything you have to give me. I am here because my wife insisted on my coming in, but I have fulfilled my errand," and out he went.

I tried to pick up the threads of the conversation and finish it, and later, as I sat thinking about him and his story, I looked out the window and saw him walking by the Joseph and Hyrum [Smith] monuments with a younger woman. I went out to talk with them. She identified herself as his wife. He had been married three times; each previous wife had died after bearing a large family.

There are two questions I asked him, which I think each person here would do well to hear answered as he answered them. I asked, in effect, how he had come to his feeling of antagonism and indifference. He told me that at age nineteen he had been ejected from a chapel by a bishop's counselor who had been summoned because of the boy's trouble-making in class. One thing that had been said, this man remembered for nearly sixty years. As he was thrown out, someone objected. The answer that came from the counselor who had the task in hand was, "Ah, let him go, he is just one kid!"

He went, and he never came back, nor was there ever any visiting, never any outpouring or increase of the love that should follow reproof, according to the Lord. He moved to another area of the land, married, had a family; his wife passed away and he married again; his second wife died after bearing a family also. He had come to Salt Lake City at the insistence of his third wife, who, having been taught by the missionaries and converted to the principles of the gospel, had brought him here hoping that somehow he might be touched—he, the member.

This also I would like to report: I asked him how many living descendants he had. He counted them and answered, "Fifty-four." I asked him then, how many of them are members of the Church, and I expect you know the answer, though perhaps not his interesting expression. He said, "Huh, ain't any of them members of the Church. They're a pretty hard lot."

This last question: Who was it the bishop's counselor propelled out the door that morning? Just one boy? Just one? This one has in his own lifetime become, in effect, a multitude, and the current has but begun to run, and every one of them denied, according to his own witness, the love of the gospel and the brotherhood of the Saints, the warmth and strength and direction of the programs of the Church.

Oh, I can understand a little more why the Lord said that one soul was precious to him.

I close with a statement Horace Mann made. This is well known also, but worth the repetition. A man questioned Horace Mann's assertion at the dedication of a boy's school, that if all the work and energy and effort and money put into the endeavor had been to save just one boy, it would have been worth it, and said to Horace Mann, "You became too oratorical, didn't you? You didn't really mean that did you?" Horace Mann answered, "Oh, yes, I meant it. It would have all been worth it, if the one boy were my son."

Every son of God is important in his eyes. Every unbaptized child, unordained boy, young man who is not in the right stage of his priesthood progression, every boy and girl not attending seminary when they can and should, every boy and girl not being married in the temple when they could— these are vitally important in the eyes of God, and should be in our eyes.

God bless us to understand the infinite importance of the one, in God's eyes, and to do all that we can to fulfill his purposes for them.

Keep a Welcome

I am deeply grateful to be invited to speak to the subject of this great crusade which the Sunday School is leading toward fellowship and brotherhood in keeping a welcome for all. I have had strong convictions about this theme all my life, it seems. I feel I have something to say about it. I would pray the Lord will bless me and give me direction and utterance as I try to do that.

We are losing some of our brothers and sisters of the Church and we want to know why. Would you continue to carry a bucket with a hole in it, spilling the water out interminably? What would happen if the Church leaders were to stand at conference and explain that 30, or 40, or 50, or 20, or 10 percent of the tithing were being consistently lost? Well, it isn't being lost, but the point is that souls are more important than money, and some of *them* are getting lost.

I have in mind a sheaf of letters that I have kept in a file over the past few years, all of them pertaining to experiences in Europe. Each is a letter detailing a sorrowful story of loss. This brief extract from one is not particularly palatable, but it is honest.

> Karen and I went to the Mormon Church Sunday morning and then to the Presbyterian Church that night. Karen either goes to the Baptist or Presbyterian Church but prefers the former.

Address given at Sunday School Conference, October 1964.

So, since she feels a little out of place at the Mormon Church and I vice versa, we are taking turns. However, I really do enjoy the Presbyterian Church. They are very friendly and make you feel so welcome. A lot more so than at the ward, I am sorry to say.

Of the many others, one will suffice. It is a letter from a mother who says:

I have a son who has been ordained to the office of priest and who has become inactive in the Church in the past two years. This is a great problem to me, and I know also it is an important problem to the Church. At different times he has gone to other churches with his girl friend. These churches have spent many hours in sending letters, cards, literature, and so forth. It seems to me that we as Latter-day Saints ought to do more of these things. Our priesthood quorums, Sunday Schools, Mutuals, our home teachers, and others should spend some time with these boys. My boy does not have a father, and he needs the companionship of an adult male more than just me all the time.

Then she tells about some things he likes to do.

I wish he had a pal or a big brother in the Church who was really interested in him and them. On occasions my boy has said, "Nobody cares whether I am there or not." I feel very strongly in this matter. He needs lots of questions answered about the gospel. I try to answer him the best I can, but I feel he needs more counseling than I can give.

This need of the member who is slipping or has slipped away is one of the motivating causes of this great program of keeping a welcome. This is the genesis of it. The genius of it will be getting Church members in general interested and active in the program. Let me try to pass on to you two basic convictions that I believe are necessary in order for a person to feel the motivation to become as concerned as he should be about his neighbor and relative and fellow Church member, and about the stranger in the gate.

First, I would like to reaffirm the vital importance of every individual child of God. And I mean *every one*. Their value in his eyes is not measurable. Every one is our brother or sister. I read again this afternoon the great poem by John Donne that talks about the bell tolling at the churchyard when one brother goes down. "It is as if a clod were dropped off the earth in the ocean," he says in the quaint English of his time. And he concludes with a colorful suggestion. "Do not ask for whom the bell tolls. It tolls for thee." He is telling us that we are so intertwined, we human beings, we children of God, that anything that happens to any of us happens to all of us, whether or not we are sensitive to the happening at the moment.

The first of two major suggestions I make to you at the outset, then, is that you do not make the mistake of under-valuing any of God's children. Do not write them off. Do not make up your mind against them. Recognize their value and their potential. This is particularly true of youth, who carry in them at the moment of your encounter the seeds of the future. For in every normal situation there will likely, one day, be those who call them father or mother. And the children are going to be pretty much like their parents.

The second suggestion is this: Please do not underesti-mate your capacity to influence them for good or otherwise. We had a bishop in one of the choice wards where we lived who somehow had gotten the vision of his own importance. Not in any arrogant sense—he was the least arrogant man around. But he was confident and concerned. Once he invited a seven-year-old girl into his office and took a card out of a little file. Then he said to the girl (who was so frightened she could hardly sit still), "Susan, this card tells me that on the twenty-second of July something important is going to happen. What is it?"

So began her first interview with a bishop. Her answer was that it was her birthday.

"That's your eighth birthday, isn't it?"

"Yes."

"What's going to happen?"

"I'm going to be baptized."

"I am sure your mother and daddy have taught you what baptism is all about," he said, "but I am your bishop, and I have the privilege of interviewing you before I give you a recommend for baptism. Let me talk to you just a minute about the purpose of baptism."

He then explained the purpose of baptism in a simple way that she could understand. She ran all the way home with her heart pulsating, her eyes large, and her breath short, to report that she had had an interview with the bishop.

I do not know how long that interview took. Probably not two minutes. But it did something so important for my daughter that I cannot be grateful enough. We have lived in other wards, and we have seen other children approach and pass that age without receiving that little blessing. I have no criticism whatsoever to offer these other bishops. In fact, I ought to be criticized because I let my tendency not to want to intrude keep me from doing what I felt like doing—keep me from mentioning to them what had happened to Susan and wondering if it could happen to the others.

Do you have an idea that you do not amount to very much in terms of your influence in the lives of young or older persons around you? Please get over it. The fact is that each of us exercises an influence, and it can be a favorable, positive, uplifting one.

At the White House Conference in 1960 I learned a lot of things, but one has stuck and I believe in it. It was the story of a man who believed in the principle I am talking about. He went to a certain large city and gave a number of grammar school teachers a big assignment. He asked each of them to take on as a special challenge four "underachieving" children. The children were not deficient mentally, not in trouble emotionally. There was no apparent reason for their difficulty, but all of them were underachieving. None was managing as he or she should the curriculum, the courses, the experience of grade school.

The teachers accepted their assignments. The interesting thing about these teachers is that not one of them was picked because he was a specialist in child guidance. The man deliberately ruled out those with special training in that field. He wanted to see what a good teacher (and this was the only criterion—that they be recognized by children and their superior officers as good teachers) could do as the special friend of some children who were on the way to trouble.

He set a time limit for his program. He came back to check up after a fifth of the time had elapsed and found, at first to his annoyance, that very little data had accumulated. He wanted some active research with an appropriate study made. But when he found out the reason for the lack of data, he rejoiced. More than half the total number of underachieving children were no longer underachieving. The reason? Although the children never knew, the teachers had agreed they would try to be the best friend of these children for the period of the program. They would try to satisfy their need for a mature, strong, concerned adult outside the home. In a few weeks, half of the students were no longer underachieving. They were doing their best work in the class taught by the teacher who was their special friend.

Can you get a vision of what could happen in this Church with the organization the Lord has given us, if each of us were to be a best friend to someone else? Begin to go down the list of auxiliaries, priesthood leadership, bishoprics, seminaries, home teachers, Relief Society visiting teachers, and all the others, and a vision of our possibilities must come to your mind. If this principle, on the scale this good man demonstrated it to be possible, were applied in every ward and branch and organization in this Church, it would produce a tremendous upsurge of love and concern which in turn would vastly improve the atmosphere of friendship and welcome in our congregations.

That application of a great, eternal principle is the most important thing I learned during a week at the White House Conference. It reinforced everything I believed.

Who are they to whom we must pay attention? Who are the ones who need our help? Let me comment briefly on some of them.

What can we do for people who are already active? These are the ones that we would normally assume would need no help. That is why a high priest in the LDS Hospital said to me one day with a smile, "Brother Hanks, I am surely grateful I have got appendicitis and have come here. Here I have had the first visit I have ever had from my high priests quorum." Why had he not been visited before? Because he was always around, and therefore presumably did not need anybody. That is a mistake. He needs someone all right. He needs to be fellowshipped. Active, functioning, effective Latter-day Saints need a welcome too. Furthermore, they are the ones who will normally pass it on with so much fervor and appreciation that our ball will really get rolling.

I cannot forget a visit to one of the stakes least blessed with membership and leadership and most blessed with problems. Everywhere I went in the Church for several years I asked in advance that the elders quorum presidency be invited to speak on a particular theme for five minutes each. I asked that the president and each of his counselors talk on the subject, "My specific responsibilities in the presidency of this quorum and what I am doing about them." It was a very interesting experience. It was remarkable how many times I heard them say, "Until I got this assignment, I never really looked at the manual. Thanks very much, Brother Hanks. This is what I *ought* to be doing. The next time you come, this is what I will have done."

In this small, struggling stake one young man stood and with strength and appreciation thanked the bishop and thanked God for that bishop. He said he had been on a United States destroyer, having been an active, alert Latter-day Saint until he had left home. But then some of the problems that occasionally befall us along the way came to him. He did not have companionship. He was all alone as far as the Church was concerned. This is what he said as he spoke to us:

> I used to sit against the bulkhead and open the bishop's letters while I was smoking a fag. I was not very proud of it, and I never answered a single letter, but I made up my mind that if my bishop cared that much about me, when I got home I would do something to pass on what he had done for me. That is why I am trying to make a success of this job as a quorum leader.

Another quorum leader had a letter from a boy who lived in the same town but who was the son of an inactive member. The boy went to another state to play in an all-star athletic contest. This second counselor in his inactive father's elders quorum presidency sent him a postcard congratulating him, and telling the boy that they were counting on him to represent the ward and the Church and his dad's quorum well. The boy's letter said:

> Brother ....: I just thought you would like to know that the day your card came was the day of the game. I appreciated it. Afterwards a lot of the fellows went out to see the town. I did not go with them. I might have but for your card. And there are a lot of them who are very sorry for some of the things they found out. They are always going to be sorry.

What can you do for the active individuals from an inactive family, who may have special circumstances, and who may not be fully fellowshipped? Well, there is a lot to be done. There's brotherhood, and fellowship, and love, and a welcome to be offered.

Let me mention the new members and the less active people. When I saw the people coming into the Church in England, I thought of the parable of the sower. There was some of the seed, as you know, that burned because it had no roots. These wonderful folks often are shallow-rooted. They need the anchors of their faith sunk more deeply. They need to know they belong to something and to somebody who will take the place of what they have given up, the associations and friendships that are behind them.

Do you remember these words from Moroni about a group of people who joined the Church a long time ago?

> Neither did they receive any unto baptism save they came forth with a broken heart and a contrite spirit, and witnessed unto the church that they truly repented of all their sins.
>
> And none were received unto baptism save they took upon them the name of Christ, having a determination to serve him to the end.
>
> And after they had been received unto baptism, and were wrought upon and cleansed by the power of the Holy Ghost, they were numbered among the people of the church of Christ; and their names were taken, that they might be remembered and nourished by the good word of God, to keep them in the right way, to keep them continually watchful unto prayer, relying alone upon the merits of Christ, who was the author and the finisher of their faith.
>
> And the church did meet together oft, to fast and to pray, and to speak one with another concerning the welfare of their souls.
>
> And they did meet together oft to partake of bread and wine, in remembrance of the Lord Jesus.
>
> And they were strict to observe that there should be no iniquity among them; and whoso was found to commit iniquity, . . . if they repented not, and confessed not, their names were blotted out, and they were not numbered among the people of Christ.
>
> But as oft as they repented and sought forgiveness, with real intent, they were forgiven. (Moroni 6:2-8.)

In this glimpse of the Nephite Church, the elements of a continuing concern and an honest, extending, enduring brotherhood are all present, based on faith, on knowledge, on regular church attendance and activity and spiritually motivating meetings.

Let me only note what a new convert said to us in the mail in England. "You feel like you never are going to be lonely again," she wrote. And she shouldn't ever be lonely again in this Church because she had become, as Paul wrote to the Ephesians, "fellowcitizens with the saints, and of the household of God." (Ephesians 2:19.)

Do you remember the words of the choice sons of Mosiah about the people they brought into the Church? But for us, they said, "they would also have been strangers to God." (Alma 26:9.)

Have you sung a song lately about strangers? I heard a man whistling one as I crossed the grounds tonight. You recognize the words, "No longer as strangers on earth need we roam." Why not? Because a connection has been made with a source of power that can heal the loneliness and emptiness and anxiety of the lost soul. But if the connection is loose, what then? There is another kind of stranger we sing about in a song. "How long we have wandered as strangers in sin." No one ought to do that in this Church if the welcome were really being kept. That means giving them friendship and instruction and activity and sincere concern. None of us is too poor to give this.

I recall something that happened to an inactive boy in England. In the Hayes Branch, not far from London, a youngster who is one of England's interesting generation of pop singers joined the Church. He is not quite as famous as some others, but he is a successful practitioner, if one can be called that, in this art—so successful that the elements of social and economic pressure got to him, and he dropped out of Church activity. Some fine people wooed him back with care and consideration. He became the first assistant superintendent of the Hayes Branch Sunday School. The Sunday School superintendent was an airman second class. The second assistant was a flight surgeon in the Air Force.

At my invitation, Brian bore his testimony shortly before we left England. He said he had told his friend that he was the first assistant superintendent of the Sunday School and explained what goes on in the Church. His friend said, "It seems that your Church is like one started by a fellow a long time ago, who called ordinary people to do the work."

Well, the activity and the concern and the brotherhood and the love have their effect. How about the nonmembers and the casual strangers? How about those who just drop in? What of those who may interfere a little with your planned program and your personal desires? In Hebrews we read, "Be not forgetful to entertain strangers; for thereby some have entertained angels unawares." (Hebrews 13:2.)

I could tell you stories of some angels. I could almost make you jealous of the blessings we have had because we have worked on Temple Square and have had a chance to entertain some strangers, sometimes at the cost of our own convenience—my wife's usually. Sometimes at the cost of the schedule we had planned.

Once this happened at Christmastime and it looked like a very unpleasant thing to do to my family, because the stranger involved was mentally upset—deeply, emotionally disturbed. She had no place to go. Her children were far away with her husband, and she had been literally cast out. I am no psychiatrist, and I am not qualified to identify mental illness, but I knew she was ill. We took her home and it did cost us a little in planned programs, and parties and convenience. But in a few days I saw a miracle happen, a miracle wrought by the love of little children who did not know that there was anything wrong. They sat on her knee and kissed her cheek and had her read stories and brought her around to a condition of stability that permitted her to go home and to be accepted. Interestingly enough in this, I suppose, rare case, she was able to maintain a stability that has persisted since.

I am suggesting that keeping a welcome is not all giving, that it contains joys for the giver that we should not be missing.

What does this all mean to us in our local situation? You can perform an illustrative experiment if you like. It may serve better than my trying to tell you what I think ought to be going on in the wards and branches of the Church.

Take a glass of clear water and an ordinary spoon. Pour in some sugar, and observe that immediately some of it is absorbed. But some of it is not. The bottom of the glass is covered to a small depth by a considerable portion of the sugar. Pour in more sugar; same results. Some of it will go to the botttom. Put in the spoon and nothing happens; but stir with the spoon, and something begins to happen. Keep stirring and the sugar will dissolve.

The glass is the ward, the branch, or the organization. The water represents its membership. The sugar is the new folks, the reactivated folks, the strangers who come. The spoon? This may be the bishop or, if there is such a thing, the coordinator, or the friendship or fellowshipping committee.

What happens when the sugar goes in the water? Some of it does not mix. What happens when the spoon is put in? A little, but not much. But what happens if the water is stirred? Just what we want to happen.

What we are really talking about is personal attitude and effort—an attitude of love and relationship and honest concern. This attitude, this effort, will get others moving. We are talking about an interest in other people based on a sound respect for who they are, or for what they can be if we can't really respect what they are. We are talking about involvement, an investment in lives.

We are talking about so small a thing as Oscar Kirkham coming to me right back here, after I had made a small contribution to a planned program, when I was eighteen, and taking my hand when all the other brethren and leaders had gone, and saying something moving to me to make me want to get back here again some way, sometime, to serve. It wasn't so much the words he said. Nobody knows any magic words (at least nobody I know) when he goes to the hospital or the house of bereavement. What we're talking about is an attitude of care, of involvement, of consideration. What matters is that we care so much that we cannot hide it.

THE GIFT OF SELF

This dimension of care and concern was stressed in a moving scripture I have saved for the last. There is to be a time when the Master of men gathers together all of his sheep, some on one hand and some on the other. And he says to those on his right hand a beautiful and wonderful thing: "Come, ye blessed of my Father, inherit the kingdom prepared for you from the foundation of the world." Then he talks about a stranger who was cared for, a prisoner who was visited, and a sick person who was ministered to, and some hungry and thirsty ones who were fed and given drink. They who receive the commendation are honest people, and they say, not remembering, "Lord, when saw we thee an hungred, and fed thee? or thirsty, and gave thee drink? When saw we thee a stranger, and took thee in? or naked, and clothed thee? Or when saw we thee sick, or in prison, and came unto thee?" The answer is well known to all of us. "Inasmuch as ye have done it unto one of the least of these my brethren, ye have done it unto me." (See Matthew 25:31-46.)

As I bear my testimony I would like to use just once more the word *concern*. I believe this word represents the love of God in a way I can understand more meaningfully than by any other word. He is so concerned that he sent his Son. His Son is so concerned that he gave his life for us. And so closely identified is he with all God's children that when anything happens to any one of them, it is as if it were happening to him.

This to me is the ideal. This is why I want to care about the individual. This is why I want to do anything in the world I can do to help him feel the dignity of his own divine heritage and his glorious possibilities.

God bless us to have a sense of relationship that will impel us, through respect for our fellowman, through love of the Church and love of the Lord, to keep a welcome.

III.
Give
Service

The leaders and teachers in the Church must give contemporary guidance to meet the needs of the day. There must be available a stabilizing, steadying influence, a force and power which will bless individuals with capacity to meet change on a foundation of things that do not change.

What Can You Expect?

We are told that this broadcast is going to beloved Britain, and so it is appropriate that I begin by noting that in the foyer of a Church building in a British city some time ago I happened by a group of older ladies who were discussing somewhat critically the behavior of several young members of the congregation who had just walked noisily by. I had observed the incident and had thought the young people a bit exuberant, but not objectionably so. The ladies disagreed. As I passed by I heard one of them disapprovingly say, "Ah, well, what can you expect from this younger generation, anyway!"

I did not agree with her implication, but I take her rhetorical question very seriously, believing that the answer is of vital significance.

What can be expected of this younger generation? There are few questions more important.

In the first place, there are so many of them. Most of us have heard the statement, sometimes uttered in solemn and hushed tones, half in apprehension, half in resignation, that soon 50 percent of the population will be under age twenty-five.

The statistic is correct, the prospect sobering. Some who speak of it do so almost as if they expected that when the

---

Address given at General Conference, October 1967.

magic mark is reached, the older generation will relinquish their responsibilities and succumb, and the young will then automatically take over! Of course, it will not happen that way. But there really are so many of them! And they are so important.

What kind of people are they?

A small, raucous, rebellious, sometimes harmless—in some cases very dangerous—minority, gets most of the publicity. The hippies, the drug adventurers, the motorcycle brigade, the flower crowd, the politically unstable, the lawless get so much press attention that there is an unquestionable effect on the style of life and the way of thinking of multitudes of youngsters everywhere.

Speaking of the discontented ones, a writer has recently said:

> So far I have seen or heard very little in the way of constructive suggestions from them. What fruitful insights and programs have they to offer us? I can't help wondering [as they criticize their adult generation] if they ever wonder what *their* children will have to thank *them* for. For fouling their chromosomes with LSD? For dropping out and copping out at a time when society was never in greater need of their participation? What are their credentials for billing themselves as the take-over generation? (Albert Rosenfeld.)

We cannot afford to underestimate or ignore their influence. But obstreperous and well publicized as they are, they constitute a small minority of the young generation.

The solid majority of our young people want to do well, are doing well, and intend to do well with the great challenges facing them.

Across the world I have found them threading their way resolutely through the maze of a civilization often characterized by conflict and inconsistency, a civilization which could not exist except upon indispensable foundations in good homes, stable marriages, happy families, exemplary parents, yet increasingly beset by disrupted family life, contention, divorce, parents who do not teach nor discipline nor set a good example. The young are sensitive; they see the gap that exists between our stated convictions and our conduct and they are bewildered, sometimes embittered. They say that the adult generation condemns a promiscuity it frequently practices, preaches peace and supports war, counsels the priority of the spiritual but in fact seeks first the material, talks of love but acts in self-interest, and generally represents a hypocrisy that cannot be admired.

In all of this our generation must acknowledge some measure of guilt.

But the young people can and do also take heart and direction from the unselfishness and sacrifice they observe in the adult generation. They see much patience and patriotism, goodness and truth and beauty and brotherly love all about them. They appreciate the value of good homes and parents who care. They love God and their country. They want to live wholesome and happy lives. Their insights are sometimes remarkable. I heard one of them say about another, "His parents don't like him. He can do anything he wants."

Let me tell you about two or three of them whom I have recently met.

Over the jungles of Vietnam a few months ago, Brother Hinckley and I sat buckled in bulkhead seats in what the flying men call the Gooney Bird—the old C-47. Alongside me was a nineteen-year-old corporal who was serving with distinction as a chaplain's assistant. He told me how he had become a member of The Church of Jesus Christ of Latter-day Saints.

> I didn't like my way of life or my associations or my prospects for the future. I knew I was missing something. So one day when I was sixteen I went into a grove of trees near my home in Colorado. I didn't know much about prayer or God. I had never heard of Joseph Smith. I just stood there and looked up and said, "God, I am ready for you if you are ready for me."

115

There was no voice, no vision, no startling experience—just sweet peace and assurance in his heart.

Within hours, through the help of the Lord, he testified to me, he was in touch with people who introduced him to the restored gospel of Jesus Christ. His life since is a stirring youthful expression of faith and great promise. He was ready for God and God was ready for him.

In Hong Kong I asked a young Mormon missionary how he was getting along in his efforts to master the difficult Cantonese language. "Just fine," he said. And when I expressed mild surprise at his optimism and faith in the face of heavy obstacles, he told me of the courage with which his parents had met a deep personal tragedy.

"With an example like that," he said, "you wouldn't expect me to whine or whimper about the blessing of learning this choice language and teaching the gospel to this wonderful people would you, Brother Hanks?"

A high school student leader was called on to speak extemporaneously in a Church meeting. He responded with good feeling and good sense. He spoke briefly about the conflict in which our country is engaged, then, with a tear in his eye, he electrified and moved us emotionally when he said—right off the top of his heart:

"If there has to be trouble, thank God, it can be in my time! I don't want my little brother or the son I hope someday to have to have to fight a war on these or other shores. If there has to be trouble, thank God it can be in my time."

Well, what can we expect from the younger generation? Everything good, creative, decent, wholesome, uplifting—if we help them, and if somehow they come to a knowledge of what makes for happiness, for joy.

Plato said, "What is honored in a country will be cultivated there." And Pericles said, "The young draw strength not from twice-told arguments, but from the busy spectacle of our great city's life as we have it before us day by day."

How can we help them?

We can be more consistent in our lives. We can provide a better example. We can repent. We can obey the commandments of God. We can teach them.

Do you remember the stirring statement of the apostle Paul to his young brother in the gospel, Timothy:

"The end of the commandment [I suppose he meant the result of obedience to the commandments] is charity out of a pure heart, . . . a good conscience, and . . . faith unfeigned." (1 Timothy 1:5.)

The promise is valid and personally relevant to all of us. Paul—he of great intellect and strong training and shattering experience; he who had persecuted, and then been turned around, and who thereafter gave his full measure to the better way—knew the really important values of life. His testimony to Timothy was that in good conscience, in wholesome, happy relationships with our families and fellowmen, and in the true faith that grants us confidence in the presence of God, lie the real blessings of life.

Is good conscience important? It is a prize beyond expression! And conscience is more than a local standard or the accumulation of the mores and traditions of a community or a society or a generation. Whatever else it is, it is the voice of God speaking to us, inspiring moral obligation. Washington called it "a little spark of celestial fire." It is true that we can desensitize our conscience, as it were. In the Book of Mormon we read of a group to whom God had spoken "in a still small voice, but ye were past feeling." (1 Nephi 17:45.) It is also said that there are those who have become "dead as to things pertaining unto righteousness." As we can desensitize a conscience, so we can prepare ourselves better to hear the voice of the Lord by stripping off what the poet called the layers of "muddy vesture and decay," by ceasing to sin and learning to obey. There is the privilege of learning true values and living to them.

Abraham Lincoln is credited with a simple summation of conscience and the way to live with joy: "When I do good I feel good, and when I don't do good, I don't feel good." No one can be truly happy who has a bad conscience, and bad conscience is the inevitable result of conduct below the level of our understanding.

We live in a universe of moral law. We can choose evil and get what we want right now and then pay for it afterward. Or we can choose good and pay for it first before we get it. So it is with a life of honesty and responsibility, of sexual purity, of integrity, of selfless service. The blessing is substantial and sweet and satisfying—worth everything, worth working and waiting for.

When Paul spoke of charity out of a "pure heart," I believe he was talking about the sense of honest, unselfish concern for others that is the mark of moral and spiritual maturity. To accept the responsibilities as well as the benefits of loving, loyal membership in a family is a high challenge to a teenager tempted on all sides by other peer and worldly loyalties. To truly care about others, to be considerate and kind and responsible reflects true maturity. The rebel group we have mentioned is expressing the selfishness of babyhood and the rebelliousness of early youth. In babies and in children, these are natural expressions of stages of living which, sublimated and disciplined as maturity comes, become appropriate self-concern and self-reliance. In a generation charged with major responsibilities amid great complexities, these unmatured characteristics are not worthy. Beyond the "give me" and the "let me alone, don't tell me what to do" stages is that level of life which leads us to ask, "How can I help? What can I do to be useful? Where am I needed?" It is on this level, we bear testimony, that the real contribution and happiness of life can be found.

I read recently of the development of "breeder reactors" which produce vast amounts of energy from a given amount of fuel, and "breed" or produce more fuel than they use while they are doing it. Life is meant to be like that. We are meant to appreciate and use the good things of our inheritance, and to leave a greater store behind us.

Along with good conscience and a genuine concern for others, we need faith in Almighty God. Jesus told the lawyer that the first and great commandment is to "love the Lord thy God with all thy heart, and with all thy soul, and with all thy mind . . . . And the second is like unto it, Thou shalt love thy neighbour as thyself." (Matthew 22:37-39.) All other commandments depend upon this.

In a generation represented by youth who refuse to whine and whimper in the face of great difficulties, who can thank God for trouble in their time if it has to come, there is great and glorious promise. But I believe the summation of the best in them, or in any of us, is in that attitude which motivated one of their number to say, "God, I am ready for you if you are ready for me."

Have you said that, in your own way, and really meant it?

The problems of our day are very great. Many of the voices we have traditionally been able to count on are silent or confused. In the world of theology and religion there is uncertainty and controversy. Faith seems to wane, spirits to sag. We worry about what men say. Perhaps it is time to cease to worry so much about what men say and ask ourselves, "What has God said?" More important than what our neighbors are doing, or what the rest are doing, is what God has done.

Long ago there was a young man who, though "little in [his] own eyes," was chosen king of all Israel. The humble Saul was ready for God, and when the prophet of God had anointed him, he "turned into another man." The Spirit of the Lord came upon him. "God gave him another heart." While

119

he listened to the Lord and his prophets, he led with great strength. When he became willful and stubborn and rebellious, he ceased to be useful and he lost his place. "For rebellion is as the sin of witchcraft, and stubbornness is as iniquity and idolatry." (See 1 Samuel 10, 15.)

A young man named Solomon loved the Lord and earnestly said to him, "I am but a little child: I know not how to go out or come in." (1 Kings 3:7.) He asked God for an understanding heart that he might discern between good and bad, and he was so blessed. Only when he ceased to listen to the Lord and became a law unto himself did he lose his gift and his place.

On the other hand, young Samuel learned and remembered all his life to say, "Speak, Lord, thy servant heareth," and became a great power for good and a chosen instrument in the hands of the Lord.

Young Joseph, sold into Egypt as a slave, remembered who he was and what he had been taught, even in the terrible temptations of Potiphar's household, and lived to serve and save his people.

A humble young Joshua presented himself to the Lord pleading for help, and the Lord said to him: "As I was with Moses, so I will be with thee: I will not fail thee, nor forsake thee. . . . Be strong and of a good courage; be not afraid, neither be thou dismayed: for the Lord thy God is with thee whithersoever thou goest." (Joshua 1:5-9.)

God has spoken and still speaks, and the message is clear.

Beyond these, and above them all, is the scriptural account of a choice Son of God knowing the need for a messenger from God to man on a mission requiring great faith and courage and sacrifice, who said to his Heavenly Father, "Send me."

He delivered his message, completed his mission, gave his life. In his moment of great agony and torment before Calvary, he laid his life on the altar, and said: "O my Father, if it be possible, let this cup pass from me: nevertheless not as I will, but as thou wilt." (Matthew 26:40.)

He was saying, as one of his humble young disciples said in a grove of trees in Colorado a little time ago, "God, I am ready for you if you are ready for me."

To the younger generation, our admonition and loving invitation is that you accept the responsibilities of your great promise. Continue to prepare for the duties of the day and the morrow. Get the help of the Lord. Appreciate your heritage. See the great goodness around you. Forgive us our trespasses and improve upon our performance. Respect our earnest efforts to protect and perpetuate the good things of life for you. Have a decent respect for generations yet unborn. Know that *your* decisions will materially affect the opportunities open to *them*. Build more strongly than we have the foundations for a decent future for all mankind. Keep the idealisms of the fathers of your freedom and the fathers of your faith. Accept the implications of your freedom: make the difficult choices when they are right, and act on them, even if you must stand alone.

Through search and service and reverence, through a life of personal cleanliness and consideration and caring, through faith and trust in God, you can be ready for him. Tell him you are, and he will surely give you the strength and courage and quality to live with contribution and meaning and with great personal satisfaction in this, his world.

Seven Points for Teachers

I truly appreciate always, and say it humbly, the blessing of association with people who, like you, teach and work with teachers of the young people of the Church. I am very sure there are other significant responsibilities which the Church has. For instance, I have much to do with and am greatly in favor of missionary work, yet of all the things the Church has to do, not one, in my humble opinion, is more important than that which you do. In a sense, all that I say today will be dedicated to that proposition.

In what I will say, there will be seven points.

1. Your job is important.
2. You can do it well.
3. It is worth doing well.
4. What to do.
5. What to teach.
6. Put your own house in order.
7. Seek the Spirit of the Lord.

As introduction, this point ought to be emphasized: One who teaches in this Church, or who works with people who do, ought himself to be clear about life. You ought to know

Address given at Primary Conference, Co-Pilot and Top Pilot Department, April 1955.

which things are important and which things are not, and your life ought to reflect that knowledge. It was the psychologist Montague who said, "The things that matter most should not be at the mercy of the things that matter least." This is important. This has relevance to everything—being a mother, being a person, being a teacher, being a Latter-day Saint. When we choose to emphasize or do some things that are *not* important, it must inevitably be at the expense of some other things that *are* important.

When you work honestly at your calling, bringing little boys to a condition of early faith, you work at a great task, for by so doing, you bring them also to a condition where they may take hold of life. The successful young man—that is, he who learns well and is faithful early—has a real start. On the other hand, the little boy, of our faith or not, who has learned certain important things about being a gentleman and being reverent and these other excellent things these sisters have been talking about, is a long way towards being a good Latter-day Saint, isn't he?

Your Work Is Important

It was the novelist Edith Wharton who said (and you will think of some people and things as you consider this), "Lots of people get themselves into the thick of thin things." This is no "thin thing" you are mixed up with. You are involved in about the most important thing you could possibly be doing, if also you are doing the other things—being a good mother, a good wife, a good friend, a good person—that are required of those who live the gospel.

Let's talk just a minute about the job being important. I think it could all be summed up, in the fact that, as Sister Carlisle was saying when I entered the other room: "You are called by God to do a very important thing for him." If God lives, if the gospel is true, this job you do is very, very important. So important that such a little verse as this would apply:

> There is waiting a work where only your hands can avail,
> And so if you falter, a chord in the music will fail.

I should like to call your attention to what the Lord has said. I will ask you to read 1 Corinthians 12:16-26. The thought of this great sermon of Paul is that no member of the body of Christ—that is, of the Church—may say to any other member, "I have no need of thee," because all the members together form the body, and no one is more important or less important than the other, supposing that each does his job well.

One verse I do want to emphasize. You might miss it, thinking that the important teaching was past. I shall preface it with the one other verse which sums up what I have just said:

> The eye cannot say unto the hand, I have no need of thee: nor again the head to the feet, I have no need of you. Nay, much more those members of the body which seem to be more feeble, are necessary. And those members of the body, which we think to be less honourable, upon these we bestow more abundant honour.

This is but to say that you in your calling are just as important in this kingdom as any other person who holds any other job. The teacher desperately needs to know this. One of the few things that upsets me a little is to hear someone say, "I am only a teacher." No one who will do his job well has any need to feel less consequential than anyone else, including the president of the Church, who has a great and important job, but in its way no more important than yours.

Let's sum this up by reference to a letter I received last summer after the visit of a good man from Hawaii, who stayed at our home a day or two. He was a Protestant clergyman whom we had known in the Islands and learned to love. He left his calling and ultimately became, after long study, a member of this Church. Two years now he has been in it, and nearly two years an elder at the time he wrote this letter.

We are still talking about point one—*Your job is important.*
Here is what he said:

> If Joseph Smith, one man committed to God, can do what
> has been done in the brief time that has elapsed, think what could
> be accomplished by a similar dedication and consecration by the
> hundreds of thousands of Latter-day Saints. Is it too much to ask:
> Is it within the realm of possibility? I, who am the least of all
> elders—less than two years old as holder of this office—feel
> that the bringing in of the kingdom of our God and his Son is
> just as much my responsibility in my office as it is David O.
> McKay's in his, or Marion D. Hanks' in his. You two bear the
> same priesthood I bear with its responsibilities. True, you have
> certain keys that an elder does not have, but the effectiveness of
> the use you make of your keys because of your office, depends
> in no small measure upon my faithfulness in my office.

He then quotes the beautiful words of Gideon: "And
they stood, every man in his place round about the camp:
and all the host ran, and cried, and fled." (Judges 7:21.)

This man has learned quickly.

One thing I would almost plead with you to know and to
pass on—your job is very important. There is an idea among
some that in the Church we have a descending scale of responsibility, that we put the president and his counselors at
the top, the Twelve, their assistants and helpers, and so forth,
and down at the bottom are the lowly ward teachers and the
lowly Primary and auxiliary teachers. Some people think that
is the way the importance slides. The fact is that many business organizations have turned their organizational charts
around. They put the workers on the top and the president
on the bottom, recognizing that the important people are
the ones who do the work, and *their* best helpers are their
supervisors, and *their* best helpers are the ones who administer, and *their* best helpers are the ones who preside. In
fact, both approaches may be misleading, for every office in
this Church is equally important if it is done well.

You Can Do It Well

This is what you need to teach some of these teachers. You can do the job if you are willing to pay the price, if you have a normal understanding of the gospel and of people. Let's just take this one idea: To do the job well one must be dedicated.

What price are you willing to pay to be a good and important Primary teacher or supervisor? Do any of you recognize the name *John Trebonious?* Anyone recognize the name *Zera Pulsipher?* Do any of you know the name of the teacher who taught David O. McKay when he was eight or nine or ten? He's talked about her many times. Do you know the name of the teacher who taught Adam S. Bennion and of whom he speaks with such great pride? You don't know the name of my teacher whom I love and revere. You don't know a single one of these names, do you?

John Trebonious was the teacher of Martin Luther. He used to take off his hat in the classroom, it being then the pedagogical custom for the professors to wear their bonnets, so-called. But he would not, and they wondered why, and Trebonious said: "These little boys will some day be men, and I do not know but that there sits among them one who will change the destiny of mankind. I take off my hat in deference to what they may become."

At that moment there sat in front of him a little boy named Martin Luther, the solitary monk who shook the world. Who is in your class whom you are trying to inspire?

We do not know much about Zera Pulsipher today. He was not destined to be president of the Church nor one of the Twelve. He was destined to be the humble teacher who took the gospel to Brigham Young and some other important people, and Brigham taught Heber, and Heber converted the thousands, and the thousands make up part of the foundation of this Church. And who knows Zera Pulsipher's name? You don't know the name of the person who taught President

McKay or these others. Their job was to do this teaching well, and they did it well, apparently.

It Is Worth Doing Well

You are familiar with Doctrine and Covenants 18:10-16. We have traditionally ascribed this reference to missionaries only, but it also applies to teachers. It is the sermon on the worth of souls in the sight of God. Here are the last two verses:

> If it so be that you labor all your days . . . and bring, save it be one soul unto me, how great shall be your joy with him in the kingdom of my Father! And now, if your joy will be great with one soul . . . how great will be your joy if you should bring many souls.

I do not know anyone this applies to so clearly as it does to a teacher.

Time and again, as we travel about the Church, we meet people of stature—a stake president, a young man being appointed to a high council, a person who is becoming a member of the bishopric, or who is one and is doing wonderful work. I have made it a special point to find out who does the best work with the senior Aaronic Priesthood of the Church. Would you guess who does? Well, they are almost inevitably men who were senior members of the Aaronic Priesthood and have been brought into activity. They are people who know the feeling of darkness and who are now in the light. How much value do you think one such man is to the Church? I shall just mention one that came to mind as I said that.

In Ogden I attended a conference where a man stood and told of his bitterness toward the Church, of his animosity and his deep desire to upset and disprove. But somehow, by being taught and repeatedly visited by people who were humble, he came around to a more careful condition, and studied and thought and prayed. He said: "I am not worthy of the priesthood I bear or membership in this Church, because I fought it." Then he told about his work as a stake missionary. He has baptized eleven so far, and is doing a tremendous job. How much value is it?

At a conference in Houston Stake I shook hands with a lady who had two boys, about eleven and thirteen. She was a lovely person, very attractive and obviously a person of character. She expressed appreciation for the experience of being there, and said something about her husband. I asked her a little about him, and she appeared to be very discouraged about the possibilities of his coming into the Church. I smiled and told her to be patient, that sometimes this takes a long time.

Later, a stake officer mentioned her, and I called attention to her two boys. He said: "You know, the day of miracles is not past. Those two kids were the meanest, toughest little brats I have ever seen in my life. They made our place a bedlam in Sunday School and Primary. I encouraged their teachers, but I went my way. I wouldn't have had their job for anything. Yet, you know, when the crisis came between the mother and father [for a crisis had come], these two little boys were so insistent, and because he loved them so much, they had brought him to a condition of at least superficial willingness that they go along." They were the quietest, sweetest, finest little boys. They didn't make a single sound through that long meeting. They sat there and listened.

The stake officer said: "A miracle has happened. They have some little problems, but they really love the gospel. They have been in the Church less than two years." Of how much worth are they?

What to Do

I am going to make nine suggestions. These nine things the teachers ought to do with their students and you ought to do with the teachers.

    1. Know them.

128

2. Understand them. I will give you this exposition of that thought: This means that if Johnny is a little bit negative and hard to get at, it may be because there is trouble in his house and his dad has a chip on his shoulder. Things may have happened which put this little boy on the defensive, made him think mankind is against him. This is not to say that you know him as Johnny Jones, who lives at such-and-such an address. This is to find out more —not pryingly, but interestedly. Be sure you give each boy individual attention.

3. This not so much different from that which I have been speaking of. Let them know you are interested.

4. Set worthy goals for them. Expect a lot from them and let them know it, and that you will not be satisfied with anything less.

5. Plan activities, including spiritual experiences. It might even amount to getting them to go out and shovel the neighbor's sidewalk. When I was a boy that was a habit around our ward. Nobody has bothered my place in the winters I have been there.

The things young people remember best from some of my classes, I have been happy to learn, were when we went and did something for somebody, or enjoyed a fine spiritual experience.

6. Prepare well.

7. Get their attention. I can hardly resist telling you the story of the donkey which one farmer sold to another. It was sold with the understanding that it was a very good-tempered, sweet, compliant donkey, but the buyer couldn't get it to do anything, so he called for the seller, and when he came, he asked, "What's the matter?"

The buyer replied, "I can't get this blamed animal to move an inch. It won't do anything."

The farmer who had owned him before picked up a two-by-four, and hit the animal in the head with all his might.

The donkey fell to the ground stunned.

At this the farmer who had bought him said, "I thought you said he was easy and compliant and willing."

"Oh yes," said the first fellow, "but first you've got to get his attention."

I am not suggesting this as a method for you to use, but I am suggesting there ought to be ways. For instance, there might be a thermometer on the wall and when a boy does what he ought to do, the indicator goes up.

8. Give them recognition. Take the time to find something good in what they are and do. I gave a talk in the Tabernacle when I was about seventeen. Three of the Brethren sat behind me, leaders of the Church. I had worked hard and I performed fairly well. I got through and, being but a boy, hoped somebody would like it, but nobody said so. The three got up and went home; they were busy.

With that experience behind me, as soon as a meeting is through I head for the kids who participate, and I shake their hands; I don't tell falsehoods, but if it is good I tell them so. If it is very good, I tell them so. It is always good, at least. If it is the best I've heard yet, I tell them that. And they are going to remember, I know. So will the ones you teach.

9. Never turn a child away.

What to Teach

Let me try to get it in just a few words. The gospel is perfect; truth is truth; but no one of us understands all about the gospel nor is fully aware of what truth is. Does your idea of God now mean as much to you as your idea of God when you were ten years old? It means more, doesn't it? Do you expect that someday you will know more than you do now? What did the sacrament mean when you were five or seven? Does it mean more now? Do you expect it someday will? What I am saying is that while the gospel is true, and while we are blessed with the gospel, we don't know all there is to know, you and I. Therefore, a teacher must be endowed with humility. There is much to learn. Never tell a child that which you

130

do not know to be true. The hardest exercise known to boys and girls is having to unlearn something taught them by somebody in whom they had faith.

I have a picture of a fine man who wears the Congressional medal around his neck. Your boys would know what that means. His name is Tom Huddleston, Yale graduate, twenty-three, with the world ahead of him. Tom Huddleston with his wingman, flew along one day in Korea. The wingman got hit and went down. Tom circled around. He saw the plane on fire, with the enemy a few hundred yards away coming toward the burning plane. There was no landing strip there, just a vacant field.

There was nothing he could really do, but he knew his wingman was being burned to death. Tom, with all the world ahead of him, set his airplane down by his friend's, got his axe, and ran and tried to tear the cowling off. That was the last they ever saw of Tom. The interesting thing is that his wingman's name was Jesse Brown, and he was then the only Negro naval pilot in the U.S. forces.

I am going to try to teach my little children that people are people, with feelings and hearts and family, worth dying for, despite the color of their skin, or who they are. This is completely compatible with Church doctrine.

Put Your Own House in Order

I wish you would see that every teacher does this. Put your *own* house in order. I will only mention the headings; you extract the lessons. Watch your appearance, your hygiene, your clothes. Be yourselves good wives and mothers; show them the good way. Be active Church participants, not just Tuesday or Wednesday afternoon for an hour. Have a sense of civic and patriotic pride—put your flag up on holidays. Pay your bills. Be consistent.

You know the story of the farmer who sold his butter to the groceryman. The butter turned out to be just a mite less than a pound and the groceryman worried about that,

131

they being brothers in the gospel. But he finally decided he couldn't sell his customers fifteen and a half ounces of butter for a pound any more, and that he had better go check. He went to the man, not knowing how to approach him, but finally determining he would talk to him as if his scales might be out of order. "Brother Brown," he said, "do you have a pair of scales you measure your butter on?"

"No, sir," Brother Brown said, "I don't, Brother Smith. To tell you the truth, I just have a balance. I weigh my butter by a pound of sugar I bought at your store."

Be consistent.

Seek the Spirit of the Lord

This is a spiritual experience in which you are involved. Bright as you are, trained as you may be, you are not wise enough to do it alone. Seek the blessings of the Lord and his favor, and you will be blessed with success and happiness, and your work will be crowned with that joy which will make it really fruitful, for God has promised his Spirit and his power to those who seek him and love him.

God bless you to believe what I have said to you about being important. You are.

Help Youth Take Sides

I honor and commend you who are here this afternoon for being here. You are associated in the most important business in this world—the business of helping boys and girls to become wholesome, happy men and women. It is my conviction that this is, in the eternal sense, the very objective and goal of God himself. We know well the scriptural affirmation that it is the work and glory of God to "bring to pass the immortality and eternal life of man."

I would like to read to you some words of Dr. Elton Trueblood, writing in the *Scouting* magazine:

> The problem of our time is whether we shall be able to develop our resources before it is too late. This is a problem for youth more than anyone else. Anyone, therefore, who gives his nights and days to the spiritual undergirding of America's youth is struggling on the front line of the battle of the century.

With all my heart I agree and believe that we are in a battle of immense significance. We are fighting for the souls of men, and our particular concern is the youth.

Let me mention several basic truths about youth:

1.   Youth has soberingly serious problems.

2.   Their problems are closely related to and often the product of adult objectives, activities, and example.

Address given at MIA Conference, June 1961.

3.   The solid majority of this generation of youth is decent and honorable and anxious to do well.

4.   They need help of a particular kind.

The problems of the young are extremely serious, but they are not unique. They are not problems of philosophical abstraction, but of purpose, of moral viewpoint, of attitude, of goals, of character, and of conduct. These are the same problems which beset adults, and the land in which we live, and our civilization. I am confident that young people will meet their challenges and do a better job of it than we have, if they get help. It is my faith that the solid majority of wonderful young people will rise if they are challenged, walk in wholesome paths if they are led, learn and possess integrity if they are taught by precept and example, act courageously if they are inspired, respond if they are called upon. But they must be taught, educated in the true sense—that is, educated not alone to letters and numbers and statistics and theories, but in terms of worthwhile objectives, wholesome conduct, responsible behavior, participating citizenship.

How can we help them? There are many ways—through the home, the community, the school, and the Church.

We must begin by identifying the adversary if we hope to defend against him. We need to learn something of his plans, his strength, and his methods of attack. This is an essential in warfare and, I remind you, we are in a battle.

In identifying our adversary and defending against him we are doing what is necessary, but this is not enough. We must take the offensive. We must make plans of our own. We must develop programs, organize our strategy, use every available resource, and be willing to give our all in the struggle.

Who is our adversary in this battle for the souls of youth?

1.   Any force, group, individual, or agency who would deliberately subvert the virtue, integrity, morals, or physical, emotional, or spiritual strength of the young.

134

2. The foolish, the selfish, the misguided, who defend evil and those who traffic in it.

3. The indifferent, who do not recognize the problem or do not care enough to do anything about it.

The *first group* is easy to identify. They are out in the open. They exalt sex and use it as a money-making device in movies, plays, recordings, books, in filth they send through the mail. They glamorize and glorify and advertise tobacco and alcohol for money. Some of them even peddle drugs to gullible young people. This adversary works through public media to make it appear that violence and dishonor and infidelity—life on its lowest possible plane—are normal and not to be worried about. They do this for money, designingly sowing seeds of iniquity in the land. They lack decency or honor or sense.

The *second group* ordinarily doesn't produce the iniquity, but they are willing to profit from it and use it. They sell it, promote it, protect it, and often defend it. They sometimes prattle about censorship and their rights as free men. What they are defending is their right to undermine and destroy the souls of young people. In this same category are those who patronize and participate in filthy things.

The *third group,* certainly the most numerous, shrug their shoulders and do nothing. They lack initiative, faith, interest, or the willingness to accept the personal responsibility to join in the war. They think that one person can do nothing or little and therefore they do nothing or little.

I repeat, the first group is easy to identify. Let me give you an example of some who are in the class of the second group of our adversaries, though they would be distressed perhaps to hear it said. There was a group of fine young people in a certain junior high school who were apprehended reading filthy literature. Their principal, an upright, decent man, took them into his office and explained what was happening to them, and then traced the source of the material. The part I do not like to tell you is that it was traced to two homes, and to two fathers who kept a stack of the stuff for private use downstairs by the furnace, or in their own dresser drawer. The kids had found it and passed it around to their friends.

The third group are all about us. I hope none of us can be counted among them. To them and to us I would say that it is time to recognize that we are in a war, a holy war for the souls of men. There never was and never will be a greater prize. Do you know the words of Theodore Roosevelt in this matter? "Aggressive fighting for the right is the noblest sport this world affords."

I believe that with all my heart. No satisfaction in my lifetime has, or in my judgment will, equal the satisfaction of loving and helping fine young men and women.

What can we do? Well, there is much that can be done, much that we must do. For one thing, let us recognize and join forces with the good people in other churches and out of churches who are aligned with us, and march arm in arm with them toward the objectives we share in fighting the adversaries of youth. One of these good folks with whom we are allied in the battle recently suggested three important measures to help the young:

1. More wholesome play and exercise.

2. Cultivation of good habits in reading, music and the arts.

3. Active worship.

Consider the opportunities in MIA and the Church for providing these important opportunities for youth! But let me center for a final moment on the second of these three thoughts.

There is so much of sublime literature available to us. There is available to us the most wonderful help in providing heroes, ideals, images, principles, leadership of the most high and important caliber for our youth. I have sat in this conference learning and appreciating our blessings. I thought of some lessons I would like my children to learn, one of them being the lesson in the article Sister Bennett wrote for the *Era of Youth* where young persons were encouraged to be dependable, to show up, to be there, to plan and perform and produce, whether it be a spectacular defense of the front line in the battle or logistics that have to go on in the rear. Young people need to learn to be there with the goods and to come through.

How can you teach the young? Through lessons? Through sermons? Through example? Yes, and through helping them discover good literature. I sat thinking this morning of the marvelous lessons of the scripture—of Naaman, who learned that in arrogance and self-sufficiency, in being vexed and turning away, there is no real satisfaction. He learned that through humility and faith God's blessings are obtainable. I thought of Paul and his bad memories and his great devotion, and of the lessons of his life. From the Book of Mormon there came flooding in the marvelous accounts of Ammon, son of a king and a great missionary, who had turned away his own kingly birthright to pursue another greater call. He went as a missionary among the Lamanites and taught them the gospel in precept and by the example of his marvelous humility and willingness to do the unspectacular task.

I thought of Alma who wished that he had the voice of an angel and could cry repentance, and then recognized where the true battlefront lies when he said, "Why should I desire more than to perform the work to which I have been called?" (Alma 29:6.)

In the Doctrine and Covenants recall the story of James Covill who covenanted to do anything God wanted him to do, and then was called to a mission he thought was the wrong one. He quit and went back to his former friends and people.

These are stories, ideas and ideals, noble characters that youth need to know. Use the scriptures, use the available literature. Don't wait another day to get into your homes the wholesome, affirmative, constructive, wonderful magazines that the Church has to offer. Use them with your own children. Use them in MIA in the classes you teach, in the talks you give. Help us to help you to help our marvelous young people in the "battle of the century."

God bless you and us to do the best that we can, for there is no time to waste, and there is no cause more important.

Church of the People

Notwithstanding the pressures of this experience, I sat yesterday afternoon almost wishing I might be called in order that I might then bear timely testimony of appreciation to the two men who offered the prayers at that session. Since we last met in conference, I have had the wonderful blessing of touring two of the great missions of this Church which are presided over by those two men, President Peter J. Ricks and President Claudious Bowman. I should like to say of them and the many like them and the thousands who serve with them through the call of the Lord, that they are common and humble men in the very finest sense of those terms, but that they have uncommon faith and uncommon courage and uncommon dignity in the great work they do. As I thought of them I thought of some words of Thomas Carlyle:

> Two men I honor and no third. First, the toil-worn craftsman that with earth-made implement laboriously conquers the earth and makes her man's. A second man I honor and still more highly: him who is seen toiling for the spiritual indispensable, not daily bread, but the bread of life.

These men and the thousands like them who preside over the wards and stakes, the branches, the districts, the missions of the Church, are men who know the task of using toilworn implements, but who know that more important even than

Address given at General Conference, April 1955.

139

this significant opportunity in God's world—the right to work for one's bread—is the great blessing and responsibility of seeking that which is spiritually indispensable, and which is the most important thing a man can seek.

I honor these men, and I feel very humble as I travel in their presence and bear witness with them of the truths God has given us to know.

I read recently out of a newspaper a few words I should like to call to your attention as an example of another great idea to which these men call my attention. Dateline, New York City, last August 7, from a press service, these words written by three ministers of Christian denominations:

> The true ministry of the layman is being rediscovered. He is now coming back to the function he exercised in the early church. There is today in the church a great resurgence of Christian interest on the part of the laity. In ancient times, in the days of Christ, there was not the marked distinction between the laity and clergy. Laity as used in the New Testament simply meant the people of God, but through the centuries more and more the work of the church fell on the shoulders of those who made it their full time profession. The liturgical movement in both Catholicism and Protestantism is winning back for the laity their ancient rights in the Church's worship life. The layman in his secular work is increasingly seeing his vocation as that of the Church's chief evangelist. He is the church in the world.

This is a truth spoken by men of good will and courage and devotion, but which has been available to the knowledge of these and other men since the days of the Prophet of God who died in the year 1844 at the hands of intolerant neighbors. The teaching, preaching, leadership of the Church should be done in Christ's Church today as it was done in his day—by the humble members of the Church, laymen holding the priesthood and authority of God. These and other truths are here available to men, and the world is beginning to learn some of them.

Last weekend, a counselor in one of the great stakes I had the privilege of visiting called attention to certain recent articles dealing with the way a chapel ought to be built, saying that in our day churches are coming to the conclusion that chapels ought to be built with classrooms attached and with recreational facilities.

I say to these good and honest people that from the beginning of the restoration of the gospel of the Lord, it has been known that the gospel was meant to take care of the full life of man; and whenever they find a Latter-day Saint chapel fully completed and dedicated, they will invariably find that there are in it classrooms and recreational facilities designed to provide for development in all the aspects of the lives of its members—physical, social, intellectual, cultural, as well as spiritual.

I read recently in one of our great national magazines a few words I thought to be highly significant about our relationship with our Father in heaven. This came from one of the great religious leaders of our day, a man whom I have revered and whose works I have read since I was a boy. Says he:

> Vital religion cannot be maintained and preserved on the theory that God dealt with our human race only in the far past ages, and that the Bible is the only evidence we have that our God is a living, revealing, communicating God. If God ever spoke, he is still speaking. He is the great I Am, not the great He Was. (Rufus Jones.)

This truth, so majestic and magnificent and basically important, is a truth which has been available anew to mankind since 1820, when a humble, simple boy had enough humility and enough real love of truth to seek from his Father in heaven a manifestation of those things he needed to know, to find his place, his purpose, and his constructive work in life.

The answer is that God does live, that the Savior is the great I Am; he has always been, he shall always be. God's truths are revealed to men when they will pay the price of seeking earnestly, and finding, being willing to accept, and accepting, then dedicating themselves consistently and loyally to him and to his cause.

I am grateful that I have been, by the providence of God, brought into an age and into a Church where the truths are known of which I am able to bear witness today: That God does live, that he does reveal his truths, that this is the Church of Jesus Christ on the earth, that we may through obedience to his word find peace, here and now, enjoy eternal opportunity commensurate with our preparation for it, and literally arrive at a reunion with him who made us and who is our Father which art in heaven.

The Teacher's Challenge

The theme assigned me, "The Teacher in the Church Today," seems to imply that to be a teacher in the Church today is different from having been a teacher in some other era of time. I am in agreement with this implication but add in the beginning that in acknowledging change we must re-emphasize the truth that there are some things that do not change.

Several weeks ago at the Air Force Academy, I listened to a talk by Dr. Ryan, executive director of the National Health Council. He said there are two key words which, if understood, would explain much of the difficulty and affliction and apprehension in this country today. He named those two words as *change* and *choice*. He noted that the multiplicity of choices grows constantly greater, and this because of the fact that we live in a world that constantly changes and becomes more complex. He noted, for instance, that the National Health Council is able to identify more than 150 careers in the field of health alone. A recent manual listed approximately 50 newly minted names identifying scientific specializations unheard of just a few years ago, and these ranged in alphabetical order from astrobiodynamics to zymocrystallography.

Change has, of course, been indigenous to every time and clime and individual; but there is in our day a much

Address given at Sunday School Conference, October 1959.

accelerated change and, therefore, a much accentuated problem. The Church is and must be aware of changes. The leaders and teachers in the Church must give contemporary guidance to meet the needs of the day. There must be available a stabilizing, steadying influence, a force and power which will bless individuals with capacity to meet change on a foundation of things that do not change.

Let me note a few of the circumstances indicating changed conditions which teachers particularly must meet. There are forces at work which threaten us and which could destroy us if we were not conscious of them and prepared to deal with them. The Census Bureau reported that between March, 1957, and March, 1958, 33 million people, or nearly 20 percent of the civilian population of the United States of America, changed their place of residence—that is nearly 20 percent of all the people in America in one year's time. This figure has increased since then. This is impressive evidence of the great need for us to teach eternal, undeviating truths which do not change, upon which all men may always count wherever they are.

Whatever the size of the building or its appearance or the classroom circumstances, the Church must always represent a sanctuary where love and peace and everlastingly stable and dependable things can be found; where there is no private interpretation; where truths that are understood everywhere throughout the Church are being taught; where the great mission of the Church is not obscured by emphasis on or argument about details which have no consequence in faith, and which have little meaning in the ultimate rolling forth of the kingdom of God. Too, there must be interest and love and welcome for the stranger. If 33 million people in America moved about in one year's time, then Church administrators and officers and teachers should be conscious that there must be a special, accelerated effort to seek out the members of the Church who have moved their place of residence and to reach out and bring them into the warmth of the brotherhood. For it may well be that many of those who have moved are the individuals most in need of our seeking and reaching out, perhaps some of them being unwilling themselves to find the place where they should be and the people with whom they should be.

Because of the startling developments in science and in space probing, etc., there has been a great upheaval in educational emphasis. During the past two years, I have been meeting with specialists in many fields across the land and have heard many facets of this problem discussed. I am aware, as perhaps many of you are, that there are some who are strongly urging crash programs of scientific and engineering education designed to rid the curriculum of courses which have no "practical value." They mean, I assume, those courses which are not likely to contribute to the capacity of men to destroy each other.

We know the absolute indispensability of spiritual, cultural, and social values. We know that a man must be fit to live as well as to think. We understand that power without ethical, moral, and spiritual strength and responsibility can lead to brutality, wickedness, destruction and perhaps annihilation. Knowing these things, it is clear to us as teachers and members of the Church of the Lord on the earth that we must be even more concerned to teach and attempt to inculcate into the lives of the members of the Church those values and virtues which will help them hasten, not the *end* of man, but the accomplishment of the true *ends* of man as civilized, sensitive, noble, loving, morally responsible sons of the Divine Father. If there is a tremendous threat in the world imposed by an atheistic people who boast that they can outproduce, outinvent and outengineer us, the answer lies not in a mad race on their terms, but in improving the quality and caliber of the individual human being to understand what life is for and what the purposeful, meaningful experience of mortality really represents. The Church with its high standards and its significant doctrine of the integrity and importance of the individual is more than ever vital.

I mention one other major change: the widespread availability of education to almost everyone who will take advantage of it. We need to face the fact that with additional widespread education comes additional conflicts. Some lose faith because religious outlook and experience have not matured with secular learning. As teachers in the Church, conscious of this circumstance, we must do everything in our power to help inspire the humility, the wonder, the worshipfulness and the sense of the eternal without which no individual's life can be truly fruitful. We must not be thought enemies to education. We must continue to encourage broad and deep education, which includes and emphasizes not alone the training and disciplining of the mind in secular matters, but gives primacy to growth and maturity in matters of spiritual significance and of service.

I know this challenge is very real, being blessed still with the privilege of some time in a classroom. We must meet it wisely, not by attempting to talk the specialized language of those who would undermine religion, but by emphasizing the contribution of the Church in matters of revealed truth, of faith, of prayer and of purposeful living. Our task is to help young people realize that if they will still seek and serve and pray and continue to grow in their understanding and mature in their experience in the Church, they will come to a stage of development when they *know* too much to believe that they have too much information to have faith.

You remember that Alexander Pope said, "A little learning is a dangerous thing,/Drink deep, or taste not the Pierian spring:" He also said, "The increasing prospect tires our wand'ring eyes,/Hills peep o'er hills, and Alps on Alps arise!" When we learn a little, we sometimes feel we know a lot; but if we earnestly continue to seek truth and are honest with ourselves, we come, after a time, to realize how little we truly do know. When one comes full circle in his searching and has gained a recognition of his limitations and his ignorance and his need for Almighty God, he is educated. John Milton said,

"The end of all learning is to know God, and out of that learning to love and imitate Him." This we must faithfully teach our young people. We must guard against drawing into our classrooms and lessons the particularized vernacular of the secular world. It would be wonderful if we were able to learn all there is to learn in every field of human inquiry, but we cannot. Our responsibility and opportunity is to teach the gospel of Jesus Christ with conviction and faith and with a sound understanding that nothing that is important and everlastingly true will ever contradict the revelations of God. We must have a recognition of our own limitations and of the need for us to remain humble and honest and respectful of the minds and contributions and agency of other men.

In truth these are days of much change; but my conviction is that the Church has the answers, the programs, the inspiration to help individuals meet the changes if we who teach and lead are alert, prepared, interested, faithful, loyal and devoted enough.

Let me read from one of the great stories in the sacred scripture. The missionary sons of Mosiah were very successful teachers. Their experience and their example can be very important to us, for the fundamentals of their successful service have changed not at all and are applicable to each of us.

In the book of Alma it is recorded:

> Yea, and they had waxed strong in the knowledge of the truth; for they were men of a sound understanding and they had searched the scriptures diligently, that they might know the word of God.
>
> But this is not all; they had given themselves to much prayer, and fasting; therefore they had the spirit of prophecy, and the spirit of revelation, and when they taught, they taught with power and authority of God. (Alma 17:2, 3.)

The sons of Mosiah had been fourteen years among the Lamanites and had undergone tremendous affliction and tribulation, "both in body and in mind," and "much labor in the spirit." Note that these teachers had the spirit of prophecy and of revelation. When they taught, they taught with the power and authority of God; and they were able to influence greatly those who listened.

My conviction is that teachers today could not fail if they possessed the qualifications which characterized the sons of Mosiah. These men were faithful in the Lord and had waxed strong in the knowledge of truth. They were men of sound understanding, and they sought and received the Spirit in their work. Having been born to kingship, they had turned from evil and unrighteousness and had given themselves to the work of the Lord. They had a sense of the importance of their assignment and gave themselves to it. They searched the scriptures diligently to know the word of God. They fasted and prayed and endured through affliction and difficulty. They labored in the Spirit and stayed with the task.

The foundations of good teaching in the Church have not changed. A teacher's attitude toward what we teach and those whom we teach is still of vital importance. Resourceful, creative, persistent preparation is indispensable. A capacity to observe in the world around us and the experiences of every day the lessons of life which can be related to the lives of those whom we teach is invaluable. Energy and enthusiasm and conviction and love are fundamental to a good teacher, and so is personal knowledge of the students and their circumstances. Binding all of these together is the teacher's testimony and sincerity and example. President McKay is quoted as having said that there are three important things about a teacher: what he *teaches,* what he *does* and what he *is.*

Do you recall the story of Don Quixote? Quixote once delivered a sermon to his groom, Sancho Panza, on the divinity within man. When Quixote finished, Sancho said: "He teaches well that lives well; that's all the divinity I can understand."

There may be some of these youngsters or adults who do not respond with spiritual maturity to the Joseph Smith story or an account of the redeeming sacrifice of Christ, but

I doubt that there is one who does not know whether his teacher is sincere and consistent in his own life.

God bless you. I believe you have the most significant and enjoyable and rewarding job in all the world—and one of the most difficult. I do not believe you can succeed in it without the Spirit of the Lord. I do not believe you can communicate conviction without paying the price to get conviction for yourself. Of all the things for which I am thankful, nothing is more important to me than having the privilege of being a teacher in the Church of Jesus Christ on the earth in these latter days—these challenging days of change and choice.

Learning Is Forever

There may be teachers who believe that the mention of current events has no place in the simple presentation of familiar gospel principles. I believe that there is a relationship between the two. As teachers, we have an insistent obligation to keep growing, to stay alert, to remain sensitive to what is going on in the world about us.

Continual growth in knowledge is vital to the gospel teacher. There are illustrations and lessons currently in newspapers and in good books that we need to know. If a book is a good book, its principles will open up new vistas of life that will reinforce, re-emphasize, and strengthen the fundamentals we are teaching.

Teachers matter, as they have always mattered. About a hundred years ago Emerson made this famous statement: "In former days we had wooden chalices and golden priests. Now, we have golden chalices and wooden priests." However Emerson may have meant it, this allegory has many applications. Certainly it can be applied to teaching. We can be golden teachers if we want to be, if we are anxious enough to learn and willing enough to pay the price.

There is a difference in teachers. Centuries ago someone said: "When Cicero speaks, the people say, 'How eloquent!'

Article printed in the *Ensign*, July 1971; adapted from a talk given to LDS seminary teachers in 1970.

150

When Demosthenes speaks, the people say, 'Come, let us march.' " Teachers matter.

We have obligation to reach and befriend and love those whom we teach. Ruskin said:

> Education does not mean teaching people what they do not know; it means teaching them to behave as they do not behave. It is not teaching youths the shapes of letters and the tricks of numbers and then leaving them to turn their arithmetic to roguery and their literature to lust. It means, on the contrary, training them into the perfect exercise and kindly continence of their bodies and souls. It is a painful, continual, and difficult work to be done by kindness, by watching, by warning, by precept, by praise, and above all, by example.

President David O. McKay wrote:

> What, then, is true education? It is awakening a love for truth, a just sense of duty, opening the eyes of the soul to the great purpose and end of life. It is not teaching the individual to love the good for personal sake, it is to teach him to love the good for the sake of the good itself; to be virtuous in action because he is so in heart; to love and serve God supremely, not from fear, but from delight in His perfect character. (*Instructor,* August 1961, p. 253.)

In the face of a great, changing world, it is our duty to teach the truth, to transmit the fine, sweet, uplifting things of our culture, and to inspire action. In order to do this, we must keep learning.

Where to discover your interest and how to amass relevant information are illustrated in the story of an obscure spinster woman who insisted that she never had a chance. She muttered these words to Dr. Louis Agassiz, distinguished naturalist, after one of his lectures in London. In response to her complaint, he replied: "Do you say, madam, you never had a chance? What do you do?"

"I am single and help my sister run a boardinghouse."

"What do you do?" he asked.

"I skin potatoes and chop onions."

He said, "Madam, where do you sit during these interesting but homely duties?"

"On the bottom step of the kitchen stairs."

"Where do your feet rest?"

"On the glazed brick."

"What is glazed brick?"

"I don't know, sir."

He said, "How long have you been sitting there?"

She said, "Fifteen years."

"Madam, here is my personal card," said Dr. Agassiz. "Would you kindly write me a letter concerning the nature of a glazed brick?"

She took him seriously. She went home and explored the dictionary and discovered that a brick was a piece of baked clay. That definition seemed too simple to send to Dr. Agassiz, so after the dishes were washed, she went to the library and in an encyclopedia read that a glazed brick is vitrified kaolin and hydrous aluminum silicate. She didn't know what that meant, but she was curious and found out. She took the word *vitrified* and read all she could find about it. Then she visited museums. She moved out of the basement of her life and into a new world on the wings of *vitrified*. And having started, she took the word *hydrous,* studied geology, and went back in her studies to the time when God started the world and laid the clay beds. One afternoon she went to a brickyard, where she found the history of more than 120 kinds of bricks and tiles, and why there have to be so many. Then she sat down and wrote thirty-six pages on the subject of glazed brick and tile.

Back came the letter from Dr. Agassiz: "Dear Madam, this is the best article I have ever seen on the subject. If you will kindly change the three words marked with asterisks, I will have it published and pay you for it."

A short time later there came a letter that brought $250, and penciled on the bottom of this letter was this query: "What was under those bricks?" She had learned the value of time and answered with a single word: "Ants." He wrote back and said, "Tell me about the ants."

She began to study ants. She found there were between eighteen hundred and twenty-five hundred different kinds. There are ants so tiny you could put three head-to-head on a pin and have standing room left over for other ants; ants an inch long that march in solid armies half a mile wide, driving everything ahead of them; ants that are blind; ants that get wings on the afternoon of the day they die; ants that build anthills so tiny that you can cover one with a lady's silver thimble; peasant ants that keep cows to milk, and then deliver the fresh milk to the apartment house of the aristocrat ants of the neighborhood.

After wide reading, much microscopic work, and deep study, the spinster sat down and wrote Dr. Agassiz 360 pages on the subject. He published the book and sent her the money, and she went to visit all the lands of her dreams on the proceeds of her work.

Now, as you hear this story, do you feel acutely that all of us are sitting with our feet on pieces of vitrified kaolin and hydrous aluminum silicate—with ants under them? Lord Chesterton answers: "There are no uninteresting things; there are only uninterested people."

Keep learning.

Why should we keep learning? Because our philosophy of education demands it, and our philosophy of life and eternity demands it.

I've outlined from the scriptures what our philosophy of education is, as I understand it. It starts with the words "commanded of God" and ends with the words, "truth demonstrates itself in right thinking and well doing."

153

Why learn? Because the world is moving, and we need to keep up with it. I mean the world of useful, productive knowledge. In three centuries, 1600 to 1900, the application of science and technology produced more changes in how men lived and worked than were produced in the previous six thousands years. More changes in how men live and work will occur during the next thirty or thirty-five years than were produced in all previous history. There is about a hundred times as much to know today as was available in 1900. By the year 2000 there will be over a thousand times as much knowledge of all kinds to record, sift, store, search out, teach, and, hopefully, use with discrimination and effectiveness. There are currently published throughout the world about seventy-five thousand scientific and technical periodicals alone, in some sixty-five languages. These contain about two million articles each year, indexed in some three thousand scientific and technical abstracting services. That will just give you an idea.

President Joseph F. Smith said:

> Among the Latter-day Saints, the preaching of false doctrines disguised as truths of the gospel, may be expected from people of two classes, and practically from these only; they are:
>
> First—The hopelessly ignorant, whose lack of intelligence is due to their indolence and sloth, who make but feeble effort, if indeed any at all, to better themselves by reading and study; those who are afflicted with a dread disease that may develop into an incurable malady—laziness.
>
> Second—The proud and self-vaunting ones, who read by the lamp of their own conceit; who interpret by rules of their own contriving; who have become a law unto themselves, and so pose as the sole judges of their own doings. [These are] more dangerously ignorant than the first.
>
> Beware of the lazy and the proud; their infection in each case is contagious; better for them and for all when they are compelled to display the yellow flag of warning, that the clean and uninfected may be protected. (*Gospel Doctrine,* p. 373.)

Jefferson said, "He who thinks a people may be ignorant and free, thinks that which is not and never will be." Why learn? There are obviously some very good reasons.

How shall we learn? I offer you five words that have evolved from a lifetime of teaching. To my great joy, on the frontispiece of an old English book on prayer I found printed what I had already learned from experience. The five words were called steps to learning: (1) *Read.* (2) *Listen.* (3) *Mark.* (To me *mark* means also copy, clip, assemble. Do it now; tomorrow you will forget where you read it and it will be gone. The kids will tear the paper up or put poster paint on it. The book you think you will remember to put the marker in will disappear, or you will forget it. *Mark* means get it in an accessible form while you are thinking about it, at the cost of some things that are less important.) (4) *Organize.* (Think and put things together. Get them cohesive, coherent. You will change them later, but organize them now.) (5) *Digest.* (As I understand it, that means getting the strength in your bloodstream, casting out the dross, and moving with energy.)

What shall we learn? I have listed four fields of knowledge in which we should keep growing. First, temporal knowledge—so-called temporal knowledge. I speak of what the scriptures themselves say in the Doctrine and Covenants, sections 88, 90, and 93, about history, other nations, languages, and so forth. Why not this instead of some of the other useless, unconstructive things we do?

Second, human relationships. We should be concerned not only with our own welfare, but also with that of others and with society as a whole. In his biography Albert Schweitzer gives this interesting example:

> To the primitive, solidarity with other humans has narrow limits. It is confined first to his blood relatives and then to the members of his tribe who represent to him the family enlarged. I speak from experience. I have such primitives in my hospital.

If I ask an ambulatory patient to undertake some small service for a patient who must stay in bed, he will do it only if the bed-ridden patient belongs to his tribe. If that is not the case, he will answer me with wide-eyed innocence—"This man is not brother of me." Neither rewards nor threats will induce him to perform a service for such a stranger. But as soon as man begins to reflect upon himself and his relationships to others, he becomes aware that such men are his equals and his neighbors. In the course of gradual evolution, he sees the circle of his responsibility widening until he includes in it all human beings with whom he has dealings.

We don't know all about human relations just by being born and living, any more than we know all about our country just by being born and living in it, or the gospel just by being born and living. Just the fact that we are teachers does not make us experts in relationships.

The third kind of knowledge is the law of the gospel and its history—the saving, central truths of life. When we have learned the message of the "prophets of poetry and music," when we have learned what the great scientists have acquired, there is another great field of knowledge that reigns supreme because it is the center of all the rest—knowledge of God and his major creation, mankind. That is what the gospel is all about. We need to teach it, and to teach it we need to learn it.

Elder John A. Widtsoe wrote:

I had studied the gospel as carefully as any science. The literature of the Church I had acquired and read during my spare time day by day. I had increased my gospel learning. I put it to work in daily life and never found it wanting.

Then he tells how detailed was his search. He wasn't demeaning science—but he thought the gospel was more important.

The fourth field we need to keep learning and growing in is the capacity to help our young people apply the great principles of truth in a strong, inspiring, motivating way.

In the British Mission I sooner or later gave every district of missionaries a unique assignment. They would come to the mission home to get motivated or inspired or instructed or counseled or interviewed. We would have a meeting, and during the meeting, when I thought we had reached the point of diminishing returns, I would sometimes say, "All right, brethren, it is ten minutes after ten. Go out on the streets in pairs. Go with a different companion from the one you came with and are working with. You can go down to the museum on the corner or stand out in front or walk through the house; but thirty minutes from now be back with a lesson of life you can illustrate from the scriptures." That was one of the greatest experiences of my life. I can't begin to tell you what I learned from these bright-eyed, alert, wonderful young people.

At the mission home I had watched the construction of a building across the street from my office, and I had heard that jackhammer going incessantly. It was supposed to be a new university building, and I looked out that window and marveled. The noise went on for years, and I said to various people, "No wonder British buildings last a hundred years. It takes them that long to put them up." This went on and on. Then one day I noticed the very famous old red-brick building down on the corner, once used by one of the most famous scientists of all time, going down, brick by brick.

One day a young missionary who had heard me complain came in from a learning-application experience wide-eyed and said, "President Hanks, have you stood in the upper stories of Hyde Park Chapel and looked across the street lately?" I said no. He said, "You should." Then he used the lesson about the whited sepulcher—you know, whitewashed on the ouside, dirty underneath. He said, "I suppose the Lord meant to tell us we misjudge when we look at facades, and when you go down there you'll understand what I mean. Behind this one little building you thought they were taking so long to build is a whole block of buildings. They were hidden by the facade of that building."

Let me tell you one of the most wonderful things I have learned recently. A perceptive man named Frehoff writes:

> Years ago I preferred clever people. There was joy in beholding a mind bearing thoughts quickly translated into words, or ideas expressed in a new way. I find now that my taste has changed. Verbal fireworks often bore me. They seem motivated by self-assertion and self-display. I now prefer another type of person, one who is considerate and understanding of others, careful not to break down another person's self-respect. My preferred person today is one who is always aware of the needs of others, of their pain and fear and unhappiness and their search for self-respect. I once liked clever people; now I like good people.

Teach the gospel, be patient, keep learning. This business of teaching the gospel, whether at home or in a classroom, is the most important business on this earth. This is God's work, and he will help us if we make the effort.

Richard L. Evans

A suitable memorial to the life of Richard Evans would require, to do him justice, the wisdom and power of the voice and pen of a Richard Evans. But there is and ever will be only one of his mold, and the voice and pen are stilled for a time, and we are left, with our limitations, to try to express our appreciation and our love.

What he did so unselfishly and so movingly for so many we attempt here to do for him. One truth qualifies our efforts —that we knew him very well, and loved him very much.

God grant us today utterance and spirit in some measure adequate in so brief an hour to celebrate appropriately the labors and life of this choice son and true servant of God.

After World War Two I became Richard's associate in his direction of Temple Square. Blessed with his friendship, I have reason to bear personal witness that he has come to this inevitable moment fully prepared and qualified to meet his Maker. He gave his "heart, might, mind, and strength" in service to God and his fellowmen. His wisdom was deep, his judgments were just and merciful, his faith unwavering. Richard Evans' nature was proof against error. The Lord has blessed him greatly in this world and in his passage from this world. His earthly experience has ended in a way suggestive of the poet's line: "God's finger touched him and he slept."

Remarks given at the funeral service of Elder Richard L. Evans, November 4, 1971.

It is so appropriate that we meet here today in this building on this, his "beloved ten acres," with this choir singing, and with his cherished associates nearby. Early and late through the years of his service he has been in this place, within these walls, at the crossroads of the West, and here his voice will ring and his memory live while time shall last.

He still lives, of course, for life is eternal and is not broken by death, not even for one parenthetic hour. "Earth's exodus is heaven's genesis," and our certain testimony is that he lives. In the economy of God, all that this man has learned and is and represents is not lost, but will be devoted, we are sure, to important creative service in the eternal kingdom of God.

The scriptures speak of "mighty" men. Richard Evans is a mighty man, gentle, kind, consistent, contributing always on the loftiest plain;
   a selfless toiler and a tiller of the vineyard,
      a worker of prodigious capacity,
         a teacher sent from God,
            a strength in time of need to countless of
               God's children, and
                  a gentleman—always a gentleman—
                     gracious and charming and
                        with a humor and wit un-
                          surpassed.

Perhaps no measure of a man's character is as revealing as his feeling for life—
   what he values in it,
      what he does with it,
         how he spends it.

Richard Evans not only won renown as a keen and perceptive observer of life, but as one who lived it warmly and wisely, and with felicity and thankfulness and faith.

His joys were in his work, his family and friends, and in the Lord.

He was famous across the earth, but he was a modest man. How many times we have watched him on these grounds meet adulation with humble graciousness, turning the conversation to the visitors and their interest and well-being. In far places of the earth we have met friends and admirers of Richard Evans, and we know personally something concerning the host of lives he has enriched and redirected, marriages that are the more solid and happy because of him, homes that are more harmonious, families more loving and united, souls to whom he has brought understanding and hope and inspiration.

Richard Evans was what the poet called a "spirit melodious, lucid, poised, and whole."

Brother Evans loved his work. His commitment was to the best he could produce. For all those years he lived under intense pressures,
>
> always fighting deadlines,
>> always meeting schedules,
>>> always facing tasks bigger than most men ever undertake,
>>>> and always performing every assignment in his special, choice way.

His efforts have been incredible, his output remarkable.

Over a broad scale of manifold talents, he gave himself without consideration for himself, generously sharing the richness of his gifts and of his love.

Of some it is said that they make the imaginary real, and of some, the real imaginary. Richard Evans made the real real.

Of his influence on others there will be no end. In the National Gallery in Washington a few years ago Richard and I read together, and I copied this truth: "The whole earth is the sepulchre of good men, and their story is graven not only on stone over their native earth, but lives on far away without visual symbol, woven into the stuff of other men's lives."

Pericles, speaking of the brave defenders of Athens, said: "In foreign lands there dwells also an unwritten memorial of them, graven not on stone but in the hearts of men."

In many nations men proudly call Richard Evans friend, and give deference to others of us because we are his friends.

In this community he was a bridge of strongest stature across the streams of differences and lack of understanding.

Among his proud associates in the Church, including multitudes of youth, he has been admired, loved, and trusted.

Charming, genuine, eloquent, he strengthened the humble and the high-placed, each feeling Richard Evans to be his own special friend.

By telephone since his passing came a call from a sorrowing lady I do not know, asking if somehow today there could be mentioned the gratitude of all the people whom he has personally helped, and the appreciation of many to his wife and family for sharing so much of him. He was a humanitarian, she said, who, far beyond their expectations, blessed needful people with acts of kindness and of love. So very busy, he took time to reach out with his special quality of concern and comfort and encouragement.

Of his feeling for his family, there is summation in the frontispiece of one of his books: "To Alice—and home and family and friends—who give much meaning to all the opportunities of time and all the assurances of eternity."

I think no man ever had a choicer wife than Alice or finer sons than Rick and John and Steve and Bill, or more loyal and loving brothers and sisters. How proud they have been of him, and he of them, and how grateful. Some of my choicest memories are the talks we had about his early life, about his mother, his father, his family.

And finally I mention his love for the Lord and his Church, love which undergirded and overarched all of his life and all that he did.

God loves us, but God needs instruments of his love, and Richard Evans had "an eye single to the glory of God." An ancient Book of Mormon writer spoke appropriately of him in words descriptive of another leader in another time:

> [He] was a strong and mighty man; . . . a man of a perfect understanding. . . . a man whose soul did joy in the liberty and freedom of his country. . . . whose heart did swell with thanksgiving to his God . . . who did labor exceedingly for the welfare . . . of his people . . . a man . . . firm in the faith of Christ . . . . [whose] heart did glory in . . . doing good . . . in keeping the commandments of God . . . [in] resisting iniquity. . . . Verily I say unto you, if all men had been, and were, and ever would be, like unto [him], behold, the very powers of hell would have been shaken forever. (Alma 48:11, 12, 13, 16, 17.)

Constantly Richard Evans wrote and spoke of faith in everlasting things; his convictions and his vocabulary were geared to values and principles and relationships of limitless, enduring, eternal quality. Early in his life his mind was made up, his course set, and there was no looking back:

God lives,
> Christ is our Savior,
>> Life is eternal,
>>> Men are immortal children of God in whose image we are made and whose plans and purposes for us are limitless and everlasting,
>>>> The gospel is restored,
>>>>> The plan of God is a plan of redemption, of mercy, and of happiness,
>>>>>> Heaven could only be heaven with family and friends.

For others of different or few or no convictions, he had great patience and great compassion and great concern. His life and teachings constantly reached out to them. To the wavering and the defeated his messages were full of love and of hope. I well remember the day on these grounds when I took counsel with him with respect to a person sorrowing for sin. The individual was not identified by name, but Richard listened quietly and said, "I have the other side of that problem." We talked, and resolvements were made. The thing I remember best about the conversation is his kindness and consideration and his emphasis on mercy, and the last words he said as we parted, "Remember, there but for the grace of God go we."

He wrote and spoke often of time, of its eternal endlessness, and of its mortal limitations. "Always," he once said, "there is less time left . . ." He wrote:

> Life is not a thing that begins and ends at two definable points. It is an eternal journey, to an endless destination; and the highest reward is for consistency of performance—not merely for occasional flashes of brilliance, or isolated acts of goodness, or brief periods of dependability. It is still true, as it was when it was anciently spoken, that he that endureth to the end has the greatest assurance of success and the greatest promise of having the labors of his life pronounced "Well done."

"Thank God," he said, "for a glorious and interesting world, for truth, for 'infinity' and for 'eternity' in which to find it—and for faith, and assurance in the limitless and everlasting future."

And thank God, I say, for Richard Evans, and his life and his contributions.

Honored and influential in the lives of multitudes of human beings as few men are in all the world—wise, just, loyal, witty, generous, full of love—he was unique—a man of honor, of integrity, of gentility, of culture, of highest character.

With us his loss is, as the poet said, "As when the lordly cedar, green with boughs, goes down with a great shout upon the hill, and leaves a lonely place behind."

We shall miss him, oh, how much we shall miss him. We shall miss the light he brought into the room, his wit, his quiet question, his eloquent prayer. We shall miss going into his office with his books and papers and mementos, and the letters and talks coming and going. But, as he said of another whom he loved, so I say of him:

> [He] is still himself, and should we ever come within reach of so high a place as where he is, we should like to take his outstretched hand and resume our talk where last we left it. . . . He was earnestly anticipating other activities and I doubt not that already he is engaged in them.

The promise of the Lord is the promise of his servant Richard L. Evans to Alice, to his family and to us all: "And ye now therefore have sorrow: but I will see you again, and your heart shall rejoice, and your joy no man taketh from you." (John 16:22.)

We shall heard Richard Evans again.

It cannot always be "in another seven days," and it may not be from Temple Square in Salt Lake City, but
as surely as the sun brings the morning,
as surely as the rivers run down to the sea,
as surely as God lives and personality persists,
and love and relationships endure,

Music and the Spoken Word by Richard Evans will be heard again by all of us who qualify, as he has done, for eternal creative work in the kingdom of our God.

IV.
Give
Obedience

The Lord wants more from us than moving expressions of conviction and covenant. He wants more than expressions of gratitude and testimony and commitment. He wants us to fear him, but to love him, to "keep all his commandments always." He wants our hearts.

God Wants Our Hearts

While the people of Israel were on the plains of Moab, in the last part of the fortieth year of the Exodus, shortly before Moses was taken from them and Joshua led them over Jordan to their promised land, Moses delivered a series of marvelous discourses to the people. He reviewed the experiences and events of the past forty years and admonished and exhorted Israel to obey and appreciate and keep faith with God, who had preserved them as a people through their wanderings in the wilderness from Sinai to Jordan. He reminded them of the magnificence of their blessings at Sinai, repeated for them the Ten Commandments and said to them:

> And it came to pass, when ye heard the voice out of the midst of the darkness, (for the mountain did burn with fire), that ye came near unto me, even all the heads of your tribes, and your elders;
> And ye said, Behold, the Lord our God hath shewed us his glory and his greatness, and we have heard his voice out of the midst of the fire: we have seen this day that God doth talk with man, and he liveth. (Deuteronomy 5:23-24.)

After bearing this great testimony, the people pledged themselves to obedience and to loyalty. They said to Moses:

> Go thou near, and hear all that the Lord our God shall say: and speak thou unto us all that the Lord our God shall speak unto thee; and we will hear it, and do it.

Address given at General Conference, October 1960.

Moses gave moving response:

> And the Lord heard the voice of your words, when ye spake unto me; and the Lord said unto me, I have heard the voice of the words of this people, which they have spoken unto thee: they have well said all that they have spoken.
>
> O that there were such an heart in them, that they would fear me, and keep all my commandments always, that it might be well with them, and with their children forever! (Deuteronomy 5:27-29.)

The scripture teaches us that on that occasion Moses "stood between the Lord" and the people to show them "the word of the Lord." So President McKay has this day stood between us and the Lord to show us his word. Our hearts have responded. Surely many of us have covenanted anew, as did Israel of old: "Go thou near, and hear all that the Lord our God shall say: and speak thou unto us all that he shall speak unto thee; and we will hear it, and do it."

And as we so affirm our faith and sustain our prophet, is there an echo in your heart as there is in mine of the voice of the Lord to Israel? "O that there were such an heart in them, that they would fear me, and keep all my commandments always, that it might be well with them, and with their children for ever!"

The Lord wants more from us than these moving expressions of conviction and covenant. He wants more than expressions of gratitude and testimony and commitment. He wants us to fear him, to love him, to keep all his commandments always. He wants our hearts.

In section 64 of the Doctrine and Covenants is recorded: "I, the Lord, require the hearts of the children of men." (D&C 64:22.) His promise to those who give him their hearts is certainly the same as it was to ancient Israel—that we may expect his blessings to be with us always, and with our children.

What a marvelous promise! What a magnificent and moving covenant God has made with us—worth everything —worth our love, our obedience, our faith; worth our hearts.

What really happens when Israel gives God its heart? What happens when men honor their heritage and divine possibilities, love him, and obey his commandments? There were certain humble Nephites not many decades before the advent of Christ who met this test, who, in the midst of affliction and persecution, followed a course and achieved the objective. I read from Helaman these moving words:

> They did fast and pray oft, and did wax stronger and stronger in their humility, and firmer and firmer in the faith of Christ, unto the filling their souls with joy and consolation, yea, even to the purifying and the sanctification of their hearts, which sanctification cometh because of their yielding their hearts unto God. (Helaman 3:35.)

King Benjamin, in concluding his magnificent sermon, pursued the course God has set out for his prophets. He instructed, he enjoined, he reaffirmed, he testified, and he promised. He said to the people:

> Humble yourselves even in the depths of humility, calling on the name of the Lord daily, and standing steadfastly in the faith of that which is to come. . . . If ye do this, ye shall always rejoice and be filled with the love of God, and always retain a remission of your sins; and ye shall grow in the knowledge of the glory of him that created you, or in the knowledge of that which is just and true.
>
> And ye will not have a mind to injure one another, but to live peaceably, and to render to every man according to that which is his due. (Mosiah 4:11-13.)

Remember God's promise to Israel? Note this:

> And ye will not suffer your children that they go hungry, or naked; neither will ye suffer that they transgress the laws of God, and fight and quarrel one with another, and serve the devil, who is the master of sin. . . .
>
> But ye will teach them to walk in the ways of truth and soberness; ye will teach them to love one another, and to serve one another. (Mosiah 4:14-15.)

171

So have come the marvelous blessings and promises of God. In 1833, in Kirtland, after a great outpouring of the Spirit at a conference held there, the Lord gave to Joseph Smith a revelation we now know as section 90. In it he gave some further counsel relevant to our theme, and a marvelous promise. He said: "Search diligently, pray always, and be believing, and all things shall work together for your good, if ye walk uprightly and remember the covenant wherewith ye have covenanted one with another." (D&C 90:24.)

Although one does not read in any one verse of scripture all that he needs to know, and although there is no simple formula of faith that is found in any one verse to the exclusion of all else, for God has given us much of his revelation, yet in this verse and in these others which reflect the promises of God, there seems to me to be the kernel of the conduct God expects of us if we are to achieve the magnificent promise he made to us. "Search diligently, pray always, be believing, walk uprightly, remember your covenants."

Now I am not one to judge my brethren of the priesthood lightly. I know to the extent my intelligence permits of the faith in you and the devotion in you and of the wonderful service you give. I therefore speak from the standpoint of appreciation when I say that there are many among us who have not invested enough of themselves in the diligent search God requires of those who know his word and therefore, living it, achieve his marvelous promises. We must search, seek, ask, knock.

Do you remember the word of the Lord recorded in the first section of the Doctrine and Covenants? He said in this marvelous preface, looking to the foundation principles of the gospel: "Search these commandments, for they are true and faithful, and the prophecies and promises which are in them shall all be fulfilled." (D&C 1:37.)

Nephi, explaining to his people why he quoted so freely from the great prophet Isaiah, said to them that he quoted Isaiah to "more fully persuade them to believe in the Lord their Redeemer," and said, "For I did liken all scriptures unto us, that it might be for our profit and learning." Again, he told them to hear the words of the prophet, and "liken them unto yourselves." (1 Nephi 19:23-24.) Surely this is one of the greatest values of scripture—that we might learn them and liken them unto ourselves, apply the lessons and instructions of the revelations to our own lives. How can we do so unless we search, seek, ask, knock, invest ourselves earnestly, diligently in the effort to acquire and organize and share a knowledge of the gospel of Jesus Christ?

The Lord said we must "pray always." His promises are wonderful. He has told us that we may receive the Spirit by the prayer of faith; that we must "pray continually," that we will not be tempted beyond what we can bear; that we must "counsel with the Lord" in all our doings, night and day; that we must "not perform anything unto the Lord" without praying to the Father in the name of Christ. His marvelous promise is that "he will direct us for good."

We are taught that we must "be believing," for all things are possible to him who can believe. I talked with a group of young people about the Book of Mormon last night and quoted to them words of the great Goethe, who said: "I can promise to be sincere, but not impartial." I am not impartial toward the Book of Mormon. We cannot be impartial toward the gospel and the Lord. If we are to get faith, we must desire faith and seek faith. We must start with an attitude of desiring faith. We must "be believing."

This also the Lord said: we must "walk uprightly." Benjamin, near the end of his great sermon, bore his testimony to the people, reaffirmed the need for faith, repentance, humility, and sincere prayer, and added: "And now, if you believe all these things see that ye do them." (Mosiah 4:10.) As Nephi bore his witness to the people near the end of his ministry, he delivered a great sermon on the first principles of the gospel, and said: "After ye have gotten into this straight and narrow path, . . . ye must press forward with a steadfastness in Christ, having a perfect brightness of hope, and a love of God and of all men. . . . and endure to the end." (2 Nephi 31:19-20.) Amulek testified of Christ, taught the first principles, admonished the people to pray, and then said: "After ye have done all these things, if ye turn away the needy, and the naked, and visit not the sick and afflicted . . . behold, your prayer is vain, and availeth you nothing." (Alma 34:28.)

We must "walk uprightly." Within the last few days I was in a meeting in an eastern city talking with a group of people about youth leadership. During the discussion one of the professional employees of the Department of Agriculture, whose civil service rating is not dependent upon who is Secretary of Agriculture, said: "We don't need to interpret human fitness to our department. We don't have to talk about it a lot. We have a man who reflects it impressively in his own life, as Secretary of the department."

This same group heard our story of the programs of the Church, of the principles upon which those programs are based, and of those who lead the programs. One said: "Yes, but your situation is not like ours. Out there you have thousands of leaders." Another person, the directing head of one of the great youth programs in our land, said: "We really can't talk about Utah in the same context with the rest of us. There is an influence in Utah not like any place else on the earth." We know what the influence is of which she spoke. It is found not only in Utah but in every place where faithful members of the Church live the gospel and exemplify its principles.

With all our protestations, sincere and honorable, with all our expressions of conviction and faith and testimony, there is required of us that we develop in us the heart that will move us to obey all God's commandments always, with the promise that things will be well with us and with our children always.

The last suggestion of the Lord in the verse quoted from the revelation to the Prophet was that we remember our covenants. We have covenanted in sacred places—at the waters of baptism, in holy houses, as we partake of the sacrament—

not alone with God but with each other. Consider again the moving charge that Alma gave the people at the waters of Mormon, that they were to "bear one another's burdens, . . . mourn with those that mourn; . . . comfort those that stand in need of comfort, and to stand as witnesses of God at all times and in all things and in all places . . . even unto death." (Mosiah 18:8-9.)

God help us, we who have been blessed with so much, to yield our hearts to him, for while men look at the outward appearance, "God looketh upon the heart."

This Is the Way

The gospel of Jesus Christ teaches us that the salvation and exaltation of men are made possible solely through the graciousness and goodness and love of God in his gift to us of his Divine Son, whose life exemplified the Father's purposeful plan for abundant living and whose sacrificial death made available to us and gave us a vision of our eternal possibilities as children of God. From the record of Nephi we read these impressive words:

> For we labor diligently to write, to persuade our children, and also our brethren, to believe in Christ, and to be reconciled to God; for we know that it is by grace that we are saved, after all we can do. (2 Nephi 25:23.)

The records of latter-day revelation, as well as those of former days, attest to the great truth that through the atonement of Christ all men will certainly be resurrected, and that all who are willing and obedient may enjoy the blessing of God's great gift of eternal life.

The Latter-day Saint understands that through the gift of God, through the great atoning sacrifice of his Divine Son, all that we might achieve is made possible for us, but he understands also that in the plan of God it is necessary that we *accept* this free gift if we would enjoy all of our eternal possibilities. For the Lord told his people through the Prophet in 1832:

Address given at General Conference, October 1956.

> For what doth it profit a man if a gift is bestowed upon him, and he receive not the gift? Behold, he rejoices not in that which is given unto him, neither rejoices in him who is the giver of the gift. (D&C 88:33.)

What must we do to "receive" his gift? The answer of the prophets has been the same, both anciently and in this dispensation, both in the eastern hemisphere and the western. Here is the answer given by Peter on the day of Pentecost to those who, having been pricked in their hearts by the witness of Christ born by the apostles, asked what they must do. The answer was clear and unequivocal: "Repent, and be baptized every one of you in the name of Jesus Christ for the remission of sins, and ye shall receive the gift of the Holy Ghost." (Acts 2:38.)

Nephi in his parting testimony expressed his feeling of compassion for his own people, for the Jew, and for the gentile, and said:

> But behold, for none of these can I hope except they shall be reconciled unto Christ, and enter into the narrow gate, and walk in the straight path which leads to life, and continue in the path until the end of the day of probation. (2 Nephi 33:9.)

And after bearing his witness of the Messiah to his people, this same prophet said: "For the gate by which ye should enter is repentance and baptism by water; and then cometh a remission of your sins by fire and by the Holy Ghost. (2 Nephi 31:17.)

In 1831 the Lord revealed to the Prophet the following:

> He that receiveth my gospel receiveth me; and he that receiveth not my gospel receiveth not me.
> And this is my gospel—repentance and baptism by water, and then cometh the baptism of fire and the Holy Ghost. (D&C 39:5-6.)

There is one other thought companion to these. Testifying that fundamental to everything we believe and hope for and have faith in is the great sacrifice of the Son of the Living God, knowing that he requires of us that we accept his great gift, there is something else necessary if we are to enjoy the high spiritual possibilities which it is within our capacity to achieve. Let me refer to the teachings of Nephi to his people after he had taught them faith, repentance, baptism, and the reception of the gift of the Holy Ghost, as previously quoted. Said he:

> And then are ye in this straight and narrow path which leads to eternal life; yea, ye have entered in by the gate; ye have done according to the commandments of the Father and the Son. . . .
>
> And now, my beloved brethren, after ye have gotten into this straight and narrow path, I would ask if all is done? Behold, I say unto you, Nay; for ye have not come thus far save it were by the word of Christ with unshaken faith in him, relying wholly upon the merits of him who is mighty to save.
>
> Wherefore, ye must press forward with a steadfastness in Christ, having a perfect brightness of hope, and a love of God and of all men. Wherefore, if ye shall press forward, feasting upon the word of Christ, and endure to the end, behold, thus saith the Father: Ye shall have eternal life.
>
> And now, behold, my beloved brethren, this is the way; and there is none other way nor name given under heaven whereby man can be saved in the kingdom of God. (2 Nephi 31:18-21.)

We accept with all our souls the absolute efficacy and essentiality of the atonement of Christ. We attest to the words of Peter and of other prophets ancient and modern that it is necessary for us to accept our Heavenly Father's gift by obedience to what we know as the first principles and ordinances of the gospel. We know also that if we are to enjoy the high possibilities for which we are created and which we might desire as children of God, we must build upon our faith and obedience with right thinking and welldoing. We must press forward with steadfastness in Christ, having a perfect brightness of hope, and a love of God and of all men. Through so doing, if we endure to the end, we shall have eternal life. There is no other way.

Free Indeed

This experience makes me feel like a Marine lieutenant friend of mine. He had been in the last war for four years and when he learned they were considering his recall to the service, he sent the board a telegram in which he said: "I desire to remind you that I spent four years in the last war, and I just want you to know I do not want to crowd in ahead of anyone else who wants the experience."

I am grateful for a great many things this morning, and especially for freedom. As a serviceman who had opportunity in an armed conflict to help defend this nation, as an American, and as a Latter-day Saint, I am as grateful for freedom as my intelligence and capacity to understand it allow me to be.

But as I look at you and consider myself, I think of another kind of freedom which is even more important than the freedom which we here enjoy to assemble and to teach and to worship. This freedom has no relationship to prison walls, or to any other aspect of physical restraint or deprivation. It may, in fact, be enjoyed by one immured in deepest dungeon, penniless and starving and in ill health. On the other hand, it may be absent from one who is not physically restrained, who has an abundance of wealth, health, prominence. I think of the freedom taught by Jesus to certain of the de-

Address given at General Conference, October 1954.

scendants of Abraham many centuries ago. Having taught
them of his Father, he gave them another great lesson, in these
words, many having believed on him:

> If ye continue in my word, then are ye my disciples indeed;
> And ye shall know the truth, and the truth shall make you
> free.
> They answered him, [angrily, you see, because they were
> already free, were they not?] We be Abraham's seed, and were
> never in bondage to any man: how sayest thou, Ye shall be made
> free?
> Jesus answered them, Verily, verily, I say unto you, Who-
> soever committeth sin is the servant of sin.
> And the servant abideth not in the house for ever: but the
> son abideth ever.
> If the son therefore shall make you free, ye shall be free
> indeed. (John 8:31-36.)

There is freedom different from and superior to even
that which we enjoy today, to meet, to teach, and to worship.
What is it? Is it, as some suppose, the right to do as we please?
Do we find this freedom in indulgence, in unrighteousness, in
sin? Do we find it in giving loose rein to passion, to emotions,
to appetites, to the unrighteous thought or act?

This freedom of which Jesus spoke does not company
with unrighteousness nor is it the product of the evil act. This
freedom, which he taught as being most important to mankind, comes to those who in righteousness have faith in God,
learn his law, and seek to understand it, and who, obedient
to it, and with responsibility, seek to do his will.

There are many among us, and throughout the world,
young and old, (though perhaps we too often confine the
lesson to the young), who have the idea that freedom, the
freedom of which we speak, can be found in unlicensed liberty.
But this freedom which Jesus taught is not the freedom of irresponsibility or unrighteousness, but the freedom which
accompanies obedience.

Is that husband free, for instance, who with disloyalty to his wife and family and with lust in his heart, entangles himself in alliances outside his own home? Is that father free who, neglecting his children, turns them away and does not love them and teach them? Is that man free who hates his neighbor, and who will not forgive the trespass his neighbor has committed against him?

Is that wife and mother free who will not perform the duties of her home with joy in her heart, realizing this to be her great calling? Is that woman free who gives her time to selfish social pursuits of doubtful worth instead of in honest service to her neighbor, her community, her church, her God, when there is so much to do?

Is that boy free who trifles with good habits, who cheats a little in school, who will not accept sound counsel and loving parental advice, but who, making his own stubborn way (for he is of the age when he thinks he knows better than they), chooses companions who are on the wrong path, goes about his activities with them, perhaps even stealing from some others the most precious things they enjoy?

Is the young girl free who thinks so little of herself that she allows herself to be handled as if she were worth nothing, or who talks with evil tongue about her friends or acquaintances; who will not be counseled, who will not be helpful or humble in the home?

The obvious answer is that these people are not free. True, they have the right to choose, but they violate their agency in choosing that which denies them the very freedom which God would have his children enjoy; for how is this freedom achieved?

Let me quote two or three verses of scripture. In addition to the words of the Lord telling us that truth makes us free, he said again as recorded in the Doctrine and Covenants, the sacred book of the restoration: "I, the Lord God, make you free, therefore, ye are free indeed; and the law also maketh you free." (D&C 98:8.)

And John recorded that Jesus said these words when he was among men: "Now ye are clean through the word which I have spoken unto you. Abide in me, and I in you. . . . for without me ye can do nothing." (John 15:3-5.)

And the Psalmist sang: "And I will walk at liberty: for I seek thy precepts." (Psalm 119:45.)

And again, James: "But whoso looketh into the perfect law of liberty, and continueth therein, he being not a forgetful hearer, but a doer of the work, this man shall be blessed in his deed." (James 1:25.)

Finally, and perhaps most importantly, out of the book of 2 Corinthians this simple statement: "Where the Spirit of the Lord is, there is liberty." (2 Corinthians 3:17.)

My humble testimony is that real freedom is not irresponsibility or license, but that real freedom accompanies faith in God, the understanding of his word, and obedience to it. (And each of us, I believe, knows personally the difference between the freedom of faith and obedience, and the bondage of sin.)

God bless us to realize as we seek to learn the marvelous principles of the gospel that he who will not in his heart forgive, he who will not be clean, he who will not repent, he who will not seek to know the truths of the Lord as they apply not only to the obedience which is a word, but also to the obedience which is a way of living, is not free.

God bless us that we may have faith, that we may learn his word and live it, in order that we may have his Spirit with us, for "where the Spirit of the Lord is, there is liberty."

Many Kinds of Voices

In this conference we have heard repeated and very impressive references to the vital importance of the home and good, loving parents who impress in that home the ideal of good example and sincere concern.

I would like to address my remarks to the place of the Church in helping to contribute to the lives of wonderful young people from such good homes and in filling a well nigh indispensable role with young people who haven't had the good fortune to have such homes.

This morning Elder Richard L. Evans referred to the suggestion of Paul to the Corinthians: "For if the trumpet give an uncertain sound, who shall prepare himself to the battle?" (1 Corinthians 14:8.)

Recently at a Church area conference I found interesting application of this sobering challenge. The choir selected to sing at the conference rose to perform that glorious hymn, "Let the Mountains Shout for Joy." Most of you will know that in that hymn there is a section where individual voices form a quartet in a beautiful refrain. The people who were singing the four parts to the quartet in this instance didn't leave their sections but sang from their same position. Because three of the singers were far from the chair where I sat, I heard them indistinctly. To the congregation in front of

Address given at General Conference, October 1965.

them I am sure this was a very well balanced and delightful presentation, but from where I sat near the alto soloist, it wasn't quite so well balanced, although it was very beautiful and very pleasant. The young lady who sang the alto part was in her teens. Her voice was strong, her knowledge of the music very good, and apparently her capacity for courage was high, because she sang through her part without a qualm, knowing that many of us near her were listening primarily to her.

That incident set me to thinking about my own and other people's children, because it illustrated a very significant, simple principle. *We hear most clearly those voices that are nearest to us, and we are inclined to be responsive to those voices.*

Do you remember what Paul wrote to the Corinthians after his allusion to the uncertain trumpet? "There are . . . so many kinds of voices in the world." (1 Corinthians 14:10.)

What are the voices to which our young people are listening? What do they hear in their homes, in the streets of their towns and communities? What do they hear over television and radio? What is communicated to them in books and magazines and photographs? What do they hear when they mingle with groups of their associates?

Well, for some the answer will be very good because there are many wonderful parents whose hearts are truly filled with a love for their young people. There are good teachers and fine, interested human beings all over the face of the earth who honestly try to be helpful to youth and to speak truly and honorably. But for many young people the answers wouldn't be so affirmative. What voices are they hearing? Very frequently commercial voices. They may be honest voices from honest commerce seeking the trade of youth. They *may* be voices of conspiring and deceitful men who seek profit at the expense of the future well-being of youth.

There are pagan voices, iconoclastic voices attacking old traditions and fundamentals, arrogantly assuring that the old ideals, the old standards, the old viewpoints of nobility and honest effort, all of these are outmoded, no longer applicable, and may be abandoned with old faith, old ways, old accepted patterns of moral behavior.

Entertaining voices come from illuminated screens, often in company with actions which are designed to emphasize that part of our nature that needs no emphasis. False voices issue from parked cars or darkened rooms, sometimes tainted with alcohol or inflamed with drugs, treacherously asking, always asking, for self-gratification. "Don't you love me?" they say. "You know I love you." Love they call it, but love it is not, and love they do not. True love "seeketh not its own." But these voices constantly sing their song of counterfeit love, always seeking satisfaction of their own lusts, never really giving or intending to give; perhaps not knowing how to give, not knowing how to truly love.

Misguided voices urging rebellion for rebellion's sake.

Beguiling voices inviting young eyes to filth or foulness, young ears to that which young ears should not hear.

Foolish voices which suggest that since most people seem to be doing it, it therefore becomes all right to do.

Cynical voices that propound moral relativism, saying that there are no virtues or principles that you can really count on any more, none that are always applicable everywhere. You make your own rules in this time and generation.

Sophisticated voices that skirt the edge of truth, telling youth, "It's your life; you live it. Never mind what parents, honest teachers, earnest adults, persons who care, have to say about it or how they feel about it. You decide; it's your life."

Peer voices, voices that are inexperienced, sometimes imitating what someone called the "imitation men" they have seen on the street corners.

Aladdin voices singing the same old strain, "New lamps for old."

Loud voices, persistent voices—persuasive, confusing.

In the midst of all this, where can young people turn to hear a voice that will move them in the direction of their dreams, their noblest and highest and most honorable dreams?

Do you remember the words of the Lord through Isaiah? "And thine ears shall hear a word behind thee, saying, This is the way, walk ye in it, when ye turn to the right hand, and when ye turn to the left." (Isaiah 30:21.)

Where can young people hear this voice?

Just last weekend, with some other choice associates I had the blessing of mingling for three days with almost three thousand wonderful young Britons, members of this Church who had gathered for a three-day festival. I wish all of you might have listened with us as these young people, who had found at least a part of an answer to that great question about where you go to hear the voice, themselves reiterated and expressed personal convictions about the message the voice had delivered to them.

A beautiful young woman, through her tears, thanked God that she now could pray, now could feel warm and good about him because she had learned that there is available in this world reaffirmation and a new witness that God lives and that Jesus is the Christ and that the will of God is being communicated to man.

The voice of a wonderful twenty-year-old girl, who had traveled hundreds of miles training youth and their leaders in preparation for a dancing exhibition, and then stood there that night conducting in her modest, gentle, beautiful way, as scores of choice young people went through the traditional dances of their nations in a dignified, pleasant, and very joyful way. They danced the modern dances, too, and they were dignified, and the feeling was strong and good.

The voice of a young Scotsman who walked more than a hundred miles with two choice associates to get to that conference, and who stood to testify of his joy in the companionship along the way, in the spiritual thoughts they had exchanged before their morning prayer together, in the company he had found at the conference. And then he bore his testimony about his own immediate future missionary opportunities.

I sat thinking, as he spoke, of another voice that had sounded, a time before but in very close proximity, the voice of a boy with, I am sure, less than favorable background and maybe less than favorable memories, who stood before a small congregation and in tears said something that constitutes as great a sermon as I have ever heard about an important subject. He said, "The way to be happy is to obey the commandments of God and not try to fix up some of your own."

The Church of Jesus Christ of Latter-day Saints recognizes the difficulties that arise in the lives of young people as they listen, often in confusion, to the strident chorus of voices of those who seek their attention. The Church seeks to provide for its youth the direction and leadership and inspiration that will help them to travel ways of integrity and honor and decency and responsibility.

If there were time to testify what we have heard these young voices repeat and reflect in their spirit and their witness, it would be a very impressive manifestation that there is a place to hear the right voice.

We met in England with a professional journalist who had lived in many parts of the world. He seemed unresponsive emotionally as he watched, and I thought maybe he wasn't responding to these choice young people. And then he sought me out to say, "Mr. Hanks, it has been nice to hear you and the others, but the thing I really enjoyed, after being in the Brighton riots and living in Asia and South America and elsewhere, is to watch these young people. They are different from any other group I ever saw."

The Church offers to its youth answers to some of their serious, sacred, spiritual questions. It offers them a guide to

187

conduct that will help them to live with meaningfulness and joy in this world, and it offers them this sacred personal commitment we call testimony that allows them to say, "I know God lives!"

Thou Art You

As I walked out of the Church Office Building yesterday morning, I heard a man say to his companion, "If I keep up this schedule I am going to end up in the grave." My immediate reaction was to feel that whatever schedule he followed, his chances of that were pretty good. But the second thought came, a thought expressed by a fine but leaden-footed youngster interrupted in the middle of a drag race by a somewhat stern officer. The boy was asked what he was doing, and he said, "I didn't want to get left in the dust." Well, he won't. No one will, and no one will end up in a grave.

The spirit of every child of God goes on living as we experience mortal death—the temporary separation of the body and spirit—and through the atonement of Christ there will be a universal resurrection. The body and spirit will be joined together again as the eternally living soul. The circumstances under which we shall live eternally—in whose presence, with what companions, and in what condition of opportunity and creative service—we are now deciding by the choices we make.

The great messages of this conference and the stirring and solemn assurances that have come have brought to our hearts renewed conviction that this is the truth. We have been teaching that truth in Europe in the past several years with many

Address given at General Conference, October 1964.

of your choice sons and daughters and their older companions. It has been a wonderful experience to see the transforming Spirit of the Lord work upon them as it worked anciently when the Savior called his apostles from the counting place and the fishing nets and bade them become fishers of men. It is an experience that we wouldn't miss nor trade for anything.

Some years ago a wonderful, successful man, who knew nothing of the Church, spent a few days with his son at a boy's camp where several of these missionaries were serving as counselors. A little time later he wrote a note to one of them. Let me read it:

> It's hard for a person untrained in writing to say what I want to and not sound a bit overboard. I think you know me well enough, though, to know that I mean just what I say. I want to tell you and the others how I feel. There is very little that I know about the Mormon religion, but this I see from my contact with you men during this camp period. In some ways it has made itself so vital to young men like you that you found yourself answering a call. You've had to do something personally because your religion is so very personal and important to you. This is a living religion.
>
> I am a ruling elder in a Protestant church, and I covet for my own church, more than I can tell you, the sort of teaching, leadership, and conviction that breathes such a vital force into its young men. We have our missionaries, of course, but this thing which you do is a different thing. It reaches out within your church in a different way, I judge, and in my humble judgment it is one of the grandest ways I have yet heard of for a fellow to repay in some measure to his God the great debt we all owe. I know that God will richly bless your mission and you. I want you to know that through you and the other men I have had a glimpse of something which to me has the possibility of being an answer to many of the problems that beset my own church and the whole world in these troubled times.

Well, I agree with Mr. Cary's generous and challenging words, his sincere words of commendation and expectation. And I agree with the wonderful implications in them for the missionary, for his younger brother and sister and his parents, for me and you, for all of us. They are to me a sobering portrait of our possibilities and our responsibilities.

As we worked with the missionaries, we worked also with wonderful members of the Church and met multitudes of choice young and older people. I see them in my mind's eye this morning in Frankfurt and Orleans and Berchtesgaden, in London and Bristol and Glasgow, and in a lot of other places. Last Sunday night at a fireside gathering in the Brigham Young University field house there were more youngsters gathered than are congregated on these grounds today. A night or two later at Utah State University I met another great group. For them and their generation, I feel in my heart strongest commendation and confidence. But they have a mighty burden to bear and a great challenge to face.

I have been thinking the last few days of the statement of the Psalmist who sang the sweet strains of heaven. "Thou preparest a table before me in the presence of mine enemies." (Psalm 23:5.) Our young people have a table prepared all right, and it is a table laden with the gifts that can make this life meaningful and happy and that can fill them in the eternal sense. But the table is, in truth (as the Psalmist said), set in the presence of their enemies.

Who are their enemies? Some of them have been spoken of this morning: men who dig gold out of dirt; certain ones who manufacture and market filth; they who, whether misguided or designing, put before our young people a picture of life as some live it, but emphasizing the least affirmative and least godly aspects of man's divine nature. The young have a table prepared for them in the presence of many enemies.

One of the enemies is, in every individual case, our own accumulated sinfulness and bad memory. We are constrained to excuse ourselves because of the failings and faults of others. We are constrained to feel that since everybody is doing it, it is all right for us to do it, and this is persuasively propounded by people in various fields who rely on the statistical method and suggest that since large numbers are doing it, then it must be all right for everybody to do it, just so long as you don't go too far.

Well, a tendency in man to excuse himself has ever been with us. Saul was sent on a great mission. Saul failed and then blamed it on his people when he was confronted by the prophet Samuel. Saul told a falsehood. He said he had performed the commandment of the Lord, including destroying certain sheep and oxen. And Samuel said, "What meaneth then this bleating of the sheep in mine ears, and the lowing of the oxen which I hear?" (See 1 Samuel 15:14.) Saul then blamed his defection on the people.

In the day of the restoration a great young prophet had to learn the lesson, too. Many of you are acquainted with the third section of the Doctrine and Covenants, this "handbook of the restoration." May I read from it a verse or two which the Lord gave to Joseph Smith after a misfortune in which he had succumbed to the pressure to do something he knew was questionable. His benefactor and friend who was helping him, providing for him, working with him, wanted some assurance for his wife and family that there really was a prophet at work, and so Joseph Smith reluctantly surrendered to him the manuscript of the then translated portion of the Book of Mormon. This came in response:

> And behold, how oft you have transgressed the commandments and the laws of God, and have gone on in the persuasions of men.
>
> For, behold, you should not have feared man more than God. Although men set at naught the counsels of God, and despise his words—
>
> Yet you should have been faithful; and he would have extended his arm and supported you against all the fiery darts of the adversary; and he would have been with you in every time of trouble.
>
> Behold, thou art Joseph, . . ." (D&C 3:6-9.)

Could there be any more sublime or sweet or perceptive answer to the suggestion, this siren song of foolishness, that "everybody is doing it"? Behold, thou art *you*. And God has given you a table, bounteously laden with the good things of eternity. Will you give it up because others are giving up? Will you surrender the sweet and sound and strong principles of this "vital force" and "living religion"?

Why is it a vital force and whence are its roots? It is a vital force because this is a vital religion. God lives. He is a living, revealing, communicating Father. Christ lives. He is the living head of this Church. There is a living prophet on the earth to whom the Father communicates and reveals his will. Man was in the beginning with God, and we are always going to live.

God bless us to choose to live in his presence with our loved ones, creatively, actively, and effectively serving and loving and learning.

Smoke and Fear

As President McKay spoke to the missionaries of the Church Friday night, I thanked God in my heart that over a large part of my life I have been blessed to serve on that interesting frontier where the Church meets the world—in the missionary cause. I rejoiced last evening as he talked of the wonderfully fine, loyal, intelligent people of integrity in the world, because though I seek premier position in few things, I would not want to be second in my appreciation of the wonderful people there are who are not of us and not like us, but who are good and decent and honest and live to the light they have received. But I confess that much as I have learned to love them, and as honest as is my respect for them and their integrity, I have recognized that their lives lack something they need and could have, and on numerous occasions I have had the blessing, with many of you, of attempting to bear witness to them of what that something is.

Why do they miss it? Why do they not enjoy it? Perhaps because they have not had a chance to learn. Perhaps because they have a seemingly satisfactory circumstance in life. Perhaps because though they may sense they miss something, the pressures and problems and influences of their lives keep them from responding, from being willing to pay the price.

I read some time ago in an eastern newspaper a little article which had no prominent place, but which represented

Address given at General Conference, April 1959.

something meaningful. It was the story of a fire in one of the clothing districts in New York City. It told of the death in this fire of more than a dozen people—fifteen, as I recall, and one sentence from the latter part of the short article was impressive and important to me. It said that these people had perished within easy access of an escape door but had not used it; rather, had huddled together and had died in the middle of the floor because of "smoke and fear." I have wondered if some one of the fifteen or so who died had been conscious enough of the door. If he had known of it and realized its importance he might have led the others through it to life.

I have thought a good deal more, as perhaps you will in contemplation, about what may have happened in that clothing factory. Apparently they had been sitting within easy access of that door (some of them at least) for years, yet had paid no heed to it. Apparently it had not meant much to them, and in their hour of extremity they were not able to find it.

There are many wonderful people in the world for whom I have personal respect and love, and whose intelligence and integrity I consider at least equal to our own, in terms of what they are willing to do for what they believe. Yet I testify with all my heart that there is something here for the finest of them, but it requires a consciousness that not all is well, that there is something to be had in the world besides social competence or other of the earthly pursuits which satisfy the ambitions of men.

"Smoke and fear" are everywhere about us. I read again this morning the vision of Lehi recorded in the eighth chapter of 1 Nephi, and then the subsequent explanatory chapter. You remember the chief symbols—the tree representing the tree of life, or the love of God; the path to it; the rod by which one, holding fast, could reach it; the chasm; the large and spacious building filled with people, old and young, male and female, their manner of dress exceeding fine, who were in the attitude of mocking and pointing their fingers toward those who had come and were partaking of the fruit. Some of those who had tasted it were ashamed because of those who were scoffing at them, and they fell away into forbidden paths and were lost. Note these words in the twelfth chapter of 1 Nephi:

> The mists of darkness are the temptations of the devil, which blindeth the eyes, and hardeneth the hearts of the children of men, and leadeth them away into broad roads, that they perish and are lost.
>
> And the large and spacious building which thy father saw [said the angel to Nephi], is vain imaginations and the pride of the children of men. (1 Nephi 12:17-18.)

My testimony and witness and the assurances of my heart are that though there are wonderfully fine people all about us, with whom I have the occasional privilege of association, some of whom I have the blessing of attempting to teach, and to many of whom I have the privilege of bearing witness, and while I have great respect for what they represent and are, there is something they are missing if they have not found that within easy access is a door leading to life, and that the Savior stands there and knocks, but they must open and walk through.

I have been deeply blessed by the great strong statements of the Brethren at this conference reaffirming that there is something in the gospel and Church of Jesus Christ which will bless the lives of the very finest of men who do not have it, and who therefore have something missing.

To conclude, I mention that such a sermon as President Richards delivered this morning is sometimes greeted by some of the people of whom I have spoken with murmurings as to arrogance and smugness, with some objection on the basis of lack of goodwill—even sometimes, they say, lack of Christianity—in such a statement. I say, and humbly, that the prophets were good and compassionate men who loved brotherhood and goodwill, yet in every instance they testified that there is a way, that men must follow that way and obey the commandments of God. In section 52 of the Doctrine and Covenants, the Prophet, under the inspiration of God, encourages compassion and love and brotherliness and prayer and humility and every other virtue, but adds:

Wherefore he that prayeth, whose spirit is contrite, the same is accepted of me if he obey mine ordinances.

He that speaketh, whose spirit is contrite, whose language is meek and edifieth, the same is of God if he obey mine ordinances. (D&C 52:15-16.)

Principle with a Promise

To me one of the most impressive sights in this world is the group at which I now look and what it represents. Interspersed among you men are many choice youngsters, and though I don't intend to talk only to them or especially to them, I would like to be able to feel that they understand what I am saying. If they do, I think the rest of us will.

Brother Hinckley gave us a wonderful sermon this afternoon. It revolved around an experience with mature, successful, effective, intelligent men in varying degrees of involvement or noninvolvement with tobacco. As he spoke, I applied the words to myself; and you who are here were doing likewise, I feel sure: "How lucky can you be."

I thought of an experience that occurred on these grounds a few years ago when an internationally known nutritionist and research scientist, who had flown here from Stockholm for the express purpose of looking at us and getting something of our story, sat across the desk with a copy of the Doctrine and Covenants open to section 89. I had asked him a question, and I was very much interested in his answer. He had been a bit combative, or at least defensive, along the route. I said to him, "Dr. Waerland, what would you think of a young man, twenty-seven years of age, who wrote that document more than 120 years ago?"

Address given at General Priesthood Meeting, April 1965.

He said, "I would say that he was 120 years ahead of his time." He then talked of some of the affirmative nutritional aspects of the Word of Wisdom. He talked of the discoveries of science and of his own researches, and said that every suggestion of the Word of Wisdom was valid.

I said again, "What would you think of a prophet who knew all that long ago, without any special preparation or training in the sense you have had it?"

He said, "I am not a religious man, and I know little of prophets, but whoever wrote that document was 120 years ahead of his time."

How fortunate can we be? Many of us may not be acquainted with the fact (though many of us are), that in this world there are many choice forces seeking the same ends we are when we teach this great principle of health. One who represented an interesting viewpoint was Thomas A. Edison, thought by many to be the greatest creative genius this world has known. He wrote these words, and I would hope that every young Latter-day Saint who sometimes feels uneasy in the peculiarities and uniqueness of his own health viewpoints would remember them or have access to them. Edison is talking about ways of living and thinking and working. He says:

> The useful man never leads the easy, sheltered, knockless, unshocked life. At thirty-six he ought to be prepared to deal with realities, and after about that period in his life, until he is sixty, he should be able to handle them with a steadily increasing efficiency. Subsequently, if he has not injured his body by excess indulgence in any of the narcotics (and by this term I mean liquor, tobacco, tea, and coffee), and if he has not eaten to excess, he very likely may continue to be achievingly efficient up to his eightieth birthday, and in exceptional cases until ninety.

He defines narcotics specifically and interestingly to include substances with which we as a Church have been at odds since God spoke to a boy prophet a long time ago.

199

I cannot forget an occasion when Dr. John A. Widtsoe, whom you will remember as a great scientist as well as a great Latter-day Saint leader, was one of a group of panelists at a university. Two others, also representing religious points of view, preceded him. One attempted to make an accommodation, to work out an acceptable approach to moderation in drink. The next was a fine young minister of the gospel, who, with measured but very emphatic phrases, objected to all that his predecessor had said, and added, "As a people, and particularly as a group of young leaders in my church, we believe alcohol to be a tool of the devil, and we are against it." When his turn came Dr. Widtsoe stood and very quietly and graciously said, "We link arms with this choice young man and those who walk with him because his view I accept and believe to be our own." Then he said, "Because I have a little time allotted and because my background happens to be the study of chemistry, let me talk to you of the nature of alcohol." He then gave a simple, strong statement concerning the chemical properties of alcohol, and its effect on the human body. I understood that he was linking arms with other good people of honest intent who are seeking to teach the truth about substances that are not good for man.

The Lord has given us a great program of health, which is based on marvelous fundamental eternal principles. You will remember that in the Doctrine and Covenants in a great revelation received in 1832, the Lord says, "The spirit and the body are the soul of man." (D&C 88:15.) A little later he revealed again the truth that the elements—that is, the elements that make up our body—and the spirit in us, when they are combined, permit us to have a fulness of joy. These are eternally important principles. They go hand in hand with the great truth that God lives, that he is the Father of the spirits of all mankind, that mortal life has a great meaning in the eternal journey man makes, and that one of the great purposes of mortal life is to take upon ourselves a mortal body (the elements), because in our eternal experience there will come a time of reunion of body and spirit.

200

You see, young men, when we die, as surely we do, the body goes to the grave. The spirit persists, it goes on, it lives. You will be you, and I will be I, each will be himself. Yes, there is a break in the eternal journey, but the break is only for the body. The spirit goes on, and then one day in God's wisdom and through his power the body will be reconstituted (in a way I do not know, and the detail is of no great consequence to me), resurrected, and the body and the spirit will recombine. That's one big reason why it is very important that we understand the fundamental principles upon which this great program rests. It is vital that we do everything we can to preserve in honor and cleanliness and integrity this mortal body. It is part of our eternal soul.

I remember reading a statement by a great person who said that this is one of the paradoxes of modern Christianity, which makes the body a very useless, negative, evil thing, and yet teaches, theoretically at least, the reality of a resurrection in which this body is part of an eternal soul. There is no such difficulty in the philosophy God has permitted us to understand. The body is a nonevil component of the eternal soul. That's one big reason why we ought to be anxious to keep it clean, anxious to keep from it the substances that would harm it. Have you ever heard these words of Goethe, the great German philosopher: "The whole purpose of the world seems to be to provide a physical basis for the growth of the spirit."

Now, in effect and perhaps with some limitations of understanding, Goethe was talking about what Paul said. Paul said that this is a temple, this body, in which the Spirit of God dwells (see 1 Corinthians 3:16)—a spirit child of God. And Paul thus expressed his understanding that it is our obligation to keep it clean and pure and, so far as we are able, free from the intrusions of that which would harm it.

Now let me say, as I conclude, one other thing. This is a principle with a promise. For years, young and some older people have been coming to me asking me to define substances which were not to be used. I have tried to reply with the words of the Lord: This is a principle with a promise. (See D&C 89:3.) What is the principle? As I understand it, the principle is that everything that God has provided for us that is good we should use with thanksgiving, with judgment, with prudence, and not in excess. Everything that isn't good for us we should leave alone. I understand that to be the heart of the principle. And the promise? The promise is that if we will obey the principle, through obedience we will get better health, greater knowledge and wisdom, and wonderful spiritual blessings.

There are so many examples of these great truths that I would like to tell you about, but let me mention one. As I walked to this building this very afternoon, I heard a man say to his companion (and I didn't recognize either, nor do I think they were part of the conference group, and I know nothing of the genesis of the statement or its circumstances, but I report accurately what he said): "When he gets a few drinks in him, he is really ugly and mean." I'm not sure anybody can improve upon that description of one who makes the mistake of getting involved in a substance that dulls his judgment, that inhibits his natural desire to control himself, that imposes upon his will.

God bless us to have the courage of conviction to live the principle and therefore inherit the promise, and to be courageous enough as we mingle with those who do not understand the principle, to appreciate their value and their worth, and share with them, as they will permit, the important reasons why we should be concerned to be obedient to this law of God.

Sincerity Is Not Enough

In our files on Temple Square we have a great many letters from people who have come to us seeking to learn something of the truths which have been testified of here. We have letters from many who have not been here but who have come in contact in some way with the Church or its principles or its people, and who have written to express (so often in almost the same words) what so many here have expressed, that they feel, they sense, they experience among the Latter-day Saints something different from anything they have ever known before.

At the opening session of this conference we had the pleasure of the presence here of a fine gentleman who had been introduced to us by letter from President George Romney of the Detroit Stake. Prior to that session and following it, we talked for some hours with this wonderful, devoted man. He had come here to learn a little about this feeling, this sense of dedication, this peace which he said he had experienced among the Mormons. He is a man of real loyalty to principle, whose mind and mouth and life are clean and decent, and who is seeking earnestly to do that which God would have him do.

He wanted to know many things about us. He knew much already. He said, "I have been an active, loyal, participating member of my church, but I am looking for something

---

Address given at General Conference, April 1956.

more." He came here to try to discover if that "something" can be found here.

May I bear witness that this experience has happened many times, and that out of it we have extracted the simple lesson that the truths of the gospel of the Lord Jesus Christ are available here to men, in reality, and that as they seek them and find them and honor them, their lives enjoy a kind of peace and fulfillment they did not know before.

I suppose it is the most fundamental and axiomatic thing we might say of religious faith that if it is to be fruitful and productive of good it has to be based in truth. The fact that there is widespread interest in religion in this nation and the world does not warrant the supposition that all those who have religious interest and religious activity will enjoy the peace and sense of purpose and the abundant life promised by the Lord to those who would find and follow his way. It is not enough simply to be "religious" or to be "sincere" in one's convictions. It is not enough to be sincerely convinced of something that is false. We must have faith in true principles and live them courageously if our religion is to help us accomplish God's purposes for us.

The call for faith comes from many quarters. Carl Jung, considered by many to be one of the most important living psychiatrists, is reported recently to have said that among all his patients over thirty-five there was not one whose basic problem was not lack of religious faith. Recently in the Christmas issue of a great magazine there was printed a statement that has much meaning to the Latter-day Saints who know the witness of the prophet Amulek, quoted in Alma, chapter 10, that the prayers and lives of a righteous remnant preserved the land, and who know also that there are other accounts of this same circumstance recorded in the Book of Mormon. Concluding an editorial, the writer said:

> No doubt most Americans are less religious than they should be. They then owe a vast and continuing debt to the saving remnant among them who do hunger and thirst after righteous-

ness and walk humbly before their God. They do not do this for America's sake, but without them America would be little more than a geographical expression.

A widely known statement made in recent years by a great military leader calls our generation "ethical infants," "moral adolescents."

We join with all those who recognize, as those quoted have been shown to recognize, the great need for honor, integrity, humility, prayerfulness, righteousness, the whole truth —all attributes and characteristics flowing from and concomitant to deep religious faith which is founded on truth.

The witness you have heard expressed here today is that God has in our day restored through living prophets, by revelation, the simple, basic, beautiful, life-giving, peace-bringing truths which men of old knew and which Christ himself came to teach in the meridian of time.

May we take time to mention three contributions that the restoration has made in supplying the deep needs of man for religious truth founded in faith? First, I note the *answers* supplied for the universal problems men have concerning God, themselves, and their relationship with their Creator. Second, the restored Church has had revealed a *program for living,* a guide to conduct, which can lead one to fruitful, satisfying, purposeful living here in mortality. Third, I speak of the spiritual conviction, confidence, assurance—*testimony,* we sometimes call it—which will motivate one to think differently, live differently, to be different than he otherwise would be.

The president of the United States is quoted as having said something last year which has special meaning to Latter-day Saints, in connection with the first contribution of the restoration we have mentioned. These are his words: "Whence did we come? Why are we here? What is the true reason for our existence? And where are we going? For the answers we have . . . the faith . . . of our religious convictions." (Dwight D. Eisenhower.)

205

One of the most important aspects of the restoration is that it supplies answers to these most fundamental spiritual questions. We may learn who we really are, and what our relationship is with him from whom we came. We are taught that the Bible may be believed when it teaches that we are the children, the literal spirit children of our Father in heaven. We have assurance that Christ was indeed the living Son of God, that he came to teach men how to live and died that we might live eternally. We know that men are free and responsible agents in a world where there are alternative forces and courses to choose among, and that we are not only free to choose but also under the necessity of choosing the path and course we shall pursue.

Man has within him, in an embryonic sense, those basic attributes which are characteristic of our Father in heaven. Man is capable of love, mercy, and justice, attributes which have their fullest development in our Heavenly Father. We have assurance through the restored gospel of the Lord Jesus Christ that we are literal children of God, that we can become like him, that the ultimate of our possibility is that someday under his guidance we may even participate with him in his great creative work.

The truths of the restoration testify that there was a plan before this world was, and that that plan contemplated our earthly existence, our freedom, and our responsibility, and that when we had left this mortal life, we should continue to live as certainly as we here exist. Moreover, they testify (and this is what first brought the Church to the attention of our friend from the East) that there is a divinely inspired program for living among us which is designed to lead men to happiness here on this earth. What is that program? You know it well. It is a program of faith, repentance, baptism, and reception of the gift of the Holy Ghost; it is a program requiring an enduring and dedicated hunger and thirst for righteousness, a life of honor and honesty, and a "love of God and of all men."

There are able and sincere persons crying out all over the world today for men to "believe." But as our friend said Friday, "They do not tell us *what* to believe or what to *do* to find happiness."

The Church of Jesus Christ of Latter-day Saints testifies to the world that the program restored by the Master of men in our day is the same program he taught men when he was among them. And as Christ taught men to have faith, to repent of their sins, to be baptized for the remission of those sins, in order that they might receive the gift of the Holy Ghost, so taught Paul and the others. Do you remember the occasion described in the second chapter of Acts, an occasion almost analogous to scenes we hear about in various parts of the world today, when the multitude, having been taught the mission and message of Jesus (but by the apostles who have been "chosen" and "ordained" by Christ so to do), found faith in the Messiah, and came to Peter and the others and said: "Men and brethren, what shall we do?" What did Peter answer? Did he tell them to go to some church, any church, and pursue any program or course they chose, whatever it might be, so long as they were sincere? His answer is recorded in the Holy Bible that all may read:

> Repent, and be baptized every one of you in the name of Jesus Christ for the remission of sins, and ye shall receive the gift of the Holy Ghost.
> For the promise is unto you, and to your children, and to all that are afar off, even as many as the Lord our God shall call. (Acts 2:38-39.)

It is revealed anew in our day that not only must a man believe, he must *believe that which is true,* and he must do that which God has commanded.

There is one final thing we spoke of: if one is to learn the answers to the basic spiritual problems of his life and is to pursue a purposeful program fruitfully and happily, he must have a motivation, an "inner aim" our friends sometimes call it, a spiritual assurance, a testimony which will inspire and impel him to learn and to live. The enjoyment of that testimony is one of the great possibilities that have come to us through the restoration of the gospel of the Lord Jesus Christ.

We testify to you that religious faith is important and urgently necessary; but it must be based in truth. The truth available to all men is that God in our very dispensation has spoken, restoring anew the ancient truths, restoring anew the only gospel, the good word of God for his children.

V. Give Leadership

---

*The answer to the problem of American youth
cannot be left with the expert and the specialist. It lies
in the hands, in the hearts, in the willing spirits
of the parents and other interested adults who can bless
them and help them meet their problems.*

Before Kings and Nobles

After that beautiful snowstorm of two days ago, I drove up streets that were littered with limbs of magnificent trees. I was fearful of what I would find when I got home, and my apprehensions were justified. Some of our lovely trees were broken. In our backyard a fence we had built to protect the neighbors while our children grew up was flattened. And I would like to tell you something serious and truthful: I haven't worried a minute about that. I have been thinking about tonight, and what we are here discussing.

We are talking about some casualties more important than broken trees, some that have happened and some that are happening, and some that we want not to happen in the future, which are far more significant. God has from the beginning been very interested in his children, those safely in the fold, some who have strayed, and those not yet in.

We are talking primarily tonight about those who are in, or some who may not be in quite as much as they should be and we would like them to be. I read again with joy what Alma the prophet wrote about some people who were far from the fold, who had once been in. He took three of the sons of Mosiah, two of his own sons, and two other converts and went to teach the Zoramites, who are described as having fallen into great error:

Address given at General Priesthood Meeting, October 1971.

211

> They would not observe to keep the commandments of God, and his statutes. . . . Neither would they observe the performances of the church, to continue in prayer and supplication to God daily, that they might not enter into temptation. Yea, in fine, they did pervert the ways of the Lord in very many instances; therefore, for this cause, Alma and his brethren went into the land to preach the word unto them. (Alma 31:9-11.)

As that happened, Alma offered to the Lord the kind of prayer which is in our hearts as we listen to these great servants of youth speak tonight:

> O Lord, wilt thou grant unto us that we may have success in bringing them again unto thee in Christ. Behold, O Lord, their souls are precious, and many of them are our brethren [I suppose we might assume he was thinking that many of them are the wives and children of our brethren now and in the future]; therefore, give unto us, O Lord, power and wisdom that we may bring these, our brethren, again unto thee." (Alma 31:34,35.)

I recently had my attention called to an excerpt from Church history that I would like to share with you in part. In the Documentary History of the Church (Vol. 5, p. 320) is "A Short Sketch of the Rise of the 'Young Gentlemen and Ladies Relief Society' from the *Times and Seasons.*" You will observe, as the annotator says, that this has more to do with youth than with the Relief Society, but that was the heading.

> In the latter part of January, 1843, a number of young people assembled at the house of Elder Heber C. Kimball [the Prophet is writing this], who warned them against the various temptations to which youth is exposed, and gave an appointment expressly for the young at the house of Elder Billings; and another meeting was held in the ensuing week, at Brother Farr's schoolroom, which was filled to overflowing. Elder Kimball delivered addresses, exhorting the young people to study the scriptures, and enable themselves to "give a reason for the hope within them," and to be ready to go on to the stage of action, when their present instructors and leaders had gone behind the scenes; also to keep good company and to keep pure and unspotted from the world.

The Prophet then notes that the next meeting was held at his house and though the weather was inclement there were many there and to overflowing.

Elder Kimball, as usual, delivered an address, warning his hearers against giving heed to their youthful passions, and exhorting them to be obedient and to pay strict attention to the advice of their parents.

The Prophet then says something that has touched me and I think will touch you who work with youth:

I experienced more embarrassment in standing before them than I should before kings and nobles of the earth; for I knew the crimes of which the latter were guilty, and I knew precisely how to address them; but my young friends were guilty of none of them, and therefore I hardly knew what to say. I advised them to organize themselves into a society for the relief of the poor, and recommended to them a poor lame English brother . . . who wanted a house built, that he might have a home amongst the Saints; that he had gathered a few materials for the purpose, but was unable to use them, and he has petitioned for aid. I advised them to choose a committee to collect funds for this purpose, and perform this charitable act as soon as the weather permitted. I gave them such advice as I deemed was calculated to guide their conduct through life and prepare them for a glorious eternity.

You see our efforts to reach youth today are not original. They are about the same, motivated with about the same sense of their need, and certainly by the same Spirit that directed those of old. This statement of the Prophet moved me because I have had the same feeling when I have stood before them. As a teacher, for years I have pondered their future as I taught them, and I have lived long enough to see fulfillment of my fondest hopes, or the beginning of the fulfillment of them, for many of them, and, I am sorry to say, the realization of some of my apprehensions. They are in fact a great and remarkable generation, yet like many of you I am well aware of the major problems confronting all of our young people, and that many of them desperately need help.

It would be an interesting experience for some of you to walk through a few days of our relationships with youth in person, by telephone, as we visit with them in interviews, by mail. It is just a few days ago that I deplaned at a major airport, met some of you leaders there, and a beautiful college-age young lady who was waiting for me. She had left her home against the wishes of her parents and others and had hitchhiked to a rock festival. On her way home from that adventure, hitchhiking now with a male companion, she was picked up by officers of the law, arrested for possession of drugs, tried and sentenced to five years in prison. Through the intervention of our local brethren, who were reached by a distraught mother through the bishop, she was given parole freedom, but the record has been made and her life is hanging in the balance. She has some decisions to make.

On my desk is a current letter, one of many, from an anguished girl crying for help. Three times the words are repeated, "Please help me!" Within hours there has been another call, from a disturbed young man seeking guidance for his friend who questions a Church position which he feels he cannot accept, which he thinks makes his position in the Church tenuous or untenable.

In my hand I hold a letter received two days ago from a faithful, brokenhearted father whose son, about the same age as the others, took his own life, notwithstanding the efforts of loving parents and a fine, wholesome family. I wish there were time to read a description of how hard these marvelous parents have tried. This is a missionary family, a committed family, a stay-together family, yet this boy, convinced of his own worthlessness, that he was a failure and that the mistakes he had made were disqualifying, took his own life. His father sent a copy of the note he left, and asked me to make such use of his letter and this letter as judgment and my feelings suggested.

What can we do? How can we help this great young generation meet the challenges of their time? I am certain that we must thoughtfully examine not only their needs and their problems, and what we have to give them, but *how* we undertake to give it, and what we appear to them *to be* as they observe it. I have been rethinking my own experience and will give you just an example or two quickly. May I do it in the spirit of a statement by Spinoza that for a long time has been very choice to me: "Neither laugh nor weep, nor loathe, but understand."

What are some of their problems? These basic observations have come from experience with youth and from their own lips and lives. I can sum them up in four or five needs.

One, they need faith. They need to believe. They need to know the doctrines, the commandments, the principles of the gospel. They need to grow in understanding and conviction. They need to worship and to pray, but they live in a time when all of this is so seriously questioned, when doubt is encouraged.

Two, they need to be accepted as they are, and to be included. They need a family, the most important social unit in this world, and even if they have a good family they need the supportive influence outside their home of others—of neighbors, of friends, of bishops, of brothers, of human beings.

Three, they need to be actively involved—to participate, to give service, to give of themselves.

Four, they have to learn somehow that they are more important than their mistakes, that they are worth while, valuable, useful, that they are loved unconditionally.

I knelt with my own family at the conclusion of a great family home evening, the night before our lovely daughter was to be married in the temple. I think she wouldn't mind my telling you that after we had laughed and wept and remembered, she was asked to pray. I don't recall much of her prayer, the tears and the joy and the sweetness, but I remember one thought: she thanked God for the unconditional love she had received. This life doesn't give one very many chances to feel exultant and a little successful, but I felt wonderful that night, and thank God that she really believes and understands what she said. We cannot, my dear brethren, condition our love by a beard or beads or habits or strange viewpoints. There have to be standards and they must be enforced, but our love must be unconditional.

I will read you just a sentence or two from the letter left by the boy who ended his own life:

> I have no hope, only dreams that have died. I was never able to obtain satisfactory interpersonal relationships. I feared the future and a lot of other things. I felt inferior. I have almost no will to achieve, perseverance or sense of worth, so goodbye. I should have listened to you but I didn't. I started using acid last summer. It's purgatory.

What a tragic story!

We need to understand their needs. They need to learn the gospel. They need to be accepted, to be involved, to be loved, and they need, my brethren (my fifth and final point), the example of good men, good parents, good people who really care.

I went to the funeral of my cousin a few weeks ago and I pass on to you something that touched me deeply there. Maybe it is the message I can share with those of us who can do something, if we will, for our great young generation. A man who served as his counselor, now himself the bishop, said of my cousin: "Every boy in his lifetime has the right to know a man like Ivan Frame."

God bless us to love these young people, to accept them, to give to them what they need in order that they may be what they want to be and give what they want to give.

The Soul of a Prophet

It is said that a great man is "one of those rare souls who sees sermons in stones and books in brooks, and the bright light of God over everything. Across a reverently gay and gentle lifetime he has had eyes to see and ears to hear music which most of us miss." It could be as well, and maybe better, said of President McKay than of any other man.

I read a little time ago the statement of one who was speaking of spiritual leadership. May it be a kind of theme for this occasion.

> I regard the problem of spiritual leadership in an age of disbelief as one of the most important of the moment. It arises because those who should lead the younger generation have either lost the gift for leadership or do not see that it matters. This is true of ministers, philosophers, poets, and artists.
>
> If we want now to know whether his leadership is genuine or spurious, we have to know what a spiritual leader is. Everything depends here on our asking the right questions. We may ask: What are the essential qualities required of a leader? This is the traditional approach which may be called individualistic, aristocratic, and isolating, because it concentrates on the "great man" in isolation from the field in which he acts. The "hero," however, does not exist in this isolation. We have therefore to go on to a deeper level by asking: What is the function of a leader in human society? And what is his relation to the field in which

Remarks given at Brigham Young University, March 19, 1968, on the occasion of the presentation of the Exemplary Manhood Award to President David O. McKay.

217

he acts? In fact, he has always to fulfill specific functions in relation to the members of the group. He has to bring light into their darkness, order into the chaos of their experience, to discover meaning, to make them feel and understand what was incomprehensible to them, to distinguish the essential from the inessential, the valuable from the valueless, and to show them the direction in which they should walk and what they should do. He must have the capacity for imparting his vision of truth to others and for inducing them to choose a specific way of life. (Frederick Henry Heinemann.)

In light of this definition or any other valid one, it may well be concluded by those who know him, his life, his teachings, his example, the power of his radiant influence, that David O. McKay has been the most significant spiritual leader of his time. To whom better than to him do the poet's words relate:

> Be such a man and live such a life
> That if every man were such as you,
> And every life a life like yours
> This earth would be God's paradise.

From another poet this worthy description of a lofty life:

> 'Tis human fortune's happiest height
> To be a spirit melodious, lucid, poised and whole.
> Second in order of felicity, to walk with such a soul.

Who has as effectively as President McKay accomplished these objectives in a lifetime? Would you hear a brief statement of the purpose of life from his own writings:

The true end of life is not mere existence, not pleasure, not fame, not wealth. The true purpose of life is the perfection of humanity through individual effort under the guidance of God's inspiration. Real life is response to the best within us. To be alive only to appetites, pleasure, pride, money-making, and not to goodness, and kindness, purity and love, poetry and music, flowers, stars, God and eternal hopes, is to deprive one's self of the real joy of living.

In the clarity of his vision, the keenness of his intellect, the scope of his knowledge, the depth of his wisdom, David O. McKay stands a paragon. Poets, philosophers, prophets, all are within his ken—their thoughts stored in his memory through hours invested and hard labors performed. His perceptive mind, his noble character, his generous nature have translated, refined, applied, made wisdom the amalgam of his learning and his love. To him the words of a friend seem particularly appropriate: "I gave it and gave it and gave it until it was mine."

What to President McKay has mattered most? Wherein has been the emphasis? Recall the teachings of his great ministry, his instructions to his people. These few I note:

Faith in God and Christ
  A Christ-like character
    Living outside one's self in love
      A life worthy of trust, a clean and wholesome life
        Nobility of soul
          Education, discipline of the mind
            Cultivation of the beautiful and the uplifting
              Wise courtship, good marriage, family unity, family prayer
                The sanctity of the home

Honoring womanhood and motherhood
  Exemplary manhood
    Honoring of parents and heritage
      Courtesy, good manners, gentility
        Hard work, service above self
          True patriotism, love of country
            Every member a missionary
              Teaching that which has come to him from God

How well President McKay has applied his ideals, fleshed in their skeleton, breathed into them the spirit of life! His ministry and his life are eloquent answer. Rather than describe, let me illustrate with these incidents from my own experience.

One morning in the temple as President McKay addressed all the Brethren who had come, fasting and prayerful, to prepare for a general conference, he calmly appraised them and then said something so simple that any one of us might have thought of it, yet none likely would have. He did, and I have not forgotten the feeling as I looked at him and heard him say (and I must paraphrase for want of specific words, but I think I have not forgotten), "We have met this morning with our bodies cleansed and clothed in clean linen, our minds prepared, our spirits subdued, to await the direction of the Lord."

Would this be a good pattern for living every day for every man?

His consideration is unfailing, his courtesy also. Recently I talked with him in his office, entering to find him seated as usual behind his desk. He had not been feeling well; he was not strong. To another person in such circumstances, it possibly would not have occurred to try to rise to greet a visitor, but I had to all but restrain President McKay as he fought to get to his feet to bid me welcome. That sweet experience brought a tear to my eye.

It led me to remember another day during the first months of my ministry when I had been asked to speak at a Primary general conference. Thinking myself to be free on the appointed day, I had accepted an invitation to address the opening meeting and was distressed then to receive an invitation to attend at the same hour the regular pre-conference meeting of the Brethren in the temple, called a little earlier than usual. When the ladies learned of this conflict they were, of course, concerned, their program having been prepared and printed, difficult to change.

I asked the counsel of several other good men, President McKay being away for the moment, and was assured by each that it was my responsibility to be at the meeting in the temple, notwithstanding my commitment to the Primary people, and I sorrowfully prepared to do that.

When President McKay returned, I had occasion to mention the dilemma to him. His immediate answer was to reassure me that I must be at the meeting to which I had committed myself, and that I should so inform the ladies.

In the temple on the appointed day President McKay arose and announced to all the Brethren in the beginning that I had been committed to a Primary appointment, and then rearranged that whole meeting in order that I, the least of them, and certainly the least important, might be in attendance for the sacred purposes that had brought us together. And then I was excused to fulfill my commitment. It seemed a small thing, but not to me; and I wondered, I confess, what other man would have been so gracious and so considerate under those circumstances.

To some, on some occasions, an interview may seem like an interrogation or even an inquisition. Occasionally honest persons are alienated because they resent the nature of the questions asked, or the attitude of the interviewer. One of the sweet aspects of an interview with President McKay, as anyone knows who has had the experience, is that while one is with him he has the full attention—the eyes, the ears, the interested heart—of a great man. I shall never forget an important interview I had with the President of the Church. I have never seen fit to discuss it in detail in public, and I do not intend to do so now, but I would simply like to note the nature of his questions and of the spirit of the man who asked them. It was a forthright and intensive interview, but it was an exchange, and the questions that brought from me what I suppose he wanted to hear were questions like this (note the nature of his asking): "Are you fully loyal to your family?" "Are there any improper involvements or alliances outside your home?" "Are there any unresolved problems in your life?" Who could resent or who could answer falsely such gracious and gentle and courteous questions?

Two other incidents bespeak clearly the wholeness, the

wholesomeness, and the inspiration with which God has blessed this great man.

I was leaving for Vietnam shortly before the Christmas season. I had a brief interview with President McKay to receive a message he wanted carried to our men in the bush and the rice paddy. He kept me longer than I had intended, anxious to hear, apparently, my plans and prospects for this mission. Interestingly, he didn't commiserate with me or sympathize a bit when he learned that the projected absence might involve the holiday season away from my family. What he said was, "What a wonderful privilege for you to be going!"

When we were through, that great hand reached out and touched me lightly on the knee, and he said something that seemed to me to summarize the glory of his ministry and a noble lifetime. "Tell them of this exchange of love," he said. "Tell them of this exchange of love."

It was not the words of love to which he was referring, but the sweetness and beauty of the feeling in his heart, which I am sure he knew was reciprocated in my own. I wonder if that isn't really what life is all about—to have the capacity to feel and the strength to communicate, to exchange love.

An appropriate estimate of President David O. McKay was given by a prominent labor leader whom I was privileged to escort to an interview with him, together with the man's wife and two daughters. It was a remarkable experience— there was laughter, good humor, sometimes conversation that seemed a little light, sometimes very serious, in this half-hour or so. There was an exchange of personal views about important matters which were affecting the country. There was the great story told by the President to this man, of the day when he and his brother Tommy had stacked the hay with every tenth load going to the Lord. Most of us know this marvelous story. President McKay told how he and his brother had taken the tenth load in regular sequence only to be challenged by their father at a certain place in the fields where the father felt the hay wasn't quite good enough for the Lord.

He wondered if the boys wouldn't like to go back to a better part of the field to get some better hay to put on the stack they were building for the Lord. At first the boys demurred, saying that the Lord should take his tenth from every part of the field. Their great old Scottish father laughed, put his arms around the boys, and told them that might be all right for others, but that for the Lord only the best was good enough. President McKay told it simply, his great hand gently touching the other on the knee to emphasize the importance of this lesson.

All of us enjoyed the interview, there was no posturing, no posing, no declaiming—just the simple, warm, generous inspired friendliness exuding and expressing itself. When we left the room, the man and his family were all in tears, and I listened to this internationally famous man say these interesting words: "I have enjoyed the experience of meeting with kings and rulers, and I have seen leaders of many kinds in many lands, but I have never met a man like that. I don't believe our generation will ever produce a man like that."

Later he repeated this statement to a group of university professors in the city, complimenting them on the blessing of living in an area near the available influence of the greatest man he had ever met.

It was said of prophets long ago, and it can be said with equal validity of David O. McKay:

> And [he] . . . did walk in the ways of the Lord, and he did keep his commandments, and he did judge righteous judgments. (Mosiah 29:43.)
>
> And they did wax strong in love toward [him]; yea, they did esteem him more than any other man. (Mosiah 29:40.)
>
> And this was [his] faith . . . , and his heart did glory in it, . . . in doing good, in preserving his people, yea, in keeping the commandments of God . . .and resisting iniquity.
>
> Yea, verily, verily I say unto you, if all men had been, and were, and ever would be, like unto [this man], behold, the very powers of hell would have been shaken forever; yea, the devil would never have power over the hearts of the children of men. (Alma 43:16, 17.)

Tradition of Their Fathers

Last evening several teenage boys spoke from this pulpit to many thousands of young and older men in a great meeting. I should like to take my theme in part from something said by one of them: "If I cannot respect Mom and Dad, whom I see, how can I respect my Heavenly Father, whom I do not see?"

To briefly establish a foundation, let me refer to a recent magazine article which began with these words: "Infant baptism is under fire." There follow several examples of this significant theological development across the world among Protestant and Catholic thinkers, and then this statement:

> Perhaps the most formidable challenge to infant baptism was made recently by Switzerland's venerable Karl Barth. . . . In his latest book, Barth argues that there is no Biblical basis for infant baptism and that the ritual is not an act of God's grace but a human response to it—which means that the individual must be mature enough to understand the meaning of such a decision. The traditional understanding of the sacrament, he says, is simply "an old error of the church." (*Time,* May 31, 1968, p. 58.)

With the substance of this we are in complete agreement. When the disciples asked Jesus, "Who is the greatest in the kingdom of heaven?" this is recorded:

> Jesus called a little child unto him, and set him in the midst of them, and said, Verily I say unto you, Except ye be converted,

Address given at General Conference, October 1968.

224

and become as little children, ye shall not enter into the kingdom of heaven. Whosoever therefore shall humble himself as this little child, the same is greatest in the kingdom of heaven. (Matthew 18:1-4.)

Then were there brought unto him little children, that he should put his hands on them, and pray: and the disciples rebuked them.

But Jesus said, Suffer little children, and forbid them not, to come unto me: for of such is the kingdom of heaven.

And he laid his hands on them. (Matthew 19:13-15.)

To this may be added the testimony of a Book of Mormon prophet: "He that saith that little children need baptism denieth the mercies of Christ, and setteth at naught the atonement of him and the power of his redemption . . . for . . . . all little children are alive in Christ." (Moroni 8:20, 22.)

In other sacred scripture we are taught that infants are "innocent before God," and then there is added this signal statement: "And that wicked one cometh and taketh away light and truth, through disobedience, from the children of men, and because of the tradition of their fathers." "But," said the Lord, "I have commanded you to bring up your children in light and truth" and to "set in order your own house." (D&C 93:38-39, 40, 43.)

It is to the phrase *because of the tradition of their fathers* that I would give special attention, and to the injunction to "set in order your own house."

Previously over this pulpit I have expressed my respect for children who have improved upon the ways of negligent parents, and my compassion for choice parents who have earnestly tried to bring up their children in the way they should go, only to have those children use their agency and individuality to follow other ways. The Lord has taught us that in his sight the son shall not bear the iniquity of the father; neither shall the father bear the iniquity of the son. Each who is accountable must ultimately account for his own decisions.

225

But multitudes of us still have our children at home, or have grandchildren, or are influential in the homes or with the children of others. Great numbers of young couples are just starting their families, or soon will be. All of us should be brought to solemn thoughtfulness by the sobering word that although children are "innocent before God," the "wicked one" is able to take away "light and truth" "through disobedience" and "because of the tradition of their fathers."

The first definition of *tradition* in a modern dictionary is: "The knowledge, doctrines, customs, practices, etc., transmitted from generation to generation."

What is the tradition in your individual home and mine? What "knowledge, doctrines, customs, practices," and so forth are being or will be transmitted from our generation to our children and their children?

God teaches us that children are to honor their parents. What in us, our lives, our character, our behavior, is *worthy* of their honor? What in us is noble, responsible, faithful, gracious, considerate? What is worthy of their respect and their emulation?

Do we teach honesty by being honest? I love to remember the story of the man who, while his little son was with him, stopped at an isolated cornfield on a remote country road, and after looking before and behind him, to the left and to the right, started to climb the fence to appropriate a few ears of the farmer's corn. Said his son: "Dad, you forget to look up."

What happens to the boy whose father boasts of the slick deal he has made in which others were outwitted? Years ago the late Joseph Welch said, on the occasion of his being named Father of the Year:

> If it were in my power to bestow on the youth of the land one single quality, I would not choose, I think, wit or wisdom or even that great boon, education. If I could choose but one, I would choose integrity. If one day my children and grandchildren say to one another, "He taught us to value integrity," I shall be content.

How is the quality of integrity passed on to the children in the home? It is passed on by living a *life* of integrity, of sober honesty, of responsible citizenship. How can one surely *fail* to pass this priceless quality on to children in the home? By being a little lawless; by being a fixer; by being a cheat and a chiseler. Not so long ago one of my two boys spoke these sobering words to me. He said, "When the two of us were young, there were times when you and Mom would obviously set out to tell us how to live the good life. We could always recognize those moments and we would close our ears and our minds. Your most influential moments were your most inadvert ones. We were apt to imitate what you really were—not what you said you were or even what you may have believed you were."

If your children are to have integrity, they must find it in the home and in you. If they live in an atmosphere of complete integrity, they will accept it as an attitude and never waiver thereafter. And having integrity, they will themselves find freedom; and having found it, gladly grant it to all others.

Every parent should ask, What ideals and values is my child learning? What is his image of himself? What is the view of others that he is developing in our home? Is his experience with his parents bringing him a growing consciousness that the "bright light of God" is over everything, and a growing confidence in the presence of his Heavenly Father?

In New Zealand, we learned an old Maori proverb: "A bird must have feathers to fly." Parents have the primary responsibility for feathering our children for flight. A child who lives in an atmosphere of disrespect, criticism, or shame will not be inclined to respect or accept himself; and of shame it has been impellingly written: "Holocausts are caused not only by atomic explosions. Holocausts are caused wherever a person is put to shame." (Abraham J. Heschel, *The Insecurities of Freedom.*)

Our treatment of others will certainly condition a child's attitude toward others. Children who see and sense in parents a genuine concern for others, expressed in acts of kindness and compassion and unselfishness, will themselves be inclined to think well of mankind and to do as the scriptures bid: to

227

"succor the weak, lift up the hands which hang down, and strengthen the feeble knees." (D&C 81:5.)

Young people so blessed may also be less susceptible to the bewilderment that confronts some in our generation's paradoxical stress on man's rights and privileges while at the same time belittling him as a creature of his environment, conditioned by sociological and psychological factors, not possessing the powers and capacities of free agency and thinking and believing, of choosing and determining, not the unique personality that God has taught us we are. The "conditioned-reflex" version of the behaviorist cannot inspire the mystery and awe and wonder which are the glory of man. To know, instead, that every individual is an eternal person, a potential god or goddess, capable of deep love and graciousness and mercy, more than human, is to prepare us to live with courage and a sense of responsibility, to inspire self-reliance, self-respect, and genuine respect for others

What is the tradition of discipline in our homes? Is our child pampered, indulged, permitted in a moment of crisis to transfer his guilt to others—his parents, peers, family, the age he lives in, society? How will he handle disappointment and failure if he is not taught to face up to his mistakes honestly? We are not talking of imposing senseless punishment. We are talking of realities, of facts to be faced, of fair rules which are understood and enforced, with sanctions consistently imposed when they are broken. "Self-respect," Abraham Heschel has said in his book quoted above, "is the fruit of discipline; the sense of dignity grows with the ability to say NO to one's self."

What shall we give to the children? Pray for a sense of humor. "Laughter leavens life" and brings a sunny spirit.

Pray also to be able to pass on the will to work, and the urge for excellence; the capacity for moral indignation, and the courage to stand alone; disdain for evil, and love of justice; the ability to love without condition or question. Do you know the story of the eight-year-old girl in an orphanage, unattractive, with annoying mannerisms, disliked by the teachers and administrators? One afternoon it was reported that she had broken a rule that would justify her expulsion from the institution. Against regulations she had been seen depositing a note in the branch of a tree overreaching the fence. The note was retrieved. It read: "To whoever finds this: I love you."

How in your home and mine is the tradition of patriotism?

On the Saturday evening just before Christmas last year, two clean, handsome young men—boys, really—their battle gear stacked nearby, stood before a large group of their comrades at China Beach near DaNang, South Vietnam, and sang "Silent Night." They had no accompaniment, and the sweet, clear ring of their voices will always be remembered, and the emotion we all felt. The next morning, before dawn, one of those young men came to my sleeping quarters to say goodbye and shake hands once more as he joined his outfit to head out into the bush on a search-and-destroy mission. It was not the Sabbath activity he would have chosen—he was disappointed not to be able to worship with fellow servicemen in our scheduled meeting—but he went his way to do his job. There is no question as to the tradition transmitted in this boy's home.

Fathers, mothers, what traditions are we planting in another generation, in our homes, as to self-control—control of our tongues and tempers and appetites? In 1884 Henry Drummond made a statement on this theme that could be read regularly with profit by each of us:

> We are inclined to look upon bad temper as a very harmless weakness. We speak of it as a mere infirmity of nature, a family failing, a matter of temperament, not a thing to take into very serious account in estimating a man's character. And yet . . . the Bible again and again returns to condemn it as one of the most destructive elements in human nature.
>
> The peculiarity of ill-temper is that it is the vice of the virtuous. It is often the one blot on an otherwise noble character . . . . This compatibility of ill-temper with the high moral character is one of the strangest and saddest problems of ethics. The truth

is, there are two great classes of sins—sins of the Body and sins of the Disposition. . . . No form of vice, not worldliness, not greed of gold, not drunkenness itself, does more to un-Christianize society than evil temper. For embittering life, for breaking up communities, for destroying the most sacred relationships, for devastating homes, for withering up men and women, for taking the bloom off childhood; in short, for sheer gratuitous misery-producing power, this influence stands alone. (Henry Drummond, *The Greatest Thing in the World.*)

What traditions are we passing on for other homes in future times that are worthy of the memories we ourselves have? On occasion through the years I have enjoyed the blessing of asking large groups of adult leaders to meditate for a moment on their conclusion to an unfinished sentence, and then share their thoughts. The sentence reads: *"The thing I remember best about my childhood at home with my parents and family is ....* "

I suspect your answers would be about the same as those that I have heard. Never once has anyone mentioned a high standard of living, or material possessions. Always they have spoken, as I would speak, of attention from mom or dad; of family associations, traditions, sacrifices, adventures together; of books read aloud, songs sung, work accomplished; of family prayers and family councils; of small presents lovingly and unselfishly prepared; of homey and wholesome and happy memories. My single question to them has always been, and I ask it today, "What are we giving our own children that they will remember with equal joy and application?"

Since our last conference my wife and I were privileged to visit Samoa and other islands in the far seas. One afternoon in the mountain tops of Upolu, in American Samoa, in the village of Sauniatu, we had a remarkable experience pertinent to this moment. The village was deserted except for a few very young children and one or two who had stayed home with them. The rest were working in the fields or at other tasks. As we walked the single lane of Sauniatu, between the rows of *falés,* from the monument toward the new chapel and school, we heard children singing. There were perhaps half a dozen of them, none more than four years old, and they were singing with the sweetness of childhood a song we instantly recognized, and stood entranced, in tears, to hear: "I Am a Child of God."

In that high mountain fastness, at the end of a long, tortuous road, on an island of the sea, we found tiny dark-skinned children, none of them having seen more of the world than their small village, singing what they had learned through the tradition of their fathers, the greatest truth in existence, save one: I am a child of God.

That other truth? That there is a God who hears the voices of his children.

God bless us so to live and teach that we may bring about a restoration of the home, the resurrection of parenthood, that the "wicked one" can never take away "light and truth" from our children "because of the tradition of their fathers."

Don't Be an Iconoclast

Some weeks ago it was my privilege to go into one of the great subterranean caverns in the southwestern part of our land. Thousands upon thousands of people visit it annually. The day I went into it, far below the surface of the earth, I was in the company of a large group, but no one whom I knew personally. The path on which we walked through this great cavern over a period of more than an hour was quite a narrow one, permitting two to walk abreast, if a bit crowded. The trail was lighted in sections as we went and was very clearly marked with white stones at the edges and with signs all along the way. We were accompanied by three park rangers and met others as we went. I walked near the front and heard some of the comments of the ranger as we were led into the magnificent scenery of this underground wonderland.

As we walked, we passed beneath a huge, high dome. Below it, appropriately named, was a deep hole called "The Bottomless Pit." There was conjecture among the people as to what might have caused this empty place in the earth. Some thought it might have been an early fossil deposit, others an area of highly soluble materials, others the result of an earth movement or some other like occurrence of nature. It was discussed for a time with no conclusion reached. The ranger informed the party that there is divided opinion on the question among the experts.

Address given at General Conference, April 1957.

A little farther along the trail we came into an area where there was another vast vaulted dome, but the debris from that cavity lay below it in a mountainous pile. Again there were comments along the trail. One said: "My, I'll bet there was a tremendous clap of noise when that fell!" An army man replied, "Do you really think there was? After all, there was no one here to hear it!"

They discussed this issue at some length, whether or not in the absence of someone to hear, noise actually occurs. I listened and said nothing, but thought of Bishop Berkeley, Irish philosopher, whose theory was that "to be is to be perceived"; that is, so-called material things exist only in being perceived. If it is not perceived, it does not exist. It is said that a group of the bishop's students at Oxford taught him the true nature of reality one very dark evening when they placed a tree stump on a certain unlighted path where he habitually walked. His perception of the stump was said to be a realistic shock to George Berkeley.

When we departed the cave, the people were still discussing whether or not when things fall there is a noise in the absence of human ears to hear it.

As I left the cavern, I thought to myself that these may be legitimate fields for inquiry, and it may be that someday someone will discover the answers, though that seems doubtful. But would it not be a most foolish thing to abandon the cave because we do not know the answers? Suppose someone should take it into his mind that all the glory of this wonder, God's handiwork, should be abandoned and never enjoyed more because those mysterious questions were not answered. Suppose one with ready access to the place and with personal knowledge of its great beauty should decide that he would never enter more because there were things he did not fully understand about it—or go about seeking to dissuade others from enjoying the majesty of it because it took effort to reach and there were certain (to him, here and now) hard-to-understand problems. Would not this be foolish and tragic?

Do you know that some of our wonderful young people of great potential intelligence and capacity and contribution are abandoning their faith and their way of life in the gospel, with all the strength and beauty of it, because they have come to questions for which they have not learned satisfactory answers?

May I read you a statement from the pen of one of the most learned among us, who left us a legacy of scientific research and useful knowledge, and of great faith. Dr. Widtsoe, after encouraging "mature examination," said:

> Wise men do not throw the Church overboard because they have not satisfied themselves concerning every principle of the gospel. Under the law of progression every principle may in time find lodgment in the inner consciousness of the seeker.

To abandon the marvelous demonstrable truths of the gospel because there are some questions one cannot satisfactorily resolve would be foolishness in the extreme. As President Clark said the other evening, "A foolish man can ask questions that the wisest cannot answer." It is no reproach to our religion or to us not to be able to answer definitively, categorically, finally, every question that can be asked. I plead with you, and I talk not theoretically but with some of your faces in mind, not to abandon all that is good in your religion because there are some things you do not understand.

I would speak now to some who influence these young people in causing them to abandon what they believe.

Along the trail down in the cavern, well marked and defined as it was, with signs and guides to make clear that we were to stay on it, some "boy play" occurred between some young Scouts in uniform who walked the trail just a short distance behind me, supervised by a Scoutmaster and several assistants. The boys were jostling and pushing each other all the way along, trying to get some adventurous, "progressive" soul to get off the trail and go out and explore a little. I watched it all and observed the instance I now think of, when a larger boy who had been tantalizing a young one, pushed him off the trail and into a dimly lighted, muddy area. The boy went near the edge of a crevice, and with an outcry that startled us all and got the rangers quickly to his side, signaled the danger he was in and the possibility that he might have perished in the darkness.

You see, along this trail at periodic intervals the ranger would stop and bend over and turn a switch which was hidden from the view of the rest of us, and an area ahead of us would suddenly become lighted. The ranger at the back, when we were safely through a certain area, would turn off the light. The youngster had gone into a section of the cave where the light did not reach.

I thought, as the lights went on and off, how realistic this experience is to life. We talk of questions, some solvable. We know that the Lord has encouraged us to seek truth, to "knock," "ask," and "search diligently." Yet there come times when we reach the end of our capacity to reason and to understand. We must learn to walk by faith. There has been given us enough light to walk the paths we are here to tread. As the Lord in his wisdom desires that we have more light, we have the assurance that it will be given. I bear my witness that from the beginning of the history of the Church the lights have come on when the need arose. It has always been so; it is so now; it will always be.

When the little boy was brought back on the trail, the ranger was very angry, chastised him severely, declared him banished from the group, and started to send him away, while the real culprit in the case stood silent. He was not going to be punished, just the boy. Then the Scoutmaster spoke up and said, "If he goes, this boy ought to go, too." He was a wise man. The ranger talked to them both for a moment and, on promise of good behavior, allowed both of them to stay. I was glad, but it occurred to me to consider the tragedy that might have taken place, and to ponder the thought that though God and wise men may forgive, there is great danger and no real happiness to be found in leaving the narrow path of gospel principle to adventure in strange paths and forbidden ways, in the enticement of dark places, in "looking beyond the mark," as Jacob said.

We left the cavern a while later. My teacher's mind and my interest in youth had brought me to some renewed conclusions, and I pass them on earnestly to mature persons who are given to assisting young people off the trail. The dictionary has a word for them: *iconoclast*. It is defined as, "One who attacks cherished beliefs as shams." What if the cherished beliefs that are attacked along the trail are true? What if they are the very beliefs that make these boys and girls the worthwhile, promising people they are? What if the foundations of their faith are effectively shaken at this crucial period, and they dangle, with no substantial footings to stand on? To quote a sentence from the economist Babson:

> Many of the most important men in America, who are what they are because of what they learned at their mother's knee, now deny their own and other people's children those same blessings, in the name of "liberalism" or "progressivism" or "emancipation."

Such men, Babson says, deny others the very blessings that made them what they are.

Do you know that when one who has influence with youth—be he teacher, leader, or parent—seriously weakens the foundations upon which a young person has built, by faith-destroying challenges the youngster is not yet equipped to meet, he fashions a disciple who has been effectively cut loose from fundamentals at a time when he needs most to rely on them? The challenger may himself be a moral, educated, well-meaning person of integrity, doing what he does in the name of honesty and truth. His own character may have been formed in an atmosphere of faith and conviction which, through his influence, he may now help to destroy in his young follower. "Disenchanted" himself in his mature years, he turns his powers on an immature mind and leaves it ready prey for nostrums and superstitions and behavior he himself would disdain.

To you who influence this boy, to "emancipate" him, in your way of thinking, may I ask you: Have you really helped him develop his capacity to contribute to the world's useful knowledge and useful work? In which particular is he a better person when you get through with him? In what aspect of life has his ability to serve been strengthened? Does he love God and his fellowmen more? Is he a more moral, clean, virtuous, decent man? Is he a more faithful husband, father, or son? Has he learned more gratefully to honor his father and mother? Does he merit their increased respect and esteem as he matures? Is his power for good increased? Has he acquired a greater influence for motivating others to constructive, participating citizenship? Is he a more worthy, admirable person to his younger brothers and sisters? Has he experienced increase of generosity, unselfishness, thoughtfulness for the needs of others through your tutelage? Is he more kind, considerate, gentle, sensitive? Does he have more sympathy, love, and understanding for those who are distressed? Does he live life more courageously, manfully? Will he endure tribulation more patiently and understandingly because of you?

I have answers to these questions. Again I do not talk from theory but with faces and lives in my mind. My experience is that when you get through with him, as fine a man as you are, as much respect as I may have for your education and your brilliance and your effectiveness and your personal integrity, you have not improved him in any of these important ways. He may be, in fact he often is, cynical, destructively critical, vain, high-minded, impervious to instruction. Quite often he has acquired attitudes toward society and habits of behavior which break the hearts of those who love him most and which you yourself would never stoop to. He sneers at his parents, at those whom he once respected, and often at God and holy things. It is quite a responsibility you have assumed.

May I commend to you what Richard L. Evans said this morning: "A teacher is responsible for the total effect of his teaching." So is it true of a parent, an official, a leader of youth. What is the total effect of your influence on the young?

I mention one other thought that came in the cavern. As we walked in that subterranean beauty, I thought what each of you under like circumstances would have thought. I thought how wonderful it would be if my lovely wife and little girls could be with me; I wanted to share with them the wonder, the inspiration, the nearness to God I felt then. A verse of scripture came to mind. It is recorded in 1 Nephi:

> And it came to pass that I did go forth and partake of the fruit thereof; and I beheld that it was most sweet, above all that I ever before tasted. . . .
>
> And as I partook of the fruit thereof it filled my soul with exceeding great joy; wherefore, I began to be desirous that my family should partake of it also. (1 Nephi 8:11-12.)

All things good and beautiful are the more so when we can share them with those we love.

I pray that the Spirit of the Lord will guide the young people of the Church as they seek answers to their questions, for this is encouraged, that they may seek "by study and also by faith"; that they may with dedication and honest effort search for useful knowledge, growing also in an understanding of God and his plan, for the Lord has said that "to be learned is good," *if* we hearken to the counsels of God.

Be Honest with Yourself

Perhaps no conference in my remembrance has devoted such effective and repeated emphasis to the home and the family, to children and youth, and to those who have to deal with them. Not attempting to correlate or specifically to fit in with what has been said, I would like today to talk not *to* the young (which I have often done), nor exclusively to their parents, but *about* the young to the adult generation in and out of the Church.

Out of my love for young people and the blessing of teaching them over the years and the association and friendship I have enjoyed with them, I have learned a few things, some of which I would like to mention today as pertinent to the general theme of home and family and the relationships of adults and youth.

About young people I have learned these things, among others:

1. That by and large they are inclined to be like their parents, to be what their parents are. There are, I am certain, exceptions, since each child, like each of us, is an agent before God, blessed with the right to choose and responsible for his choices. They, like we, must choose, and therefore some of them are not like their fine parents, while some improve upon their parents. But we may repeat with absolute assurance that by and large they are inclined to be like their parents.

Address given at General Conference, April 1958.

Now this characteristic of youth can result in great good or in great trouble, depending upon what parents are, what kind of example and precept they present.

2. They can be tremendously influenced by interested adults other than their parents—by teachers, leaders, counselors, bishops, by interested adults who will take time to love and give attention to them, to have confidence and faith in them—because young people, like the rest of us, respond to those who show interest in them. They love those who love them, trust those who trust them, and in general can be counted upon to respond to the type of adult who is interested in them.

Of course, this can be a good or bad thing, depending upon the kind of adults who show interest, and what their motivations are.

3. A third thing I have learned about the young: They love an ideal. They are great followers. Their ideal may be a singer, an actor, a teacher, a parent, an author, an explorer, a scientist, an athlete, but they are inclined to choose someone to idealize. Usually it is someone older than they, but not always.

This, like other characteristics of the young, can be good or bad, depending upon the persons whom they choose to idealize.

4. I have learned about the young that they can be taught, that they are responsive to the atmosphere and environment of the world around them. They respond to advertising and example, to filth and evil and degradation and bad influence, and they will respond likewise to virtue and decency and integrity and honor, if these qualities are manifested to them in ways they can understand. They can be taught.

This can be good or bad, depending upon the fare their minds and eyes are fed upon.

5. I note about the young that they are not easily misled as to individuals. They can often detect quickly one who

seeks to deceive them. They can uncover in interested adults with questionable motivations the real purposes of their interest. Again and again I have seen it demonstrated that they can spot one who tries to deceive, who pretends to represent virtue and integrity and does not. It is also true that young people sometimes are more willing to follow an openly evil or cynical person than one who is not what he should be and pretends to be. Therefore, it matters a great deal that we be genuine and earnest and honest in our relationships with them.

Believing that the young can be taught, and desiring to surround them with virtuous and uplifting and ennobling ideals, the Church has endeavored to provide experiences and influences and opportunities in the lives of the young which will bring into their beings, their minds, their very souls, the high and noble and decent things which will motivate them to contributing, participating citizenship in the world and in God's kingdom.

For that purpose, the Brethren have provided a series of small cards and large posters, with a general theme, "Be Honest With Yourself," and some magnificent contributions have been made to the young, contributions with which I am sure every right-thinking adult, in or out of the Church, would be sympathetic. My experience as I have traveled the country and passed on the idea to others not of the Church is that they have responded with great interest to the program.

Now, I have one serious question to ask. I have talked about the young, and have said of them that they are going to be like their parents, but that they will respond to interested adults outside of the home; that they are responsive also to ideas and ideals; that they can be taught; that they are quick to discover hypocrisy; and that we are attempting to get them to "be honest" with themselves. The question I ask is: Are we, the adult generation, honest with ourselves and with them?

Is it possible that in our approaches to the youth we are missing the significance of the opportunity to teach them that is ours? Could it be that Thoreau speaks of many of us when he says there are "thousands hacking at the branches of evil to one who is striking at the roots"?

I read a statement by an interested modern observer a time ago, which is a little harsh, perhaps, but which I repeat because I am sure it has some truth in it. He says:

> Youth has more to teach its parents than to learn from them. The real savages are the old, not the young. Much of what the young learn from their elders they acquire at their peril. The world's tragedy is that it must be grown up—in other words, that it must be run by men who, though they know much, have forgotten what they were in their youth.

And as a key to what I am hoping to suggest to you, these words of Quarles:

> Thou canst not rebuke in children what they see practised in thee. Till reason be ripe, examples direct more than precept. Such as is thy behavior before thy children's faces, such is theirs behind thy back.

May I point out an example or two. The Lord has given us counsel about the significance of this magnificent machine, the body, with which we are mortally blessed, and has taught us that the body is an eternal component of the soul—that "the spirit and the body are the soul of man." We teach the young that their bodies matter, and that their care of them is important.

On an airplane a week ago last Friday headed toward the East, I read out of the same section of one newspaper two interesting items—one a statement by a director of the American Cancer Society that if Americans would stop smoking it is likely twenty-five thousand of them would be saved from certain death by lung cancer in the next few years. And in the same section, the notation that in 1957 Americans smoked 409 billion cigarettes, an increase of 4 percent and more over the year before. Can you say to a youngster, "Be Honest With Yourself," in a world where this goes on? Do you yourself contribute to the confusion that must result in his mind?

I read in that same newspaper (out of one edition in one day) another interesting item—a statement about a sixty-two-year-old practicing attorney in a Midwestern city who had given himself up under the pressures of a tremendous man hunt for a hit-and-run driver. A prominent leading citizen, he confessed that he had a hazy notion of having hit something on his way home from a cocktail party. The something he hit was a thirty-one-year-old father of five children, a Scoutmaster who died on the street where he was hit. In newspapers and magazines on the airplane were the blandishments of the liquor trusts, encouraging youngsters to be like certain "men of distinction"—like this man, perhaps.

When we cry to the young to "be honest" with themselves, let us consider what goes on in the world around us— the movies and television, the books and plays, the advertising in the newspapers we read—that so pervert the great creative capacity of man, given us of God in order that we might find a partner, get married in his appointed way, establish a home and build a family, an outpost on earth of heaven's promise. Can we with honor and honesty tell the young to "be honest" with themselves, knowing that they are responsive to the example we interested adults set?

It is so with us—we who claim to be followers of the risen Christ and yet do not obey his commandments. It is so especially on this significant Easter day. He said: "I am the way, the truth, and the life: no man cometh unto the Father, but by me." (John 14:6.) Yet there are those preaching in his name who are willing to be quoted in the newspapers as saying that they prefer not to have the term *Christian* applied to themselves, for Jesus Christ, to them, said one recently, was a folk tale like Santa Claus.

I say to you that there are those who know for certain for themselves that God lives, that Jesus is the Christ, and that living his commandments and being honest with ourselves is the only way really to motivate the young to do what we would like them to do.

The Needs of Youth

Perhaps many of you did not hear President McKay's stirring declaration of faith and confidence in youth at the beginning of this conference. To no message could I have more sincerely thrilled and responded. I add my testimony of joy and confidence in them. I am one who earnestly believes that teaching them and seeking to help them and bearing witness to them is as important as any missionary work being done in the world today.

This morning Brother Petersen delivered to the nation a moving expression of his conviction that in the parents and homes of America lies the basis of much of the problems of our youth. To this I add my testimony. I believe that there is no force so vital in helping to shape the lives of the young, for good or ill, as the influence of parents and home.

I would testify of another truth: In my judgment there has never been so great an opportunity or so urgent a need as there is today for this Church, its members, families and homes, to share great and vital principles, programs and inspiration with the youth of the Church and the nation. I believe we have an unparalleled opportunity for leadership and contribution. I would like to witness to you that our much-discussed, terribly-tempted, often troubled, frequently under-valued, but wonderful, solid, promising youthful generation

---

Address given at General Conference, April 1961.

has knowledge of its needs and says to us, sometimes in the very words we have said to them (when they have a chance to say it and be listened to), that they know their challenges and would like us to help them meet them.

Problems of Youth

There are very tragic problems involving many of the youth of the land. I confess that I still wonder at the propriety of quoting statistics that are unpleasant on the face of them and in their implications, without time to properly consider backgrounds and circumstances, but I believe that we have no time to lose and that sometime, someplace, parents and other adults must be confronted with the facts. Let me give an example of what I mean.

The United States Navy a time ago instituted a program of morale-building among its personnel, a wonderful program based on fundamental principles of morality and responsibility and patriotism with which the Church has always been concerned and which are in operation among us. The results of the Navy program are reported to be excellent, but let me report a few of the sobering statistics that motivated the institution of the program and which still reflect at least in some measure the existing circumstances. During one six-month period, it was reported in public print, the Navy brig population totalled enough men to man the entire submarine fleet of the nation. The Navy was starting a new court-martial every two and a half minutes of every single working day. Enough men were deserting each year to man twelve guided-missile cruisers, enough being dishonorably discharged to man twenty destroyers, and enough being hospitalized for neuro-psychiatric reasons alone to man five Forrestal-type carriers.

The American Social Health Association estimates an annual venereal disease-infected population in the United States of 200,000 under twenty years of age. In any one year, fewer than 50,000 of these are reported. Most of the remainder are undiscovered, many until they make their mark in

245

tragedy in the lives of unsuspecting family or others. It is also noted that there were 207,000 illegitimate births recorded in this nation last year.

These statistics are startling enough, but they are indicative of another problem which especially alarms some knowledgeable observers. Note this recently published statement:

> As we fail to reverse the rising trend in juvenile delinquency, we approach a critical situation. Our national resources for detention, treatment, or rehabilitation of the pre-delinquent or the delinquent child are already inadequate, unevenly distributed and severely strained. They will be unable to cope with further increases in our youth population and with the rise in delinquency.

In plain words, this notes the apprehension in the hearts of many who believe that we cannot possibly produce specialists, experts, guidance counselors, psychologists, social workers, fast enough to meet the increasing need for them. Obviously, then, the solution lies elsewhere. There has to be another answer. We do not minimize the work of the experts and trained workers. While the Church is primarily interested in prevention, the message of the gospel is one of restoration and rehabilitation also. The first principles of the gospel are faith and repentance, based in the love of God and fellowman.

The answer to the problem of American youth, however, cannot be left with the expert and the specialist. It lies in the hands, in the hearts, in the willing spirits of the parents and other interested adults who can bless them and help them meet their problems—this great solid majority of wonderful young people who want to do well, who are not now in trouble and do not want to be, but who need help if they are to become the constructive, contributing, wholesome human beings they would like to be.

What are the needs of youth?

Young people need the love and approval of their parents and of others whose lives influence them and who are important to them. They need to be accepted as they are and in light of what they can become, and they need to be motivated through love to want to be the very best they are capable of being. They need a feeling of belonging, of solid attachment to something stable. They need the confidence and the respect, the faith and the high expectations of their elders. Let me quote again the marvelous words of Goethe: *"If you treat an individual as he is, he will remain as he is, but if you treat him as if he were what he could be and ought to be, he will become what he could be and ought to be."*

I have in my possession a copy of a letter written from the plains by a pioneer mother who had just buried her husband. Brokenhearted, she took her children and continued the journey with the great faith that had moved her from Europe across an ocean and now moved her to cross a continent. In that letter she calls her husband her "best friend," her "dearest friend."

Is it not true that the best friends we have in this world ought to be those of our own household? What kind of an atmosphere would youth grow up in if that feeling were in the homes of the Latter-day Saints and perhaps through us in the homes of a great many good, faithful, loyal people in this nation and the world? How would it be for the spiritual prosperity of the young if they were assured of a love that endures and inspires and allows for imperfections and failings and mistakes and for repentance?

I do not think I will hear anything in this world more sweet and moving, and to me as a parent, more satisfying, than some words I heard from the tongue of a four-year-old in the middle of the night some years ago. There had been a childish infraction which was somewhat serious since it involved the use of a butcher knife between two little children, and since I have normal love for them and some normal anxieties for their future, I had interfered. There was a period of instruction, some discipline to emphasize it, a few tears, some explanations, and a time of self-examination. We were awakened very early the next morning to hear the two little girls talking. The three-year-old was in bed with the four-year-old, being comforted from some nocturnal fright. We heard the four-year-old say to her: "Don't be frightened, Nancy. You will be all right." And then, "Do you know something, Nancy? Do you know that Daddy and Mommy love us even when we are naughty? They're 'dis trying to help us."

Oh, the Lord help us to have wisdom enough and faith enough always to help them believe it and to make them know that their Father in heaven feels this way also, that it is to us and to him they must turn in repentance, in faith, and in humility.

With this love and affection and confidence, young people need to be instructed. Someone once said that we habitually underestimate their intelligence and overestimate their experience. We expect them to act like miniature adults and yet often we do not teach them.

What is it that we need to teach them? We can be sure of their perceptiveness. We can be sure that they will see and hear and absorb and imitate, and therefore it is vital that what they see and hear and absorb is worthy of imitation. We need to teach them, as the Lord has taught us to teach them, the first principles of the gospel. We need to teach them prayer. We need to help them get a sense of their relationship with their Heavenly Father that will make them want to walk uprightly before him, that will help them to seek objectives and goals that go beyond the material. We should endeavor to teach them to want to educate and discipline their minds and to keep their bodies clean and healthy. In their youth they need to be taught that there are things worth sacrificing for; they need to learn good citizenship, patriotism, respect for others, honor and honesty, courage. They need to be taught to love good literature and beauty and God's world.

There is an enlightening, if somewhat sobering picture of what our young people need to learn, in the words of a

Red Chinese intelligence officer describing captured American soldiers:

> He has weak loyalties to his family, his community, his country, his religion, and his fellow soldiers. His concept of right and wrong is hazy. He is basically materialistic and he is an opportunist. He is ignorant of social values . . . There is little or no understanding, even among university graduates, of United States political history and philosophy or of their own freedom's safeguards and how these allegedly operate within their own decadent system.

Our young people need to be taught many basic things which we cannot assume they will acquire outside the home. We need to teach them there, and then to seek to spread our influence and effectiveness into the schools, the neighborhood, the community and the nation.

I love some words attributed to Samuel Taylor Coleridge concerning what we should teach our children. It is said that a man widely known for his productive acres, sculptured gardens, and bright children, announced in the presence of Mr. Coleridge that he would not prejudice his children toward religion but would leave them to decide when they grew up. Coleridge is reported to have said to him:

> Bravo, this is a very progressive idea. Why do you not apply it to your fields and orchards and gardens in the future? Do not prejudice the soil to seed or weeding or cultivation, the trees to pruning or thinning, the gardens to bulbs or planting. Why not see if they will just grow up and decide to be what you hope they will be?

Young people need to be taught.

In addition to these fundamentals, youth needs discipline, guidance. They need to be made accountable for their actions. They deserve to have fair rules established which are understood, and then to have the rules consistently, fairly, and firmly administered.

Youth needs high ideals and to be somehow moved to want to have the willpower and the resoluteness to identify with them and to serve them. We talk here of character, of the convictions and courage and conscience which combine to produce and preserve much that is good about mankind.

A conference or two ago President McKay made a statement which has been echoed all over the nation, and I suspect beyond its borders, when he said that flabbiness of character and not flabbiness of muscle lies at the root of many of the problems of American youth.

Young people need to know that self-esteem is a prized possession and that self-esteem comes only when we live a life consistent with honor and with high principles which we know to be good. As a boy I had the blessing of a wonderful mother who moved me to read and to memorize. One of the most fruitful sources of wisdom that I found were the writings of Seneca, a Roman senator. Then one day I read the life of Seneca. Until then I had thought him to be one of the strongest and finest and most admirable men with whom I had become acquainted through literature. But I read in that book how Seneca, lacking the courage of his convictions, had stood on the floor of the Roman Senate and justified Nero's murder of his own mother. I fell out of love with Seneca at that moment. I admired him no longer. My experience and witness is that youth generally have little admiration and confidence for adults who say one thing and do another, however superior their intellect may be.

Activity is one of the pressing needs of youth everywhere. They need to be permitted to express themselves freely, creatively, responsibly, in wholesome action, under good leadership, in favorable circumstances, with worthwhile companions. I listened to a discussion between two wardens in our city at a convention. They agreed that there were two things invariably true about the inmates under their charge: First, they had never had a chance to take part in organized activity under good leadership. Second, they had never learned responsible attitudes toward others.

Well, someone has to be the Scoutmaster, someone must be the quorum adviser, someone needs to lead the chorus and be the coach. Someone has to be interested enough if they are going to get what they need to mature happily. There has to be someone to lead them. Perhaps it is not inappropriate to quote some words already alluded to in this conference, *"If not by me, by whom?"*

Young people need to be blessed with the opportunity to work. They must learn that there is no excellence without labor.

Young people need to find faith in God and immortality, in the purposefulness of life, and the perpetuation of human personality beyond the grave. They need to know that families can be eternal. They need to know for themselves the sacredness of service and the holiness of prayer. People who really know youth and who have had reason to assess some of their problems are saying wherever I go that what the young lack most importantly is faith and courage, faith and courage— ingredients with which they may best be endowed in the home, tools which are not passed out in college, weapons which are not to be discovered in any military arsenal.

Finally, I mention that in all of these things, and in every other worthwhile objective for them, youth needs the example of adults whom they can honor and revere. In listening to young people all over the land I have heard very few references to the missile gap. It is not this gap that worries youth, but the gap between precept and performance, between knowledge and conduct, between ritual and righteousness, between what the adults say and what the adults do. Youth, after all, is responsive to the values which the adult generations in fact—not in theory—exalt. Said Plato, "What is honored in a country will be cultivated there." And, we might add, in a home and family, in a neighborhood, a community, a church.

God bless us that we may recognize their great value and potential, that we may understand their problems, and that we may offer to them, out of the sincerity of our love for them, what they need.

The Most Important Assignment

In the early days of my service in the First Council of the Seventy I observed in the records of a stake to which I was assigned that this stake had a very strong elders quorum. I was anxious to discover why. I asked the stake president in advance if we might hear from the three members of the presidency of that quorum at our Saturday night meeting. This was arranged. The quorum president who spoke was a professional man who had been very faithful in the Church but whose duties had made it difficult for him to devote time to active leadership, and so he had really never before held an office. Now he had been called to be the president of the elders quorum by a wonderful man who believed in him and his potential, and he took the assignment. He wanted to succeed in it, so he worked and prepared himself and got some good help and started out. He told us how he had divided the elders quorum area into certain segments. He and a companion had taken segment one; his counselor and a companion another segment; the other counselor and the secretary, each with a companion, also taking a segment of the quorum area.

They decided that an occasional visit would not do the job, because this quorum was quiescent to say the best. In fact, when the leaders were chosen, there were scarcely any others they could count on. So the president and his counselors with companions visited these homes, humbly and earnestly

Address given at General Conference, October 1966.

trying to get involved in the lives of the men and their families. At the end of the quarter they shifted areas, so that at the end of the year (they hadn't quite finished the year actually) all the members of the presidency had become deeply identified with every man in that quorum.

This choice leader bore his testimony of gratitude for the opportunity he had had and sat down in tears. I leaned to the stake president and said, "I understand." He said, "Wait a minute."

The first counselor was a young sales executive who had invested great imagination and creative energy in his leadership. He was charged under the program with the responsibility of the Church service of the men, and this meant temporal and religious activity projects. Their temple attendance was high, their quorum attendance uniquely high, their sacrament meeting attendance wonderfully strong. They had projects of all kinds. I remember his mentioning one. They had assigned every man in that rural stake to grow a little porker to sell, but the market went down. He turned around and said to the president with a smile, "I forget how much money we lost on the project, President, but every single man in the quorum responded to the challenge and was involved."

When he sat down, I thought I knew why this quorum was what it was, so I leaned to the president and said, "I understand." He said, "Wait a minute."

He then called to the pulpit a young farmer, married, with several children, I suppose not as much formal education as his companions, but with a kind of Abraham Lincoln honesty about him that communicated quickly, and what he said I don't think I will ever forget. He said, "When the stake president asked me to be the second counselor in this quorum of elders, I said, 'Who are the others?' He said, 'Brother .... and Brother ....' And I said, 'I don't know those fellows very well. Do they intend to succeed, or are they going to fail?' The president said, 'We assume they intend to succeed.' And I said, 'Don't assume it; ask them.

If they intend to succeed, I will take the job. If they are going to fail, I don't want anything to do with it. I am not about to get associated with an outfit that starts out to fail.'

"Well," he said, "the president asked them and they said they intended to succeed so I took the job.

"Now," he said, without the trace of a smile (and I think it was really a guileless statement, although all of us laughed a little), "I want to tell you that these are great, successful priesthood leaders, and the reason they are is me."

He wasn't being immodest or arrogant. The people responded. They knew him. They knew he meant it and how he meant it.

In those days his assignment would make him chairman of a committee called "fact finding and statistical" or "reporting," as we came to say. I wonder how many of you would get the fire charged in your veins with that nomenclature. Somehow it did his. He really believed that his assignment was the most important in the Church. He knew that successful priesthood leaders can't really do their job unless they have a clear concept of where they are going, and a foundation of facts upon which they may move. He supplied that. He knew more about the men in that quorum, I feel quite certain, than almost any other comparable officer in a quorum in the Church. And it expressed itself, this concern, with a quorum that had come alive almost as Nehemiah led Jerusalem to a rebirth long ago.

Now I would like to bear a testimony of appreciation and deep respect for you wonderful brethren and sisters who serve in the Church, who have the courage and the faith to face up to circumstances that are often quite difficult, maybe even depressing, but you do it. God bless you to remember that while the results may not be as spectacular as in this choice quorum, it is a certainty that if you, with honesty and integrity and a sense of your commission, seek to do the job the Lord has called you to do, wonderful results will occur.

VI.
Give
Love

Mature love provides a climate of wholesome, repentant, forgiving consideration. It listens. It hears and senses the needs of another. It can never be separated from character, from unselfishness, from good humor and from every tender virtue. Love is unconditional.

Special Needs of Others

It is my purpose today to bear testimony to some who have special needs, and to those who have accepted commission from the Lord and covenanted with him to try to help satisfy those needs.

As Christ taught the gospel to the people of this hemisphere, he asked them, "What manner of men ought ye to be?" and answered, "Verily I say unto you, even as I am." (3 Nephi 27:27.)

As Christians, we accept that instruction reverently as our guide and our goal.

We know that Christ loves his Father. He came into the world to do the will of his Father, knowing the part he was to play, the price he would have to pay. He loves us, and for us he fulfilled his mortal mission after suffering so intense and so deep as to cause him to bleed at every pore. With his blood he bought us, brought us the gift of immortality, and made possible for us all good and lovely things now and eternally.

He was gracious but he was not timid. He taught men the truth about his Father, the living God, and testified of him, and of his own atoning mission, even though many who had followed him thereafter no longer walked with him. He cried repentance and was baptized of John in Jordan, and

Address given at General Conference, April 1973.

taught all men to do likewise, and promised the obedient and faithful the blessing of the Holy Ghost.

Christ knows the worth of souls.

He came as Isaiah had prophesied and as he affirmed in the synagogue in Nazareth, "to preach the gospel to the poor . . . to heal the brokenhearted, to preach deliverance to the captives, and recovering of sight to the blind, to set at liberty them that are bruised." (Luke 4:18-19.)

He taught the parables of the lost sheep and the lost coin and the lost son, and he lunched with accused Zacchaeus, and admonished men to emulate the compassionate act of the demeaned Samaritan—"Go thou and do likewise." He exalted the humble publican who, in contrast to the self-righteous Pharisee, "would not lift up so much as his eyes unto heaven, but smote upon his breast, saying, God be merciful to me a sinner" (Luke 18:13), and he confronted the accusers of the repentant woman.

So closely is he tied with his fellowmen that in one of his most powerful parables he taught that bread given to one of the least of his brethren is bread given also to him, and so is any kindness or act of grace or mercy or service. To deny help to one of the least of his brethren, he said, was to deny him.

His message is one of hope and promise and peace to those who mourn the loss of loved ones—"And ye now therefore have sorrow: but I will see you again, and your heart shall rejoice, and your joy no man taketh from you." (John 16:22.)

To the lonely and the hopeless and those who are afraid, his reassurance reaches out: "I will never leave thee, nor forsake thee." (Hebrews 13:5.)

Christ understands.

> Wherefore in all things it behooved him to be made like unto his brethren, that he might be a merciful and faithful high priest in things pertaining to God, to make reconciliation for the sins of the people. For in that he himself hath suffered being tempted, he is able to succour them that are tempted. (Hebrews 2:17-18.)

For we have not an high priest which cannot be touched with the feeling of our infirmities; but was in all points tempted like as we are, yet without our infirmities; but was in all points tempted like as we are, yet without sin. (Hebrews 4:15.)

He prayed to the Father for those who were not obedient, and he wept. He called little children to him and blessed them, and wept. He taught us to pray. These and much more he taught and did. They represent the manner of person he was.

Of course he was more: he was the Divine Redeemer, the Savior of all mankind, the Firstborn in the Spirit and the Only Begotten in the flesh. He was the Prince of Peace. He "came into the world . . . to be crucified for the world, and to bear the sins of the world, and to sanctify the world, and to cleanse it from all unrighteousness; that through him all might be saved." (D&C 76:41-42.)

What he did for us we could never do for ourselves, and his example of love and service and sacrifice and seeking first the kingdom of God is our guidestar and our path.

What does he expect of us?

At his call, commissioned with his holy priesthood, being his agents, on his errand, we are under covenant to represent him faithfully and to do the will of the Father.

All about us are opportunities.

There came the other day the story of the small boy who had lost his pet and who in tears beseeched his anxious mother for help. She reminded him lovingly that she had tried as hard as she could to find the pet without success. "What more can I do, son?" she asked. "You can cry with me," he said. "Bear ye one another's burdens, and so fulfill the law of Christ." (Galatians 6:2.)

A cherished friend who works with little children who have difficulties told me recently of a nine-year-old girl who has lived in seventeen foster homes. She needs someone to cry with her, and laugh with her, and teach her, and love her.

There are so many who are not—or feel they are not—understood. Recently our family visited with a dear friend, Sister Louise Lake, who has lived her gracious, sharing life in a wheelchair for more than a quarter of a century. Perhaps because our twelve-year-old son was with us Sister Lake told us of another twelve-year-old with whom she became acquainted in a rehabilitation center in New York where she was working. The boy had been blind and for most of his twelve years had lived a sad existence, thought to be uneducable, incapable of learning. Then he was given a chance, and, thank the Lord, a marvelous spirit and fine mind were discovered. He told his friend that he had thought all his life that being blind was the worst thing that could happen to one —until he met Campy. Campy was Roy Campanella, great athlete, who at the height of his career was rendered physically helpless in an automobile accident. The blind boy said he had decided after meeting Campy that his condition was worse than not being able to see. "But there is something even worse than that," he said. He talked of feeling his way down the hall at the hospital, hearing the scuff of feet as people passed him by. "There is something worse than being blind or crippled, and that is to have people not understand you," he said. "I guess they think that because I am blind I can't hear or speak either."

There is one who always understands, and those who seek to become the manner of person he is must seek to understand. We are never really alone when we love God and accept the friendship of his loving Son. I think of the mother of fourteen children who was asked if she had a favorite. "Well," she said, "if I do, it's the one who is ill until she gets well, or the one who is away until he gets home." So it seems to be with the Lord.

After a meeting with our servicemen at DaNang in South Vietnam, we talked with a senior pilot who had come very close to death that day and who was still shaken. He had a request to make, and he made it shyly, not wanting to impose. "I wonder if you might have just a minute when you get home,

Brother Hanks, to call or write a note to my twelve-year-old son to tell him that I am all right and that his dad is thinking about him. He was ordained a deacon last Sunday without his father there, and I want him to know how much I love him."

Those nearest us need love also.

There are so many who grieve and are weighed down because they have not behaved in a way their own conscience can approve. To them the Lord still speaks through his prophets ancient and modern. Recall the words of Jacob to his brethren: "And now, my beloved brethren, seeing that our merciful God has given us so great knowledge concerning these things, let us remember him, and lay aside our sins, and not hang down our heads, for we are not cast off." (2 Nephi 10:20.)

In the last recorded letter of the great prophet Mormon to his son Moroni are written the lamentings of the prophet over the wickedness of the people, described in the record to be "without principle, and past feeling." Mormon's final testimony to his beloved son included this marvelous admonition and explanation of the effect Christ's gifts should have in all of our lives:

> My son, be faithful in Christ; and may not the things which I have written grieve thee, to weigh thee down unto death; but may Christ lift thee up, and may his sufferings and death [and his resurrection], . . . and his mercy and long-suffering, and the hope of his glory and of eternal life, rest in your mind forever. (Moroni 9:25.)

Christ in our lives is not meant to grieve us or weigh us down unto death because we have been imperfect. Through him we may be *lifted up* by accepting his gifts and his mercy and long-suffering. These blessings we must seek to keep in our minds always. "For how knoweth a man the master whom he has not served, and who is a stranger unto him, and is far from the thoughts and intents of his heart?" (Mosiah 5:13.)

261

They who would follow him and be the manner of person he is will, as he did, lift up the repentant who suffer and sorrow for sin, and bless them with love and forgiveness.

Of course, all honest men on occasion feel their weakness and groan in the face of their inadequacies and ignorance and pride. Even Job, that good and godly man who possessed a faith which all his afflictions could not shake, bore this witness at the conclusion of his ordeal when, seeing God, he said, "I know that thou canst do every thing, and that no thought can be withholden from thee. I have heard of thee by the hearing of the ear: but now mine eye seeth thee. Wherefore I abhor myself, and repent in dust and ashes." (Job 42:2, 5, 6.)

But Christ will lift us up and help us to become as he is as we do as he did; as we love our Father and give him our lives; as we love each other and all men, and learn and live and teach his word; believe in the worth of souls and let our lives be the warrant of our earnestness; mourn with those who mourn, and bring hope to them; understand and comfort those who weep; cry unto the Lord.

> Yea, and when you do not cry unto the Lord, let your hearts be full, drawn out in prayer unto him continually for your welfare, and also for the welfare of those who are around you.
>
> And now behold, my beloved brethren, I say unto you, do not suppose that this is all; for after ye have done all these things, if ye turn away the needy, and the naked, and visit not the sick and afflicted, and impart of your substance, if ye have, to those who stand in need—I say unto you, if ye do not any of these things, behold, your prayer is vain, and availeth you nothing, and ye are as hypocrites who do deny the faith. (Alma 34:27-28.)

May we look up and look around and kneel down, and may God bless us to be worthy, and to become the manner of person he is.

Moving into Marriage

In coming back to Britain, Sister Hanks and I have had an experience as sweet as anything we might prayerfully anticipate in the awaited reunions of the eternal world. It has been one of the great satisfactions of our lives to find so many of you whose lives we saw changed as you came in touch with the gospel, or developed in it, now holding such important and marvelous callings in stake and mission presidencies and bishoprics, in district and branch presidencies, high councils, auxiliary leadership, and in many other important assignments in the kingdom. We congratulate and commend you and pray God to bless you and invoke his spirit upon you and the generation arising, that there may come from this conference that stimulus of spirit and commitment to service which will commend you to the merciful intervention of the Lord in your behalf and in behalf of those who may be touched through your service.

I have thought and meditated and can come up with no better word than that given by one of the good men of this land to express in reaffirmation the testimony I have had the blessing of bearing in Britain many times. C. S. Lewis wrote some words I quoted to your outstanding student leaders two days ago. I would like to make them a keynote of my brief remarks this afternoon. He said, "I believe in Christianity as

Address given in Area Conference at Manchester, England, August 1971.

I believe that the sun has risen, not only because I see it, but because by it I see everything else."

Recently I had an experience that tied together the marvelous *fruits* of the gospel with its *roots*. I attended the funeral of a cousin who was the eldest grandson of my grandfather, Archibald Frame who joined the Church in Lanark, the only one of ten in his family to do so, and then was rejected by his family. My grandmother joined the Church in Glasgow and was disowned by her family. I was fifteen when she died at age ninety-four, and the sweetest memory I have of her is her description of that rejection. When her beloved father, her noble father who in her eyes could do no wrong, learned she had joined the Church, he said that he had no daughter Helen any more. Years later as a mature woman she returned as a short-term missionary to teach her own family. Her father, then in his nineties, stood at the corner of the picket fence, his white hair blowing in the breeze and wept, saying, "Helen, my Helen."

A week ago Friday morning in the Salt Lake Temple I saw the product of Archibald Frame and Helen Duff, and the other good grandparents who came from Gloucester under a little more favorable circumstances, when I had the blessing of performing the wedding of our eldest daughter. The night before in our home we had our last family home evening as a group before Susan left us to form a new family of her own. There was laughter, and there were tears; there were recollections and tributes and a family prayer led by the daughter who was moving into her new life. Then I had the marvelous blessing of laying my hands upon the head of my child to give her a father's blessing. I have never had and do not expect to have a more sacred, sweet or satisfying experience in this life.

I would like to bear my testimony to you, my beloved brothers and sisters, that the roots of the gospel are firmly planted in sacred principles which are eternal. The fruits of the gospel are the product of those roots. They cannot be enjoyed any other way.

I know from personal experience the difficult circumstances under which so many of you live the gospel. I know how earnestly you pray and how desperately you try to bring unity in a home; or if not that, at least some kind of forbearance in order that you might worship as you would like. I know the price some of you—many of you—have paid. Not only are the stories appropriate to the days of the early brethren or Brother Hinckley's day or mine; but your days also see much of sacrifice for what you believe.

For you who suffer under less than perfect circumstances, and many of you who enjoy beautiful relationships at home, and particularly a whole generation looking ahead to the establishment of homes, I offer my testimony that it is vital as we marry, or in marriage, or as we look forward to a marriage which may seem a little distance ahead, we understand how very significant our relationships in marriage are.

Marriage is a sacred covenant. The scriptures are plain: "Marriage is ordained of God unto man." It is a sacred union into which the Spirit and power of God should come and will come if we do all we can to lay proper foundations as we proceed in or toward this union.

But marriage is more than an ordinance. It is a partnership of two persons who come together as they are, imperfect. Marriage doesn't meant two perfect persons join together and live happily forever after. The process is one of effort—honest, earnest, unselfish work. The union of marriage is so important, so total a commitment, so intimate a relationship. In it he has major responsibilities and she has major responsibilities. Those responsibilities can be described in words as sacred as any I know, tied together with all the other sacred words I know: wife, mother, homemaker, heart of a home; husband, father, protector, provider, head of a home.

Marriage is a partnership. The properly authorized priesthood officer (and other authorized persons out of a temple) can pronounce a wedding. No one, however full of love and good wishes, can pronounce happiness. It must be brought

265

about by two persons who care, two mature individuals who try.

Marriage is a companionship. It is meant to be a warm, sweet, wonderful, sympathetic, gracious, tender relationship. It is meant to bring to those in marriage the security that can only come when one is loved unconditionally, surrounded with an atmosphere, a climate, a sensitivity so that all one wishes to become she will be helped to become, he will be aided to become.

Marriage is a friendship, and marriage is a love affair.

I keep in my office desk one sweet, gentle letter written in 1848 in cultured hand, in cultured terms, from a place called Honey Creek, Missouri, by a pioneer mother who, like my grandmother, left this land as an emigrant. She spent many days at sea and then to her heartbreak found her husband to be seriously ill. He died two days away from the new land. She had to see to his burial upon arrival, and then at Honey Creek sat down to pen the letter which was sent back to England to his mother and sister notifying them of his death. That letter changed my life. I offer it to you today in the hope that it may change or direct some lives here. This beautiful young convert, a thousand miles away from the salt desert which was to be her home in a new country, in a new Church, with new associates and few resources, wrote these words to his mother and sister:

"Dear Mother and dear Hannah: Your dearly beloved son and my best friend has gone the way of all the earth. Dearer to me in life than life itself, he is gone. Oh Mother, Mother, what am I to do?"

She talked of their three little boys and her determination to rear them in the nurture and admonition of the Lord to be like their daddy, to serve God, to bear the priesthood and magnify it with honor. Three times in that one heartbroken little note she referred to her husband as her "dearest friend," her "best friend," her "most loyal, loving friend."

266

Oh my wonderful young brothers and sisters, move into marriage with someone with whom you can be best friend, good companion, honorable partner, sweetheart, and true servant of the living God. I could sum it all up in a sight I saw in the Hotel Utah awhile ago. At President McKay's invitation I went for some words of counsel prior to departure to an Asian area. He wanted something said to the servicemen and gave me a message. While I was there the photographers arrived to take pictures which would announce the celebration of President and Sister McKay's wedding anniversary—sixty-six or sixty-seven years together. They were posed, the picture planned. They were seated on a small sofa holding hands, jollying and talking together; and then at the moment when the picture was snapped, without premeditation or any instruction, Sister McKay raised that great, strong hand to her lips. The bodily powers were long since dissipated but the love affair had been getting better all the time! It is meant to be, for marriage is ordained of God. We who are married and you who will marry, establish relationships that are respectful and honorable, worthy of men who hold the Holy Priesthood, worthy of women who are choice queens, the daughters of God. Look forward to and plan for a marriage of that kind.

Practicing What We Preach

My theme this morning is practicing what we preach. I suppose everyone understands what that means. Last Sunday in Logan I heard a choice teacher report her conversation with a little girl in a class. She had asked the little girl, "What does it mean to practice what you preach?" "Oh," said the youngster, "that means writing your talk and saying it over and over again before you give it in church."

I would like to say a few words this morning about the more conventional interpretation of practicing what we preach.

I visited the hospital the other evening to see my desperately ill sister, and found her family surrounding her bed, holding their family home evening, led by her fourth missionary son just returned from foreign fields. I joined them and then went home rejoicing and thanking God for that kind of example, and met my own family who were waiting, and prayed that we might do a better job of practicing what we preach.

What do we believe that we should be practicing, or practicing more effectively, many of us? What is our duty? What are we commanded? What do we preach?

Well, one important thing we preach is that parents are to love and teach their children and set an honorable example before them, and that children are to honor and obey their

Address given at General Conference, April 1971.

parents. Parents are to love and cleave to each other; and children, as King Benjamin said, are to "love one another and serve one another." We are taught to meet together in a weekly family home evening, to pray together as families, to give an account together of the tithes we pay, to attend sacrament meeting and worship together as a family. We are expected to fast together and to give an amount equivalent to the cost of what we did not eat to the bishop for the care of those who have needs. As a family we are to greet the home teachers and respond to their instructions and inquiries. Motivated by the lofty stature of the family in Church belief, we should be reading and learning together, working together, having pleasant, happy occasions at our meal times, supporting each other in school, Church, and civic involvements. We should be planning and enjoying projects together, building our customs and traditions into a continuity of generations. All of this we are taught and encouraged to do.

But it is not of duty or commandment or admonition that I wish to speak this morning, cherished and holy as those words are. I would like instead to speak of invitation, of opportunity, of privilege, of love, of gratefully taking time while there is time to enjoy the blessing of our family and home.

How much joy are we missing that we could be having and are meant to have, joy that we could experience only in our own home and no other place, only with our own family and with no other group?

It is instructive to look at the music we sing. Our little ones sing, "I am a child of God, and he has sent me here, has given me an earthly home, with parents kind and dear." Our wonderful young people sing, "We'll build on the rock they planted . . . the rock of honor and virtue, of faith in the living God." From our singing mothers comes the great strain, "Love one another," and all of us sing, "Love at home." Our ties with God and each other are everlasting. Our homes are sanctuaries from the things and cares of this world. Our family is the heart of our eternal hopes. Our love is the tender thread

269

that ties us to an endless, creative, increasing union. These are the things we believe and preach. Can we do more to enjoy the blessings of such concepts in our lives, in our homes, in our families? Can we do better while there is time at practicing what we preach?

Matthew Arnold wrote, in Empedocles on Etna:

> We would have inward peace
> But *will* not look within.

May we for a moment this morning, each of us, look within himself and home and family as I offer a happy example or two of what I am talking about.

About twelve years ago I had a call early in the morning from a beloved friend who is a physician. He asked me to come to the hospital to administer with him to his infant son, just born and fighting for his life. We reached our hands into the incubator and laid them on this tiny boy and prayed, and then sat and waited with Larry's mother while he took a turn for the better. We were there when the pediatrician came to announce that he was going to make it. He came through that difficult ordeal with a fine mind and a strong, indomitable spirit. Only a pair of legs that are not quite as strong as they one day will be remain to remind Larry how blessed he is to be alive.

Recently this little boy's big brother returned from having served an honorable mission for the Lord abroad. A perceptive uncle, observing the reunion at the airport, wrote a letter to Larry which I had the privilege of reading. I asked if I might have permission to quote it and have been given that permission. I would like you to know about a Latter-day Saint boy just ordained a deacon who tries to practice what we preach.

Dear Larry,

Yesterday I got a lump in my throat without even swallowing a frog; and I got a tear in my eye without even inhaling a hippy's breath! More than that I got a picture tattooed on my memory that I'll never forget.

It's only right that I thank you for the lump, the tears and the picture, for a handsome boy named Larry Ellsworth gave me all three of them . . . and he didn't even know it or ask for a receipt.

It started when he stood waiting for his brother to return from serving our Heavenly Father as a missionary for two years in a far-off land named Chile. You could see that the two years had been longer for this boy than for anyone else. He was so intense, so pale, so absorbed with just watching and waiting.

Then to see his face light up when he saw his brother again! It was like a flashlight in a dark room.

Someone whispered that this wonderful boy had been saving his nickels, dimes and quarters for two years to buy his big brother a basketball . . . a more than $30.00 "best there is" basketball because he loved him! He wouldn't let anyone else contribute. It was his idea and his gift . . . the best way, out of money he could have spent for himself but chose not to because he loved someone else so much!

Then I watched this fine boy stand without saying a word at the side of his brother, happy just to look way up at his face, hold on to his leg, and see him home again.

I have a special love and admiration for both of those boys: the giant who went far away all alone to do what was right, and the little brother who waited and planned and remembered.

Larry, you're a fine boy. I'm sure that you'll be a great man . . . for you have a big heart and a tender conscience. Some can run faster, jump higher, walk farther, play longer just because they had an easier time getting born into this world. That's no credit to them. But you have more than most to be thankful for, because Heavenly Father sent one of his favorite sons to live in your body . . . and it's who lives in a house that makes all the difference. Thanks, Larry, for the lesson an old dumb uncle learned yesterday just by watching.

Love, Uncle Dick.

A few weeks ago I listened to a stake president exhort his people to build strong families and to enjoy them. It was a great sermon, and the high point of it for me was his account of the family skiing trip when a four-year-old wanted to go to the top with the rest of the family and ski down. When they arrived it was discovered that he had to snowplow all the way down because it was just a bit too tough a run for his age and experience. The mother started to accompany her four-year-old son down the hill but her teenage son voluntarily took over and lovingly shepherded his little brother down instead of swooping down himself as he could have done. He cheerfully sacrificed one swift run down the mountain, and blessed a whole family with a sweet spirit of love and concern and appreciation.

Among many who do wonderfully well at practicing what we preach there is one other I would mention. To our home periodically over the past several years has come a special kind of man as our home teacher. He has brought with him a dear son who, like Larry of the letter, had a difficult time getting born and has had some major problems to contend with. The father and son have sat many times side by side in our home, hands gently clasped or arms intertwined, or a hand on a knee, communicating, always expressing without language, an exchange of love. How we admire this man and his beloved son.

These are some of the simple chords of melody that make a home harmonious and happy. Kindness, consideration, courtesy, care, laughter, unselfishness, prayer, thoughtfulness, doing things for each other, forgiving each other, sustaining each other, loving each other—these are notes happily enjoyed and eternally remembered.

If a family loses its cherished human values and deteriorates into only the form of a family, it has lost what a family is for. Whatever changes are said to have occurred in our time, there is left to the family the most important purpose of all—the satisfaction of the basic emotional and spiritual needs of its members. In any era, one has written, society is a "web of which the family forms the central strands." In home, family and love lie the resources that fulfill the life of the individual and the life of the community, indeed the resources that would redeem our troubled world and bring it lasting peace. Children must be safeguarded and reared. Only in the home can children be assured of the love and direction they need to live life, and only parents who genuinely love can meet those needs. But it must be more than a preached or pronounced love; it must be love that takes time, makes the effort, listens patiently, gives freely, forgives generously, "provides the amenities that will grace and adorn and make beautiful the relationships of family life."

But I must add today that I do not speak *by* authority or *from* authority, but *with* authority, for I myself know these things to be true. I know them to be true because I have experienced them, I have lived them, I have been there.

The home I grew up in had the kind of love of which I speak, though it had little of material things. I hope and pray that our happy home has done as well. Of course I have said what I have said today in part for myself and our own family, for we still have the privilege and blessing of seeking to improve. I am grateful to thank the Lord for that. I do not know a greater accolade in this life, and believe there is none, than a note from a six-year-old who writes: "Guess what, Mom, I love you," or from a teenager's gracious gift: "Dad, you are my friend and I will love you forever," or from a dad or mom to a choice son or daughter: "I love you. I am proud of you."

Does not this motivate us to want to be what we can be?

Jesus said, "As I have loved you . . . love one another."

God help us, parent and child, to accept the opportunity while there is time, in our homes and families, to practice what we preach.

Where Art Thou?

Great emphasis is being given these days to programs designed to preserve and develop physical fitness. This morning my wife read to me a quotation that emphasizes other aspects of fitness even more important: "There is no exercise better for the heart than reaching down and lifting people up." I pray for that spirit of uplift in these few moments.

In the writings of a great modern religious figure is the story of a conversation between a persecuted saintly rabbi of the late eighteenth century and his jailer in Petersburg. The jailer asked, "How are we to understand that God, the all-knowing, said to Adam: 'Where art thou?' "

Having obtained from the jailer his assent that "the scriptures are eternal and that every era, every generation and every man is included in them," the rabbi said:

> In every era, God calls to every man: Where are you in your world? So many years and days of those allotted to you have passed, and how far have you gotten in your world? . . . How far along are you?
>
> In so asking, God does not expect to learn something he does not know; what he wants is to produce an effect in man which can only be produced by just such a question, provided that it reaches man's heart—that a man allows it to reach his heart. (Martin Buber.)

Address given at General Conference, April 1968.

We know that much that demeans man and keeps him from finding himself and his place, and from developing his great potential, comes from his efforts to hide himself from his Father, as Adam did, and from the love, the relationships, the service, and the vicissitudes that the Father has sent him to this earth to experience.

A thoughtful editor has recently written these words:

> The human potential is the most magical but also the most elusive fact of life. Men suffer less from hunger or dread than from living under their moral capacity. The atrophy of spirit that most men know and all men fear is tied not so much to deprivation or abuse as it is to their inability to make real the best that lies within them. Defeat begins more with a blur in the vision of what is humanly possible than with the appearance of ogres in the path or a hell beyond the next turning. (Norman Cousins, *Saturday Review*, February 6, 1965, p. 18.)

We know well that character is an achievement, not a gift; yet all men to some measure, most of us to some considerable measure, and too many of us to a tragic measure live below our moral capacity, are willing to accept a plausible lower view of mankind and of ourselves than we should or need to, and fail to "make real the best that lies within" us.

The Lord wants us to be our best; he wants us to achieve our highest possibilities. This is the purpose of the gospel. He died to give us that opportunity. What principles are involved in our succeeding? What problems keep us from it?

Recently I read a brief newspaper account of a survey made at a great American university among many thousands of students over a period of several years. With access only to the article and not to the study itself, let me briefly paraphrase, to some measure quote, and add some of my own words to the four conclusions that came out of that study, which coincide with what I also have observed and experienced in some years of working with youth. While this study dealt basically with college-age students in our current generation, what it notes is significantly applicable to our culture in general:

1. They are looking for a faith, but are skeptical of all faiths, being disposed and encouraged to question everything and to doubt the established ways.

2. They are looking for a community to which they can belong—for a family, a group, a society—but they are skeptical of all organization. They see institutions as authoritarian, threatening their identity and individuality. Many feel that the family has failed them. Disorganization and resistance give them a chance for preservation as persons, so they sometimes favor chaos over order.

3. They know they need to think beyond themselves and to give service, but they are frightened by the commitment service requires.

4. They want to love and be loved, but their image of self is poor, and they are not sure they are capable of love or worthy of being loved.

In summary, the problems revealed by the survey are in *believing, belonging, giving* and *loving*. These happen to be the basic ingredients essential in the development of the human potential. They are pivotal principles of the gospel of Jesus Christ. Let me speak of them briefly, primarily in illustration.

What does it matter to our happiness or to the development of our character whether or what we believe?

Before Joan of Arc was burned at the stake, not yet nineteen years of age, having saved her country, she was offered her freedom if she would repudiate her vision and her faith. Maxwell Anderson's great play *Joan of Lorraine* has her answering:

> Every man gives his life for what he believes. Every woman gives her life for what she believes. Sometimes people believe in little or nothing . . . One life is all we have, and we live it as we believe in living it, and then it's gone. But to surrender what you are, and live without belief—that's more terrible than dying— more terrible than dying young.

The apostle Paul spoke of "faith unfeigned." (1 Timothy 1:5.) It is not, of course, lip service or eye pleasing of which he spoke. It is not to know everything, or to understand perfectly. Recall the wonderful answer of a loving father who sought the help of the Master for his afflicted son. Jesus asked him if he believed, and the agonized father, his son's life in the balance, was supremely honest: "Lord, I believe; help thou my unbelief." (Mark 9:24.)

Faith is not rooted in perfect behavior, though it inspires us to desire it, to seek for it. Consider the parable of the Pharisee and the publican. The Pharisee boasted of his righteousness; the publican (who the Savior said went down to his house justified, rather than the other) "would not lift up so much as his eyes unto heaven, but smote upon his breast, saying, God be merciful to me a sinner." (See Luke 18:10-14.)

Faith is to know that he will not reject us. From the Book of Mormon: "And now, my beloved brethren, seeing that our merciful God has given us so great knowledge . . . let us remember him, and lay aside our sins, and not hang down our heads for we are not cast off." (2 Nephi 10:20.) From the Bible: "Therefore will the Lord wait, that he may be gracious unto you, and therefore will he be exalted, that he may have mercy upon you." (Isaiah 30:18.)

Faith motivates us to yield our hearts to him, truly yield our hearts. It motivates honesty to acknowledge limitations and vulnerability, willingness to learn, humility to seek help, courage to act, simplicity to trust. It is to have confidence in the presence of God. Faith is, as it has been well said, "a condition born [of the Spirit] in a mind that has looked at all of the available evidence and discovered in it a meaning with which the soul can live at peace. It is not appalled by an invitation to think." (Guy Wilson.)

Recently in Vietnam I learned again of the need for men to believe. A choice friend was serving as the commander of a helicopter gunship unit. They had suffered many casualties and much damage, but miraculously no deaths in their highly dangerous work. The morning before I talked with him in DaNang my friend, a wonderful servant of the Lord, was standing by his ship preparing to lead his group on another difficult mission. The blades of the whirlybirds were rotating when the major was approached somewhat hesitantly by a young enlisted man from one of the aircraft. The commander impatiently asked the boy what he wanted.

"Some of us were wondering, sir," he said earnestly, "whether you've had time to say your prayers this morning."

Humbled by the nature and spirit of the question, the commanding officer replied that he had had time to talk with the Lord.

"Thank you, sir," said the young man, smiling, relieved. "The guys and I didn't want to take off on this mission until you'd had time to pray." (*Improvement Era,* May 1968, p. 39.)

There had been no overt prayers before the group and no sermon or lesson on the subject, but somehow the word was out among the men that their outfit had something special going for them because their commanding officer was a man who prayed.

The most urgent need of our time is to understand spiritual truths and apply them to our lives. It has been said— and I think well said:

> Our age has tried sophistication and intellectualism, but these have given no peace. Psychology and sociology, humanism and rationalism have given us not a fraction of the abiding joy and calm our fathers knew through their faith. For still, there is the devastation of doubt and fear and envy and greed and guilt. (Rev. Massey M. Heltzel.)

We have learned again in this conference that the most significant confrontation to be experienced in this world is with Jesus Christ, and yet many still turn from him without knowing him or opening their hearts to him.

A marine in Vietnam said it impressively for his generation in a poem published recently in the Era of Youth:

SOUL SURVIVOR

Last night, on our perimeter,
A man fell in the barbed wire coils
And, in his delirium,
Sobbed these words:
"Oh, dear Christ—"

I thought with him: the blood was flowing;
Far away from homeland, injured,
Tired from the all-night guarding,
Weary from the sandbag filling;
Emptiness walked all around him,
Caused by missing many loved ones,
Caused by worried fears of dying,
Worrying more about worrying them.

Yet, in his one time of trial,
Still, the mighty hope remained—
The faith in higher strength, in mercy;
Then I thought, "Just how can I,
Even at my most content,
Ever turn my back on Jesus?"

(John Blosser, *Improvement Era*, March 1968, p. 53.)

He who believes knows that he belongs. But he also needs
to feel himself an important and accepted part of a group.
Young people want and deserve parents and a family they
can be proud of. Their capacity to become worthwhile persons
is strongly affected by the absence or presence of such a family
and by their own acceptance of the challenge to be a contributing, responsible member of it. The influence of a good
family is well captured by this account from an unidentified
source:

It was a gorgeous October day. My husband Art and I were
down at the boat landing helping our friend Don drag his skiff
up on the beach. Art remarked wistfully that it would be a long
time before next summer, when we could all start sailing again.
"You folks ought to take up skiing like our family and have fun
the year round." Don said.

279

Doesn't that get pretty expensive?" I asked.

Don straightened up and smiled. "It's funny," he said. "We live in an old-fashioned house—legs on the tub, that sort of thing. For years we've been saving up to have the bathroom done over. But every winter we take the money out of the bank and go on a couple of family skiing trips. Our oldest boy is in the army now, and he often mentions in his letters what a great time we had on those trips. You know, I can't imagine his writing home, 'Boy, we really have a swell bathroom, haven't we?' "

In the love of such a family is the climate most suitable for the growth of quality and character and moral capacity. If there is added to this the strengths of good companionships, commitment in a truly living church, involvement in a community of enlightened and mutually concerned persons, responsible citizenship in a great country, young people will have the ideal atmosphere for growth. When they do not have, or could have had but do not choose or appreciate these blessings, they are suitable subjects for small vision, inadequate self-discipline, and a flabby sense of responsibility.

The strengths and problems of our youth were illustrated in an experience our teenage daughter had recently. Backing from a driveway onto an unlighted street, she dented the fender of an automobile parked across the narrow road. Flustered and upset by the incident, she yet took time to leave a note on the car identifying herself and accepting responsibility for the damage. She then came home and acquired a parent and the two returned and knocked on the door of the home of the owner of the car and made arrangements with him. She was praised for her direct and uncompromising honesty.

That very night while leaving the public library she and a friend saw a fur-coated lady in an expensive car seriously damage a parked automobile and then speed away without a glance or effort to make the thing right. Feeling at home in a society including this kind of experience is understandably difficult for some young people.

With believing and belonging, we need to learn to give and to serve if we are to live up to our moral capacity.

I have referred before to the development of a "breeder reactor" — a variety of machine that will produce vast amounts of power at a low cost, and in the process will actually create more nuclear fuel than it burns. A life patterned on the way of Christ would be like that, and every life should be. It is our blessing to use, thoughtfully and thankfully, all that is provided for us from the past, and to leave behind us more and better materials with which the generations ahead can work. In faith, freedom, wisdom, beauty, in material blessings, we should add to and not consume our heritage.

Recently I learned of a meeting at the University of Pittsburgh where twenty-five hundred senior honor students from the high schools of Pennsylvania gathered. At the podium was a man who stood in braces, on crutches. He was a medical researcher who had worked on the polio vaccine project. He left many of those bright shining faces wet with tears when he said to them, "Our generation couldn't find the answers in time to save itself. Thank God we found them in time to save you."

What a significant challenge to youth to make real the best that lies within them! Yet someone has called ours the "age of the shrug." I hope and believe this is not so.

Do you recall the words of Marshal Petain after the fall of France? Sobering words: "Our spirit of enjoyment was stronger than our spirit of sacrifice. We wanted to have more than we wanted to give. We tried to spare effort and we met disaster."

Contrasting this is the statement of a noble man near the end of a rich life of contribution. Asked how he could account for his wide acquaintance with and memory of the poets, the philosophers, and the prophets, he smiled and said, "Well, I had to work hard to learn it, and then I gave it and gave it and gave it until it was mine." (Attributed to Dr. Howard R. Driggs.)

What of loving and being loved? Perhaps the most serious problem of many young people and of their adult generation is their poor self-image, a conviction that they are worthless. To be able to truly love God and his neighbor, one must esteem himself. Everyone needs to love and to have the assurance that he is worth loving and that he *is* loved, beyond "demand or reciprocity, praise or blame." No mere tolerance or indulgence can take the place of such love, which does not come from sermons or resolutions, but only from persons who can give it, and from God.

It is written: "You cannot love another person—that is, behave toward him so as to foster his happiness and growth unless you know what he needs. And you cannot know what he needs unless he tells you—and you hear him."

So much that is spurious and counterfeit is spoken and done in the name of love. Hear the word of the Lord: "By this we know that we love the children of God, when we love God, and keep his commandments." (1 John 5:2.) That charity which is defined by the prophet as "the pure love of Christ" (Moroni 7:47) is described clearly by the apostle Paul:

> [It] suffereth long, and is kind; . . . envieth not; . . . vaunteth not itself, is not puffed up.
>
> Doth not behave itself unseemly, seeketh not her own, is not easily provoked, thinketh no evil;
>
> Rejoiceth not in iniquity, . . . rejoiceth in the truth.

Such love, said the apostle, "never faileth." (See 1 Corinthians 13:4-6, 8.)

The major source of our self-image should be our Heavenly Father, whose children we are, in whose image we are made, whose attributes and qualities we have within us in embryo. He it is who loved us so much that he sent his Only Begotten Son to show us the way and to die for us. We are his children, worthy of love, and we have in us the capacity to love. We must learn to love even as we are loved by him.

Let me conclude with this prayer and earnest hope: God help us, and help us to help younger generations, to make the choices that will qualify us as worthwhile people, to make real the best that lies within us, to live up to our moral capacity, and to accomplish what is humanly possible, through believing, belonging, serving, and loving, even as the Son of God has taught us. God help us to be able to answer in good conscience when he asks: "Where art thou?"

Give Them Memories

It is a very pleasant and humbling and uplifting experience to look at your faces in this congregation, and to remember with gratitude and affection the gracious kindness with which you accept our humble efforts in your stakes and missions as we go on assignment there. I know that many of the problems you deal with, many of the most difficult ones, involve homes and families, and it is of this that I would like to speak. Few other subjects seem to me so urgently important in our time or to have such eternal relevance.

I speak to those who have children at home, and to those who have influence in homes where there are children, as well as to the great generation represented by this marvelous chorus who are making decisions now that will effectively influence their future homes and families.

In offering my witness about the home and family, I renew my expression of deep respect for children who wisely choose the better way, often in improvement upon their parents, and my deep compassion for good parents who strive earnestly to bring up their children in the way they should go, only to have those children use their individuality and agency to follow other ways. The Lord has forcefully taught us that in his eyes "the son shall not bear the iniquity of the father, neither the father bear the iniquity of the son." (Ezekiel

Address given at General Conference, April 1970.

284

18:20.) Each accountable person must ultimately answer for his own decisions.

It is our individual responsibility, parent or child or parent-to-be, to make decisions that will improve upon the quality of our homes and our relationships within them, and each of us should be anxious and honest in his efforts to do that.

William Thayer wrote: "As are families, so is society. If well ordered, well instructed, and well governed, they are the springs from which go forth the streams of national greatness and prosperity—of civil order and public happiness."

In the early days of the restoration the leaders of the Church were instructed to "set in order your houses." The Lord gave clear and explicit instructions to the Brethren and certainly to all the members of the Church that they be "more diligent and concerned at home, and pray always." (D&C 93:50.)

The wise men of the world have added their witness to the importance of doing this. Let me quote one, Martin Buber:

> If we had power over the ends of the earth it would not give us that fulfillment of existence which a quiet, devoted relationship to nearby life can give us. If we knew the secrets of the upper worlds, they would not allow us so much actual participation in true existence as we can achieve by performing with holy intent a task belonging to our daily duties. Our treasure is hidden beneath the hearth of our own home.

It is on this strong affirmation, which I believe with all my heart, that I offer five specific suggestions as to how we may find and multiply the treasures hidden beneath the hearth of our own home.

First let me mention *family associations.*

What other families does your family know well? What other fathers and mothers do they see in action? Do your children ever sit at the table or in family home evening, or kneel in prayer with another family?

Parents should be deeply concerned to build friendships with other families who have wholesome ideals, whose family life is constructive and strong. Children can greatly profit through exposure to other homes, parents, and families where there is good disposition, pleasant attitude, good fun, good humor, good literature, respect and discipline and cleanliness and prayer, where there is devotion to serving the Lord, where the gospel is lived.

With children, as all of us know, life is often a matter of following the leader, and wise parents will want their children to enjoy the influence of other families whose convictions and example will offer them strong incentives to build happy relationships in their own homes.

As parents we have been very grateful for the wonderful neighborhoods in which we have been privileged to live, and for the strong families in whose homes our children have visited as friends or baby tenders. Many religions and viewpoints are represented among our neighbors, and our children have profited greatly and have been greatly strengthened in their gratitude for their own home and faith from seeing the quality of the homes and families of the good people who live in our neighborhood.

Across the street, for instance, is a wonderful Latter-day Saint family into whose home I have always been grateful to have my youngsters go. The mother is a warm, gracious friend and homemaker, whose surroundings reflect her own character. Her husband is a special kind of man who has inspired our children and others in the neighborhood with his creative efforts to encourage patriotism and learning and appreciation of our historical heritage. There have been contests and essays and quizzes, serious celebrations along with the parties and fun on special holidays.

That leads me to the second suggestion. Families thrive on *traditions* and the *special rituals* of family life. Celebrating special days and seasons in special ways, working together, enjoying family home evenings and family councils and conversations, deciding upon and preparing for and enjoying holidays together, family meals and prayers—there are so many significant ways to build family traditions that will be remembered.

With all else that is sacred about Christmas, for instance, it can mean a beloved white star on the chimney, that symbolizes the season. It may also mean that special time together on Christmas Eve, carols sung at each home in the neighborhood, up and down the block, fun and music, and the involvement of others from outside the home. Everyone participates, but especially the guests who share the experience, who takes part, who read and contribute some special thought of Christmas. The Bible teaches us that we must not be forgetful to entertain strangers, for in so doing many have entertained angels unaware. The custom of having honored guests with us in our home has given us that experience every year for many years at Christmas and other times.

Let me be personal enough to mention that the choicest memories of recent years, as we talk of ritual or celebration at our home are the times we prepared as a family to bid a precious child farewell on her way to school. We celebrated the sad/happy event, and joined our hearts together as the head of the home gave her a father's blessing and invoked the Spirit of the Lord upon her. Twice we have had that glorious privilege, and pray God that we may enjoy it with each child.

It is of such simple but significant things that family traditions are built, and unified families with them.

All of us turn reflectively to the sweet memories of our childhood at home, and each of us, now blessed with families or looking forward to that privilege, should be thinking about the memories we will provide for their future.

Third let me mention *family values*. What gets major attention in our homes? What do we really care about, take time for? What is worthy of our consideration, our attention, our money, our efforts? What of books and reading them? What of thoughtful acts of kindness, of sharing, involving the whole family within and without the home? What of prayer and conversation and genuine concern with each other?

In 1926 the *Improvement Era* carried a memorable statement by a college senior concerning thoughts of home and relationships there. Let me read a part of what he wrote about his good home:

> 1. I wish I could remember one circus day, or one canyon trip, in which my father had joined us boys, instead of giving us the money and equipment to go, while he and mother stayed home, and made us feel guilty by working while we played.
>
> 2. I wish I could remember one evening when he had joined us in singing, or reading, or tussling, instead of always sitting so quietly with his newspaper by the reading lamp.
>
> 3. I wish I could remember one month, or week, or day even, when he had made purposeful work out of drudgery by planning the farm work with us, instead of merely announcing each morning what the day's work would be.
>
> 4. I wish I could remember one Sunday when he had bundled us all into the buggy and taken all to Church together, instead of staying home while we went in the morning, and leaving us home while he and mother went in the afternoon.
>
> 5. I wish that I could remember just one talk in which we had discussed together the problems and facts that trouble every growing boy, on which his clear and vigorous viewpoint might have shed such light and comfort, instead of leaving me to pick up the facts haphazardly as I might, and to solve the problems as best I could.
>
> And yet my conscience would cry shame were I to blame him, for no man could ever be more devoted to his family, more anxious for their welfare, more proud of their successes. His example has been a beacon to us. He just didn't know—and there is the pity of it to me—he just didn't know that we needed HIM. He didn't know that we would rather have his companionship than the land he could leave us—that some day, maybe, we might make money for ourselves, but that never can we make ourselves the memories that might have enriched and molded our lives. I can't see a fathers' and sons' outing without a lump in my throat.

Fourth I speak of *discipline* in the home, and of course I am not talking about harsh punishments but of fair rules, understood and enforced with sanctions consistently imposed when they are broken. I am thinking of realities, of facts to be faced, of a future of attitudes toward law and rules and personal responsibility being learned. Samuel Johnson, the great British literary genius, said that he would never permit his children to "deny him"—that is, to deny to callers that he was at home when he was, busy as he was. He said, "If I teach my children to lie for me, I may be sure that they will soon conceive the notion of lying to me."

Discipline involves adult solutions to the problems that arise in living together. Wise parents do not subject each other or their children to emotional poisoning. Disagreements are handled maturely and constructively and not destructively.

Discipline begins with concern and commitment and example, like that other word that comes from the same root: *disciple*.

Children need standards, need guidelines of behavior, and limits. They need models who care, who are firm and fair and sensitive and consistent. Wholesome discipline can be gentle and sensitive, but often it isn't.

A daughter and I were recently discussing her return home at an hour that seemed questionable to me. I shared with her an experience with my wonderful mother. I had spent some years away at schools and missions and wars, and the two of us were now alone at home. I returned from an appointment one evening at midnight to find the light still on in Mother's little bedroom. As I had always done, I reported in to Mom, sat on her bed, and kidded with her a little. I asked her why she was still awake. "I am waiting for you," she said.

I said, "Did you wait for me while I was on a mission, Mom, or at sea, or in battle?"

Her answer was calm and sweet. She gave me that little pat on the knee that reflects the mature compassion of the wise for the ignorant, and said: "No, that would have been foolish. I just knelt down here by my bed and talked to the

Lord about my boy. I told him what kind of man I believed you to be and wanted you to be, and prayed for his watchful care of you, and then left you in his hands and went to sleep. But now you are home," she said, "and you can count on it that I will be interested in you as long as I live."

She is gone now and it is remarkable how often I get the feeling that she is interested still, and forever will be.

Finally I mention *family love,* expressed in so many wonderful ways. Someone once said, it's been often quoted, that the best thing a father can do for his children is to love their mother. I believe this, and that the strongest and surest base for loving others is to love the Lord and to bring the binding and blessing balm of that love into all relationships of the home.

Children have the right to learn that love is the foundation of a good family and that love cannot exist apart from such qualities as respect, consideration, responsibility and loyalty. Love is not self-centered and is not self-serving, but is concerned with the well-being and happiness of others. It is providing for our loved ones an atmosphere of warmth and kindness which accepts and preserves the uniqueness of each as an individual person while building the unity of the home.

Love means friendship and companionship and partnership and unity. It expresses itself in modesty, in generosity, in sensitivity, in courtesy, in counsel, in appropriate compromise. It inspires affection and confidence and trust and self-control.

Love, mature love, provides a climate of wholesome, repentant, forgiving consideration. It listens. It hears and senses the needs of another. It can never be separated from character, from unselfishness, from good humor and from every tender virtue. Love is unconditional.

It must be strongly said of each of these avenues to family felicity that it does not just *happen*—it must be brought about by people who think and care and make the effort.

God help us to be more concerned with a high standard of life than with a high standard of living. God help us, while there is time, to take time to do everything we can to bring about now, or in the family we will one day have, by making wise choices now, the unity and strength and sweetness that a home is meant to have. I believe we can do that, or materially move toward bringing it about, through thoughtful family associations, memorable traditions, correct values, wise discipline, and great love.

What will we give our children to remember?

It is likely that what they will remember best is the treasure we unearth from beneath the hearth of our own home.

Friends of the Master

After a meeting with a group of students recently, one young man waited to ask a question. "Elder Hanks," he said, "what are *your* goals? What do *you* want to accomplish?" I observed his seriousness of purpose and answered in the same spirit that my strongest desire is to qualify to be a friend of Christ.

I had not responded to such a question just that way before, but the answer did put into words the deep yearnings of my heart.

In ancient times Abraham was called the "friend of God." Jesus, shortly before his crucifixion, said to his disciples, "Ye are my friends, if ye do whatsoever I command you. Henceforth I call you not servants . . . but I have called you friends." (John 15:14-15.) In 1832 to a group of elders returning from missionary service he repeated the message: "From henceforth I shall call you friends." (D&C 84:77.)

Today I would like to speak of one lesson among many that he taught us and that you and I must learn if we are to merit his friendship.

Christ's love was so pure that he gave his life for us. "Greater love hath no man than this, that a man lay down his life for his friends." But there was another gift he bestowed while he was on the cross, a gift that further measured

Address given at General Conference, October 1973.

the magnitude of his great love: He forgave, and asked his Father to forgive, those who persecuted and crucified him.

Was this act of forgiveness less difficult than sacrificing his mortal life? Was it less a test of his love? I do not know the answer. But I have felt that the ultimate form of love for God and men is forgiveness.

He met the test. What of us? Perhaps we shall not be called upon to give our lives for our friends or our faith (though perhaps some shall), but it is certain that every one of us has and will have occasion to confront the other challenge. What will we do with it? What *are* we doing with it?

Someone has written:

> The withholding of love is the negation of the spirit of Christ, the proof that we never knew him, that for us he lived in vain. It means that he suggested nothing in all our thoughts, that he inspired nothing in all our lives, that we were not once near enough to him to be seized with the spell of his compassion for the world.

Christ's example and instructions to his friends are clear. He forgave, and he said: "Love your enemies, bless them that curse you, do good to them that hate you, and pray for them which despitefully use you, and persecute you." (Matthew 5:44.) What is our response when we are offended, misunderstood, unfairly or unkindly treated, or sinned against, made an offender for a word, falsely accused, passed over, hurt by those we love, our offerings rejected? Do we resent, become bitter, hold a grudge? Or do we resolve the problem if we can, forgive, and rid ourselves of the burden?

The nature of our response to such situations may well determine the nature and quality of our lives, here and eternally. A courageous friend, her faith refined by many afflictions, said to me recently, "Humiliation must come before exaltation."

It is required of us to forgive. Our salvation depends upon it. In a revelation given in 1831 the Lord said:

> My disciples, in days of old, sought occasion against one another and forgave not one another in their hearts; and for this evil they were afflicted and sorely chastened.
>
> Wherefore, I say unto you, that ye ought to forgive one another; for he that forgiveth not his brother his trespasses standeth condemned before the Lord; for there remaineth in him the greater sin.
>
> I, the Lord, will forgive whom I will forgive, but of you it is required to forgive all men. (D&C 64:8-10.)

Therefore, Jesus taught us to pray, "And forgive us our trespasses, as we forgive those who trespass against us." (Matthew 6:12, I.V.)

Does it not seem a supreme impudence to ask and expect God to forgive when we do not forgive—openly—and "in our hearts"?

The Lord affirms in the Book of Mormon that we bring ourselves under condemnation if we do not forgive. (See Mosiah 26:30-31.)

But not only our eternal salvation depends upon our willingness and capacity to forgive wrongs committed against us. Our joy and satisfaction in this life, and our true freedom, depend upon our doing so. When Christ bade us turn the other cheek, walk the second mile, give our cloak to him who takes our coat, was it to be chiefly out of consideration for the bully, the brute, the thief? Or was it to relieve the one aggrieved of the destructive burden that resentment and anger lay upon us?

Paul wrote to the Romans that nothing "shall be able to separate us from the love of God, which is in Christ Jesus our Lord." (Romans 8:39.) I am sure this is true. I bear testimony that this is true. But it is also true that we can *separate ourselves* from his Spirit. In Isaiah it is written: "Your iniquities have separated between you and your God." (Isaiah 59:2.) Again, "They have rewarded evil unto themselves." (Isaiah 3:9.) Through Helaman we learn that "whosoever doeth iniquity, doeth it unto himself" (Helaman 14:30), and from Benjamin, "Ye do withdraw yourselves from the Spirit of the Lord" (Mosiah 2:36).

In every case of sin this is true. Envy, arrogance, unrighteous dominion—these canker the soul of one who is guilty of them. It is true also if we fail to forgive. Even if it appears that another may be deserving of our resentment or hatred, none of us can afford to pay the price of resenting or hating, because of what it does to us. If we have felt the gnawing, mordant inroads of these emotions, we know the harm we suffer.

So Paul taught the Thessalonians that they must "see that none render evil for evil unto any man." (1 Thessalonians 5:15.)

It is reported that President Brigham Young once said that he who takes offense when no offense was intended is a fool, and he who takes offense when offense *was* intended is usually a fool. It was then explained that there are two courses of action to follow when one is bitten by a rattlesnake. One may in anger, fear, or vengefulness pursue the creature and kill it. Or, he may make full haste to get the venom out of his system. If he pursues the latter course he will likely survive, but if he attempts to follow the former, he may not be around long enough to finish it.

Years ago on Temple Square I heard a boy pour out the anguish of his troubled heart and make a commitment to God. He had been living in a spirit of hatred toward a man who had criminally taken the life of his father. Nearly bereft of his senses with grief, he had been overcome with bitterness.

On that Sabbath morning when others and I heard him, he had been touched by the Spirit of the Lord and in that hour the pouring in of that Spirit had flooded out the hostility that had filled his heart. He tearfully declared his determined intent to leave vengeance to the Lord and justice to the law. He would no longer hate the one who had caused the grievous loss. He would forgive, and would not for another hour permit the corrosive spirit of vengefulness to fill his heart.

295

Sometime later, touched with the remembrance of that moving Sabbath morning, I told the story to a group of people in another city. Before I left that small community the next day, I had a visit from a man who had heard the message and understood it. Later a letter came from him. He had gone home that night and prayed and prepared himself and had then made a visit to the place of a man in his community who had years before imposed upon the sanctity of his home. Because there had been animosity and revenge in his heart and threats made, that evening when it was made known that he was at the door his frightened neighbor appeared with a weapon in his hand. The man quickly explained the reason for his visit, that he had come to say that he was sorry, that he did not want hatred to continue to consume his life. He offered forgiveness and sought forgiveness and went his way in tears, a free man for the first time in years. He left a former adversary also in tears, and shaken and repentant.

The next day the same man went to the home of a relative in the town. He said, "I came to ask your forgiveness. I don't even remember why we have been so long angry, but I have come to tell you that I am sorry and to beg your pardon and to say that I have learned how foolish I have been." He was invited in to join the family at their table, and was reunited with his kin.

When I heard this story I knew again the importance of qualifying ourselves for the forgiveness of Christ by forgiving.

Robert Louis Stevenson wrote:

> The truth of Christ's teaching seems to be this: In our own person and fortune, we should be ready to accept and pardon all; it is our cheek we are to turn and our coat we are to give to the man who has taken our cloak. But when another's face is buffeted, perhaps a little of the lion will become us best. That we are to suffer others to be injured and stand by, is not conceivable and surely not desirable.

So there are times when in defense of others and principle we must act. But for ourselves, if we suffer injury or unkindness, we must pray for the strength to forbear.

Christ gave his life on a cross; and on that cross he fully, freely forgave. It is a worthy goal to seek to qualify for the friendship of such a being.

More than 250 years ago Joseph Addison printed in *The Spectator* a paragraph of sobering thoughtfulness:

> When I look upon the tombs of the great, every emotion of envy dies in me; when I read the epitaphs of the beautiful, every inordinate desire goes out; when I meet with the grief of parents upon a tomb-stone, my heart melts with compassion; when I see the tombs of the parents themselves, I consider the vanity of grieving for those whom we must quickly follow; when I see kings lying by those who deposed them, when I consider rival wits placed side by side, or the men that divided the world with their contests and disputes, I reflect with sorrow and astonishment on the little competitions, factions, and debates of mankind. When I read the several dates of the tombs, of some that died yesterday, and some six hundred years ago, I consider that great Day when we shall all of us be contemporaries, and make our appearance together.

God help us to rid ourselves of resentment and pettiness and foolish pride; to love, and to forgive, in order that we may be friends with ourselves, with others, and with the Lord.

"Even as Christ forgave you, so also do ye." (Colossians 3:13.)

Index

INDEX

INDEX

302

INDEX

INDEX

INDEX

308